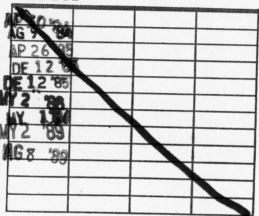

CONGRESSIONAL STAFFS

Capitol Hill, Washington, D.C.

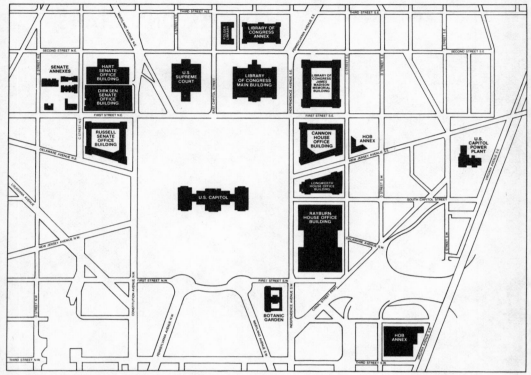

Source: Adapted with the permission of The Architect of the Capitol, George M. White, FAIA.

CONGRESSIONAL STAFFS

The Invisible Force in American Lawmaking

Harrison W. Fox, Jr.
and
Susan Webb Hammond

THE FREE PRESS
A Division of Macmillan Publishing Co., Inc.
NEW YORK

Collier Macmillan Publishers
LONDON

The Free Press
A Division of Macmillan Publishing Co., Inc.
866 Third Avenue, New York, N.Y. 10022

Collier Macmillan Canada, Ltd.

First Free Press Paperback Edition 1979

Library of Congress Catalog Card Number: 77-72041

Printed in the United States of America

Casebound printing number

  3 4 5 6 7 8 9 10

Paperbound printing number

1 2 3 4 5 6 7 8 9 10

Library of Congress Cataloging in Publication Data

Fox, Harrison W
  Congressional staffs.

  Bibliography: p.
  Includes index.
  1. United States. Congress--Officials and employees.
I. Hammond, Susan Webb, joint author. II. Title.
JK1083.F68   328.73'07'6   77-72041
ISBN 0-02-910420-3
ISBN 0-02-910430-0 pbk.

The extracts on page vii were reprinted from Rowland Evans, "The Invisible Men Who Run Congress," *Saturday Evening Post*, June 8, 1963, p. 13; Samuel Jacobs in Lewis A. Dexter, *The Sociology and Politics of Congress* (Chicago, Ill.: Rand McNally & Company, 1969), p. 222; and Senator Dick Clark in Spencer Rich, "An Invisible Network of Hill Power," *The Washington Post*, March 20, 1977, p. E 5.

To Lynn and Bob

"... of all the sources of power in Washington today, the most nearly invisible—yet in some ways the most influential—is the congressional staff ... a staff of professionals is no less essential to the care, feeding and orderly operation of Congress than Merlin was to King Arthur or Cardinal Richelieu to Louis XIII."

Rowland Evans

"You know, one of the things you should study is the staff here on the Hill. It's very interesting business."

Samuel Jacobs
Staff of Senator Patrick V. McNamara

"Dependency on staff is great. Domination, no. Dependency, definitely. There is no question of our enormous dependency and their influence. In all legislation, they're the ones that lay out the options."

Senator Dick Clark

Contents

Preface and Acknowledgments

For a number of years we have observed, studied, and at times participated in the work of Congress. We find the legislative process endlessly fascinating and challenging. The United States Congress, responding to currents of change in our society, has become a specialized organization handling a heavy and complex workload.

And like other institutions, it makes increasing use of professional experts for assistance in legislative decision making. Assistants on committees, on the personal staffs of Senators and Representatives, and in central support groups make up what some observers are calling the congressional bureaucracy. But given the nature of legislative decision making and the nonhierarchical structure of Congress, staff jobs are, in general, not typically bureaucratic. Little has been known about the staff who fill the professional positions on Capitol Hill. They are, by and large, an anonymous community. Because staff do much of the work of Congress, it seemed important to us to describe and analyze their background, tenure, and activities and roles. We focus on answers to the questions: Who are the staff? Where do they come from? How long do they stay? What are their jobs? How are staffs organized, what are their sources of information, what are their relationships to each other and to the principal actors of Congress, the Senators and Representatives? In short, what do staffs do and what difference do they make?

The book is not about the Congress as an institution but about a subpopulation—professional staff. The major focus is on the professional non-elected persons in Congress. From a quantitative perspective the numbers and frequency of staff activities were recorded as well as organizational character, committee patterns, and committee and personal office output. From a qualitative or attribute view, detailed material on personality types, educational background, sex, and personality characteristics are presented.

The data are comparative in an individual (person-to-person) sense and on the office or committee level, although detailed comparisons across all variables for each committee and personal office were not possible. Minimal reference is made in the text to the tables in the Appendix. Those interested should consult the tables for further data.

The study presents data on the major professional groups within the legislative branch including committee, personal, and support agency staff. Over 800 staffs and Congressmen responded to questionnaires and/or were interviewed, resulting in an accumulation of data that provided the base both for the tables (see Appendix) and the analysis presented in the text. Particularly because the study covers the major professional groups on the Hill participating in the legislative policy process, it provides an overview of staffs which can be used as the base for cumulative research on legislative staffing.

As this book goes to press, a word about present activity of the Senate and the House relating to staffing will be useful.

Recommendations made by the Temporary Select Committee to Study the Senate Committee System were adopted in part by the Senate in early 1977. Some committee jurisdictions were shifted, and as a result some committee staffs were combined.

The Senate, during consideration of the FY1978 Legislative Appropriations Bill, voted to combine allowances for S.Res.60 staff with clerk-hire allowances, effective at the start of the 1978 fiscal year on October 1, 1977.

In the House, The Task Force on Work Management of the Commission on Administrative Review proposed recommendations for consideration by the full Commission in September, 1977, to slow the growth of committee staff by requiring approval of a specific number of nonstatuatory staff slots each year; for cumulative clerk-hire allowances during a calendar year; and for some mechanism giving individual Representatives more assistance on committee work—either through designation of a personal committee aide or through increased flexibility in office allowances. Commission recommendations did not reach the House Floor for debate.

We have incurred many debts during the course of preparing this book. We are particularly grateful to a number of friends and colleagues who read and commented on earlier versions of the manuscript, particularly Carl Akins, Janet Breslin, Lewis A. Dexter, Bruce F. Norton, Jeanne B. Nicholson, and Thomas O'Donnell. We want especially to thank Milton C. Cummings, Jr. and Robert L. Peabody, both of Johns Hopkins University, who helped us with critical advice and comments as the study was designed and moved to completion.

A number of congressional staff have endured long discussions, given interviews, and generally expanded our understanding of the legislative process and the role of staff. Our debt to them is great. And finally, we want to thank the many Senators, Representatives, and congressional staff aides who agreed to our requests for interviews and responded to our questionnaires. Although they have been promised anonymity, this book would not have been possible without them.

A special thank you is in order for Bill Brock, Senator from Tennessee, 1971–1977, whose fundamental belief in reform provided a work setting for Harrison Fox that allowed this work to continue.

Bruce Chase, Charles Colloruli, Richard Moraski, and Pamela Neff assisted in tabulating some of the data. Deborah Mitchell, Gayle Fitzpatrick, and Hilda

Stephens typed the manuscript with speed and dispatch. And our editor, Tita Gillespie, assisted immeasurably in the intricacies of moving from manuscript to book.

Of course, any errors are ours. We hope we have contributed to a better understanding of one of our favorite institutions, the U.S. Congress.

Harrison W. Fox, Jr.
Susan Webb Hammond

Washington, D.C.

List of Abbreviations

AA Administrative Assistant
LA Legislative Assistant
EA Executive Assistant
CRS Congressional Research Service
GPO Government Printing Office
CBO Congressional Budget Office
OTA Office of Technology
    Assessment
GAO General Accounting Office
DSG Democratic Study Group
ADA Americans for Democratic
    Action
ACA Americans for Conservative
    Action
OMB Office of Management and
    Budget
FY Fiscal Year
H.R. House bill
S. Senate bill
S. Res. Senate Resolution
H. Res. House Resolution
H. Con. Res. House Concurrent
    Resolution
S. Con. Res. Senate Concurrent
    Resolution
J. Res. Joint Resolution

H. J. Res. House Joint Resolution
S. J. Res. Senate Joint Resolution
Pub. Res. Public Resolution (no longer
    in use)
PL Public Law
Stat. United States statutes at large
S. Rept. Senate Report
H. Rept. House Report
CQ Congressional Quarterly
NJ National Journal
(D.-Fla.) (Democrat-Florida) (Political
    party-abbreviation for state)
(R.-N.J.) (Republican-New Jersey)
    (Political party-abbreviation
    for state)

OFFICE BUILDINGS

LHOB Longworth House
CHOB Cannon House
RHOB Rayburn House
DSOB Dirkson Senate
HSOB Hart Senate
RSOB Russell Senate

CONGRESSIONAL STAFFS

1. The Staffs of Congress: An Overview

Staffing is power. But how much power is involved? "This country is basically run by the legislative staffs of the Members of the Senate and the House of Representatives," so Senator Robert Morgan (D-N.C.) told his colleagues.[1] Congressional staffs, both committee and personal, are an increasingly vital resource to Members of Congress. As legislative decision making has become more complex, existing staffs have expanded and the distribution of staff has changed. New staff support groups have been established. Congressmen have come to view staff assistance as important to policy formulation, to constituent service, and to the power acquisition that is central to congressional activity.

Congress includes structures—the Capitol and Taft Bell Tower, for example—but it is the activity of the people working on Capitol Hill that best represents the Federal legislative branch. In other words, the essence of Congress is people at work, and most of these people are staff, not elected representatives.

The key aspects of what makes Congress run—activity, communication, organization, and community—in large measure involve staff. Many congressional outputs can be traced back to staff activity, where they conceptualize, write, type, and finally communicate a message. Constituent-service activities are almost always performed by staff. Investigations, general oversight, foresight, and program evaluation are again supported by and often carried out by staff. Certain legislative activities such as voting, chairing hearings, marking up a bill, are almost always acted out by Congressmen. But exceptions can be found even here. For instance, one of the most important recent congressional reform measures, the Congressional Budget and Impoundment Control Act of 1974, was marked up by groups of staff and given final approval by the Members. In this instance we may be seeing a departure from traditional procedures, illustrating a further erosion of one of the Members' roles.

This is not a book about Members of Congress. It is a study of their staff. Our primary purpose is to describe and analyze the work of congressional staff in the legislative and policy process. Our focus in this study is on staffs working on congressional matters—committee, personal, and central staffs of the two Houses, and support agency staff. Within these groups, our central concern is

1

with professional staffs active on constituent, legislative, and oversight matters. This emphasis on staff and the constellation of factors characterizing them includes describing their attributes; reviewing staff activity; examining committee and personal office organization; discovering communication networks; and determining staff impact, through their roles in the congressional functions of constituent service, legislative development and policy making, and oversight. The discussion covers the aide as individual, and comparisons of staff as groups in their personal office and committee settings.

Our purpose is to contribute to increased understanding of the legislative process; in focusing on the staff person, our vantage point differs from that of most books on Congress. Staff are part of the currency of the legislative system. Without staff as a medium of exchange, as a resource and as a point of interaction between Congressional actors, the system would play a very different role in our government.

Thus, the message is that staff do much of the congressional work and that, in many instances, this work could not be done without staff. A case can be made that staff have too much influence, authority, and power. Based on a detailed examination of the staff's current roles, this book helps shed light on this dilemma with the hope that independent judgments can then be made about the part they play in government.

Legislative aides have the capacity to significantly influence congressional decision making. Their expertise and judgment are often critical. For instance, staff exercise control over communications into and within a committee and personal office. They participate in identifying issues and developing legislative positions. They conduct research, gather background data on specific legislative matters, and draft legislation. They prepare testimony, speeches, Floor statements, explanations to constituents, and reports. Increasingly, they coordinate legislative strategy. They brief Congressmen on pending legislation. Most important, they are expected to offer their opinions and act as a ''sounding board'' for Senators and Representatives.

Factors which may affect a staff member's influence are the Congressman's information channels, control of committee resources, constituency characteristics, as well as the Congressman's perception of his role. The personal relationship between aides and Congressmen also have a bearing on staff role and function.

Congressional staffing continues to be highly personalized, but it also reflects the change toward a more complex and institutionalized Congress. Indeed, the demands for professional information analysis and the accompanying pressure for more personnel conflict (to an extent) with the traditional emphasis on close personal relationships and the generalist orientation which have been the hallmark of congressional activity.

CHANGES IN THE STAFFS OF CONGRESS

The Legislative Reorganization Act of 1946 marked a major change in congressional staffing. Although various themes have recurred before and since 1946, and although the trend toward larger staffs has been continuous since the mid-nineteenth century, the provisions approved in 1946 for professional, specialized staff laid the basis for the present congressional system.

In the years before 1946, congressional staffs had increased slowly in number and activity. Legislation subsequent to 1946 provided for more rapid increases in the size and pay of committee, personal, and support staff. Each house of Congress presently has a body of staff aides divided among administrative staff, committee staff, and Members' personal staff. In addition, supporting agencies such as the Congressional Research Service (CRS) of the Library of Congress and the General Accounting Office (GAO) are technically part of the congressional support staff. Table 1 (Appendix) identifies the wide range of members within the congressional staff system.

During the past decade congressional staffs have increased rapidly. The Legislative branch in 1976 employed over 38,000 persons, including 3,000 on committees, about 10,000 on personal staffs of Senators and Representatives, and 17,900 in supporting agencies such as the Library of Congress, the GAO, and the Government Printing Office. It should be noted that many of the employees of the support agencies serve persons outside Congress.

The effect of a growing congressional bureaucracy[2] has received relatively little scrutiny as compared to the attention focused on Presidential staff and the consequences of the institutionalization of the Presidency. And yet the resources represented by additional staff capability affect congressional operations: staff expertise may alter the content of specific legislative products, affect strategic maneuvering, or enhance the constituent-representative link. Staff resources are often representative of a Member's power. Through their position in the congressional structure and their participation in the legislative process, staffs influence the larger political system.

It has generally been accepted that committee staff play a significant role in the development of legislation and in the exercise of legislative oversight. Our study of personal staffs made us more aware of the interrelationship of personal and committee staff aides. Professionals on personal staffs of Senators and Representatives often make an extensive contribution to oversight and policy formulation. Increasingly, staff aides, personal and committee, operate as independent professionals in a complex environment.

The job of a congressional aide, whether on a personal or committee staff, is a peculiarly personal one—based on mutual trust, confidence, and loyalty to a member. Analogous jobs in the Federal government are the White House staff, personal assistants to Presidential appointees, and clerks of judges. These jobs are expected to terminate after a time. On the Hill, if a Senator or Representative continues to be elected, jobs which in any other branch of government would be of short term may last for a number of years. We suspect that the conditions of employment, such as lack of tenure and a clearly defined career pattern, as well as the required role anonymity, contribute to the preponderance of relatively young and short-tenured Hill aides. Employees work in a situation in which personal relationships are significant, and the universalistic personnel rules of bureaucracy do not apply.

Staffers from a wide range of offices emphasized to us the personal nature of staffing—"staff revolves around the Congressman and hence, reflects his interests and his style," one aide said. Another added, "and different constituencies allow you to act differently." But the similarities are also evident: common administrative problems and a shared need for expert assistance in the performance of congressional functions.

Long-time staff members agree on the increasing congressional workload, the growing complexity of legislative decision making, and the greater number of demands on staff today. One aide said:

> "My Congressman's predecessor had two girls on his office staff when he first came to Congress—no AA. He supervised the office himself, and gave whatever had to be done to the girls. He also might end up typing something himself. He *never* sent out press releases."

Another long-time aide described office work over a period of thirty-five years:

> "Why, the previous incumbent, who served for eighteen years, replied to his letters by longhand. . . . Now, government is much more complicated and people are baffled—but they are also much more sophisticated and conscious of pending legislation. The staff *has* to act as liaison with them."

Congress has been ambivalent about adding staff, and has done so with some uneasiness. Most Senators and Representatives agree that staff bring a needed expertise and assistance to busy Congressmen, but they are concerned that increasing specialization brings bureaucratization and accompanying staff management problems.

In 1946, Congressmen appeared with constituents before executive branch departments and agencies; they were hesitant to delegate this activity to aides. Today aides handle most constituent casework and Federal projects work and now Congressmen worry that they spend too much time responding to staff, and not enough listening to each other and exchanging ideas.

Senator Ernest Hollings (D-S.C.), in an exchange with Senator Mike Gravel (D-Alaska) during hearings on the FY (Fiscal Year) 1976 Legislative Appropriations Bill, said:

> "There are many Senators who feel that all they are doing is running around and responding to the staff. My staff fighting your staff, your staff competing with mine. It is sad . . . .

"Everybody is working for the staff, staff, staff; driving you nutty. In fact, they have hearings for me all of this week. . . . Now it is how many nutty whiz kids you get on the staff to get your magazine articles and get you headlines and get all of these other things done."[3]

Expertise is viewed by some with distrust. For example, Congressman Clarence Cannon (D-Mo.), when he became Chairman of the House Appropriations Committee in 1951, discharged a research staff built up by the previous Chairman, Congressman John Taber (R-N.Y.). According to one observer the new Chairman did not use outside experts but rather, had had any investigation and research done by executive branch employees on temporary loan.[4] Congress has always been a generalist-oriented institution and has had a verbal culture; therefore experts bring a new dimension.

Some feel that there are already too many aides: they are ubiquitous, and perhaps lazy. They take up too much space and they insulate Senators and Representatives from direct participation in decisions and debate. In short, too many aides interfere with the efficiency and effectiveness of the Congress. Senator Herman Talmadge (D-Ga.), during debate in June, 1975, explained how Senators could do their jobs more efficiently:

"If we would fire half the Senate employees we have, fire half the staff and not permit a paper to be read on the floor of the U.S. Senate, we would complete our business and adjourn by July 4th. (Laughter)

"The Senator from Georgia knows that when you get more staff and more clerks they spend most of their time thinking up bills, resolutions, amendments. They write speeches for Senators, and they come in here on the floor with Senators. Unanimous consents are obtained for so-and-so to sit. He is there prodding, telling the Senator how to spend more money."[5]

This uneasiness about staffing has been evident over many years and persists today. We will return to it later, when we discuss current trends in congressional staffing. There are tensions, to some degree inevitable, between various congressional norms and traditions and the needs and demands of a technological age with complex and interdependent problems.

STUDIES OF STAFFING

In recent years a steadily proliferating literature has made use of the latest developments in a variety of disciplines to delineate an increasingly sophisticated picture of Congress. The application of quantitative methods in, for example, roll-call analysis, the use of social science methodology, direct observation, and participation have been employed as research tools.

In this array of literature, little attention has been given to congressional staffs and no systematic analysis made of their role in the legislative process.

Scholarly interest in Congress has most generally focused on the central actors in the legislative drama, the Senators and Representatives, or on case studies of a particular piece of legislation or an issue. Journalistic accounts have often treated the abuses or one aspect of staffing, such as pay.

We are left with the somewhat surprising situation of a major congressional group whose numbers and influence are increasing but of whose characteristics and activities little description or analysis is available.

STUDY DESIGN

This book grew out of studies of the jobs and roles of Senate and House professional staff aides in personal offices and on congressional committees. A major objective of these studies was to determine the staff effect on legislation and policy through description and analysis of recruitment patterns, staff attributes, office organization, communication networks, and staff activities. In addition, we have analyzed our data in accordance with the hypothesis that variables significant to other congressional operations—party, region, seniority, and policy attitude—might affect staff use and staff impact on the policy process.

The initial research on professionals serving on personal staffs was conducted during the 92nd Congress. The research in the Senate was mainly based on two questionnaires sent to all or subpopulations of professionals on the personal staff of Senators in January, 1972. In addition, interviews were later conducted with a dozen of the respondents. Both questionnaires and interviews dealt with office organization patterns, sources of information, and communication networks. The central focus of the Senate study was on role activity, attributes, interpersonal relations, values, and attitudes of professional staff members.[6]

Seventy-two interviews with Congressmen and professional staff in twenty-five randomly selected offices form the prime source of data on personal staffs in the House. A pilot study of four offices (of two Republicans and two Democrats) was conducted during the 91st Congress (1969–1970), to test some assumptions and to aid in the design of research in this topic. These findings were helpful in delineating both hypotheses and methodology of the present study.[7]

The House sample was stratified by party, region, and seniority and closely reflects the party ratio and seniority distribution of the 92nd Congress. By region, the sample slightly underrepresents the East and South, and slightly overrepresents the West and Midwest.[8] Research was directed at examining the activities of personal professional staffs in the policy process, and what variables might affect their role. Interviews yielded data on office organization, job specifications, staff background, and activities of staff, including information sources and communication channels. Even though research on personal House and Senate staff was performed independently, we have been struck by the similarity of our findings. The modes of analysis also illuminate differences between staff groups and add depth to our analysis.

The committee staff research was conducted during the 93rd Congress. A questionnaire was sent to all committee professionals, of which 313 (31 percent) responded. The respondents were roughly representative of staff division between House and Senate and between legislative and appropriations committees. The survey questionnaire responses were later supplemented by interviews with a small group of respondents during the 93rd and 94th Congresses.

Additional sources of data include published documents such as committee hearings, calendars, and reports, the *Congressional Record,* and mimeographed material from subgroups in each House. *Congressional Quarterly's* voting indices were also drawn on. Payroll records were obtained through the House Disbursing Office and published records from the Secretary of the Senate. Both authors have served as aides on Hill staffs.[9] And since the data collection, there has been continuing contact with staff and Congressmen on the Hill.

Capitol Hill is described by participants and observers as a community, a governmental "subculture." In this study we describe several subcommunities on the Hill (the professional personal staffs of Senators and Representatives and professional committee aides), examining factors involved in congressional activity. Where there is a community, we can expect to find role expectations (norms), role behavior, and output.

Attributes

Staff background—education, training, previous employment, and state of residence—are examined in Chapter 3, as are personality characteristics of aides. Do professional staff members tend to come from the same states as their members? What are their social, experiential, and educational backgrounds? Do men dominate the top positions? Are there differences between Senate, House, and committees? Answers to these questions are a first step in the description of professional staffs.

We are able to analyze attributes by job and by staff group—House, Senate, or committee. It is possible to draw a profile of a typical Congressional aide. We can delineate some of the linkages to the wider political system and draw some inferences as to the impact of these attributes on congressional activity.

Recruitment and Tenure

Little has been written about prerequisites for professional legislative staff positions. Is entrance into a staff position a function of the opportunities for action provided and the skills of the potential staff member,[10] so that both political opportunities and professional skills may determine if a candidate for a staff position will be successful?

Staff members serve at the pleasure of their Congressman.[11] Turnover varies in different positions among offices and some staff stay on long after an initially planned departure time. The occupational mobility of staff before and after their congressional careers is of interest. We examine recruitment and tenure patterns of Capitol Hill aides, comparing and contrasting the different staff groups. Consequences of frequent turnnover and of protracted tenure among staff aides are also discussed.

Organization

The United States national legislative bureaucracy is unique. No other legislature, national, state, or local, has the quality or quantity of staff assistance found within the U.S. Congress. Various factors which affect staff organization, both personal and committee, and the implications of certain typologies of office organization for decision making and policy outcomes are examined. Congress is a decentralized institution. With over 535 separate personal offices and at least 100 committee groups, legislative secretariats for each house, and support organizations, Congress qualifies as a complex organization. Within this complexity is found both diversity and similarity. Every personal office has similar furniture, square footage, is within a few minutes of the Capitol, and has access to many of the same resources. In these areas the difference is marginal. Some Congressmen have offices with a view of the Capitol. Others have extra space in an annex.

But there are a number of dissimilarities that affect the operation of the various offices, committees, and other organizations on Capitol Hill. For example, in an hierarchically organized office or committee, communication between staff and Member is through a staff director or administrative assistant (AA); in coordinative offices, two persons coordinate the work of staff and serve as the link to the member; in the individualistic organizations, at least three and up to a dozen professional staff report directly to the member. Determinants of congressional behavior, such as a member's seniority, party, background, region, and policy attitude are important to the personal office organization and its predisposition to respond. Other factors that make a difference in the organization of offices and committees include workload, changes in office priorities, expectations and perceptions of interpersonal relationships, and the way staff view their member in terms of authority, power, and influence. The latter factors help to explain the relationships between a member and his staff.

Activities

Legislative staff activities are varied. Numerous factors, including staff perceptions of their jobs and Senators' and Representatives' perceptions, affect the specific mix of staff activity. Chapter 6 describes the activities of staff and variations within different types of offices. A comparison of activities in House, Senate, and committee offices enables us to analyze the work of specific subgroups of the congressional system.

Increasing professionalization is evident, in training, previous employment, and tasks performed. Although Congress continues to be a milieu that encourages generalists, specialization is nevertheless increasing: there are more press secretaries and research assistants than ever before on House personal staffs. A number of House offices employ more than one legislative assistant, making possible area or functional division of the workload, as has been the practice in the Senate for some years. Within the relatively small House staffs—up to eighteen employees, divided between Washington and district offices—tasks must continue to be somewhat interchangeable. Nevertheless, a rough division of function has come to prevail at the professional level. On committees, too, the trends are similar. For example, an increasing number of subcommittee chairmen have been hiring trained professionals. Overall, Congressmen seem to be learning to use staffing resources more effectively.

Communication

Communication is central to the operation of Congress and critical to congressional outputs. What sort of communications networks exist in Congress? Are they inherent in office and committee structural organization? Do all staff groups participate? Is informal behavior a significant factor? We describe and analyze staff contact and information exchange in order to delineate congressional staff communication patterns. Particular attention is paid to internal and external communication linkages and information sources among staff and their support persons and groups.

Professional staffs come in contact with a wide variety of individuals. Within each Senate office, for instance, professionals interact with their Senator, other professional staff, nonprofessional staff, volunteers, and interns. Interaction on the extra-office level with constituents, executive department personnel, committee staff(s), other parts of the legislative bureaucracy, lobbyists, newsmen and commentators, judiciary, and citizens who are not from the home state are common occurrences.

A professional staff member establishes a certain type of interpersonal relationship with his Senator, Representative, or the members of his committee, and with those in his office.

Impact of Staff

Limitations of organizational resources—time, staff, money—can restrict the effectiveness of an office or committee. Restrictions on any one of these three resources may foreshadow limitations on at least one of the others. For instance, if a Senator does not have enough staff to deal with his constituents, then he often may devote more of his time to these efforts. His allocated salary allowance determines to some extent the quality and quantity of the staff he may hire. Other limitations may relate to staff training, to office workload, and to a Congressman's or staff aide's perception of the job.

Constraints on staff affect organizational behavior within the office. Such constraints as legislative norms, office leadership, staff organization, and specialization affect office output. Constraints on the behavior of professional staff members contribute to staff professionalization and vary among different offices.

In the end, the question must be what differences do staff make? Our focus will be on the roles they play in constituent service and policy matters—planning, performing research, and formulating statements; legislative development; and control and supervision of the executive (oversight).

Questions relating to staff's operation, changing potential, and role in Congress are examined: For instance:

What types of people do the constituent and legislative staff work?

How are the operational units, committees, and personal offices of the legislature organized? Related to this, is staff affected by party, seniority, policy attitudes, region, and background of the member?

Is there a common personality type among staff?

How does the staff member view his relationship with his member in terms of influence, power, and authority?

How are members of this community recruited and what is their tenure?

Do members of this community see their jobs as a career?

Are staff members partisan?

Is there a staff bureaucracy?

With whom do staff communicate and exchange information?

The answers to these questions help provide the basis for determining the effect of staff activity.

NOTES

1. *Congressional Record,* September 8, 1976, S.15432.
2. Staffs are indeed larger and require the application of management skills, but some of the norms which are understood as common to bureaucracies, in the Weberian sense, are not found in congressional offices. (See Chapter 10, below.)
3. Hearings before a subcommittee of the Committee on Appropriations, U.S. Senate, 94th Congress, 1st Session, on H.R. 6950, Legislative Branch Appropriations, FY 1976, April, 1975, p. 1221.

4. Committee on Expenditures in the Executive Department, U.S. Senate, Hearings on Evaluations of the Effects of Laws to Reorganize the Legislative Branch of the Government, 82nd Congress, 1st Session, May, 1951, p. 42.
5. *Congressional Record,* June 9, 1975, S.10131.
6. See Appendix for further discussion of the Senate research.
7. Susan Webb Hammond, "The Office of the Congressman: Organizational and Recruitment Patterns," unpublished M.A. thesis, The Johns Hopkins University, 1970.
8. The choice of the sample and the methodology of the study are discussed in the Appendix.
9. Harrison Fox has served on House and Senate personal staffs, Senate committee staffs, and the Senate personal committee staff. Susan Hammond has worked with House and Senate members and with the Commission on the Operation of the Senate and the House Commission on Administrative Review.
10. Donald R. Matthews, *The Social Background of Political Decision-Makers* (Garden City, New York: Doubleday, 1954), p. 11.
11. Several unsuccessful attempts have been made to bring personal staffs into a Civil Service system. See, for example, discussion in Lindsay Rogers, "The Staffing of Congress," *Political Science Quarterly,* LVI (March, 1941), pp. 16–17; *Hearings,* Joint Committee on the Organization of Congress, 1965; Debate on H.R. 17654, Legislative Reorganization Act, Sept. and Dec., 1970.

2. The Growth of Congressional Staff

Legislative decision making is generally incremental, and changes in congressional organization and procedures are no exception. Even major internal "reforms" tend to occur following a number of incremental changes and often consolidate existing practices. Staff changes are also typically incremental—an extra aide is permitted or there is a slight increase in staff allowances from time to time. The additive effect of these changes has been significant. Sizable staffs, capable of sophisticated services, now exist within Member offices and committees.

Staffing changes also reflect the broader systemic changes occurring in the congressional environment. In the House, for example, decision making on personal staff allowances has become more automatic, universalistic, and less divisive, both reflecting and contributing to the increasing institutionalization of that chamber.[1] Gradually, less House time has been devoted to debate on staffing, and votes are less closely divided. The decision arena has shifted from the Floor, with its opportunities for parliamentary maneuvering, to procedures which rely primarily on committee decisions.[2]

Patterns of change with regard to staffing have tended to recur according to a cyclical pattern. Committee staff changes have generally preceded those for Senate and House personal staffs, setting significant and important precedents. And, Senate action on personal staffing tends to precede House action.

The first groups in Congress to obtain staff were the committees. Clerks for individual Senators were then authorized in 1885 and for Representatives, in 1893. Similarly, committees first obtained specific authorization under the 1946 Legislative Reorganization Act for professional staff. Shortly thereafter, administrative assistants were authorized for Senators, but not until 1970 were professional aides to House Members formally recognized. Today, committee staff continue to include a larger number of professionally trained aides than House personal and most Senate personal staffs.

Personal staffs were first authorized for the "have-nots" in the Congress, the Members who did not hold committee chairmanships and hence could not hire clerks to assist them. Initially, clerks could be employed only during the session; later this was extended to the full year. The 1975 resolution (Senate Resolution 60), permitting Senators who do not control committee staff to hire personal legislative aides for assistance on commitee work, was a similar effort to allocate resources more equitably. Concerns of Congressmen about staffing are also recurrent. For many years recognizable themes have run through debates on staffing:

1. The problems of an increasing workload;
2. Sensitivity to constituent reaction to an increase in congressional expense, particularly expenses which can be attached to separate individuals and which may be interpreted as a salary increase for the Congressman;
3. A strong minority argument that there is no need for increased staff;
4. Staffing as part of congressional reform;
5. The importance of efficiency and economy in the operation of government and disagreement as to methods of achieving both;
6. The expense of added staff.

These themes were voiced in 1893, when the House first authorized funds for personal "clerks" to Representatives (clerk-hire), and continue to appear in a 1976 debate when clerk-hire and office operations allowances were modified by the House.

There has been increasing flexibility in staffing and office operations allowances. Early legislation was often written for a specific number of clerks at specific salaries. Today, each Senator and Representative is allotted a total amount for salaries of personal staff, with House staffs limited in size. Committees are authorized a core staff of permanent employees, with additional "inquiries and investigative" funds for staff authorized each year.

A number of the practices of earlier years have been modified by law or experience. Statutory prohibition against nepotism and the requirement that personal staff work in either state (or district) or Washington, D.C., offices are responses to specific abuses. The employment of the same clerks by executive departments and Congressmen no longer is possible, although committees do obtain the assistance of executive branch personnel "on loan." Similarly, there is far less mixing of committee and personal office matters than occurred in earlier years, when clerks to committee chairmen also handled personal office business, and committee records were mixed in with the chairman's personal office files. And finally, staff is more expert and professional, although the term "clerk-hire" for staff salary allowances continues to reflect the early days of congressional staffing, when committee and personal staff jobs were clerical and Senators and Representatives handled their own legislative work.

Change has occurred most rapidly in recent years. But the pattern of change remains that established during the 1800's: authorization for added staffing in response to congressional demands; gradual appointment of the maximum number of authorized staffs and a buildup of demand for increased assistance; subsequent authorization of staff increases.

By and large, the debates on staffing which occur in Congress today do not have high visibility and center on marginal matters of numbers and dollar allotment. Only on occasion do staffing provisions become highly controversial and divisive, as in the 1975 Senate debate on S. Res. 60 or the 1976 debate in the House on staff and office allowances. When prolonged debate occurs, the underlying issue is one of power and authority.

Control of staff resources may enhance or hinder the effectiveness and the power of individuals or groups. Senators pushing for more staff in 1975 argued for greater equality in the allocation of Senate resources; freshmen Senators working within the constraints of personal staff allowances and without control of committee staff felt at a disadvantage in carrying the Senate workload and, ultimately, in their ability to make an impact on congressional outputs. A major element in the brief House debate in May 1975 on procedures for setting office allowances was a protest against the growing power and authority of the Committee on House Administration and its then Chairman, Representative Wayne Hays (D-Ohio).[3] Congressman Hays had used the committee's jurisdiction over internal housekeeping matters and his chairman's position to enhance his place in the House power structure.

The 1946 Legislative Reorganization Act (P.L. [Public Law] 79–601; 60 Stat. 812) is a watershed in the area of staffing, as well as for other aspects of Congressional reform. Section 202, providing for professional committee staffs, was the first formal Congressional statement of the principle of professionalization and specialization for staffing. A core of permanent committee staff, from which larger committee staffs could be built, was established for all committees.

1946 also appears to be important in the transformation of staffing from a conflict issue to one on which most Congressmen agreed on basic premises. A number of significant steps which had already been taken by Congress served as a base for developing the present large, somewhat specialized personal and committee staffs.

By 1946 clerk-hire paid for by government rather than from personal funds, with payment made directly to the employee rather than in the form of an allowance to the Congressman, had become accepted practice. The form of the staff allotment for personal staffs had also been set: a gross allotment for salaries, a maximum salary limitation, and in the House a ceiling on staff numbers. Office facilities were also accepted as a necessary adjunct to the Congressional function: the Cannon House Office Building had been completed in 1908, the Senate (Russell) Office Building in 1909, and the Longworth House Office Building in 1933. There was some agreement that within specific parameters, those who need staff should be able to hire persons to fill their needs. This point was made explicitly in the House for the first time in 1939 during debates on personal staff.[4] When the parameters become too wide, potentially divisive Floor debates on staffing occur.

EARLY STAFFING PRACTICES

Staffing began in both Senate and House as clerical assistance. For many years (1885–1946), Senate legislation authorizing personal staff read, "For clerks. . . ."[5] And the appropriation continues to be referred to as "clerk-hire."[6]

A brief survey of patterns of staffing prior to the 1946 Act, with personal staffing in the House of Representatives as a case study, will serve to illuminate some of the consensus and practices of the pre-1946 Congresses. The discussion will, in turn, highlight changes since 1946 which help to explain current staffing practices.

Prior to the 1840's, members of committees handled committee matters without paid assistance. After that time committees in both houses were authorized to hire, at first, part-time help. In 1856, full-time clerks for the Committee on Ways and Means and the Senate Finance Committee were approved. Thereafter, committee staffs became increasingly accepted, and the number of clerks employed increased gradually. By 1924, 120 committee aides were employed in the House and 141 in the Senate. At the time of the Legislative Reorganization Act in 1946, committees such as Appropriations had a history of expert, nonpartisan staff—a tradition which did not extend to most other committees.

The House in 1902 eliminated the distinction between committee chairmen and members for purposes of personal office staffing. But as recently as 1931, Senate provisions of the Legislative Appropriations Act (FY 1931) provided clerks for each category of Senators separately. Also in the Senate, committee and personal staff of committee chairmen were not distinct: Appropriations measures directed that personal clerks of chairmen should be "ex officio clerks . . . of any committee of which their Senator is chairman."[7]

Senators were first authorized to employ personal clerks in 1885; the Legislative Appropriations Act (FY 1886) of that year provided "clerks to Senators who are not chairmen of committees at six dollars per day during the session."[8] The House passed similar provisions eight years later, in 1893.

Before 1893, Representatives who were not committee chairmen either managed without personal assistance, or paid "secretaries" with personal funds. Often, Congressmen wrote letters longhand during Floor debate, or at their rooms in the evenings. Committee chairmen had authority to appoint clerks to assist on committee business, and, as the debate on the 1893 clerk-hire bill makes clear, those clerks were often expected to assist on the chairman's district business as well.

Prior to 1893, pressure had been building for authority to employ personal staff. In the 49th Congress, 2nd Session (December 6, 1886 to March 3, 1887), H.R. 10078, providing clerks for Representatives who were not committee chairmen, had been reported out of committee, debated by the House, and then "laid on the table" rather than passed. Similar legislation was introduced in succeeding Congresses. On March 3, 1893, J. Res. (Joint Resolution) No. 21, authorizing the use of government funds during the Congressional session to pay for clerks appointed by Congressmen who were not committee chairmen, was approved by the 52nd Congress.[9]

The 1893 Resolution, and debate over its passage, is instructive not only for the light shed on the early years of clerk-hire, but also for certain provisions and themes which continue thereafter. It illuminates both Congressional and issue continuity in an uncertain world; indeed, this may be part of Congress's strength as an institution.

The 1893 law limited the amount available to the Representative for clerk-hire—a constraint ever since—although it did not limit staff number, authorizing that the member should be reimbursed for ". . .one person or persons" hired. (In fact, most Congressmen hired one clerk; a few hired two.)

The use of government funds to pay Congressional clerks was approved. The issue had been discussed in the House for a number of years prior to actual passage.

Themes voiced in the 1893 debate—of expense, constituent reactions, increased workload, congressional reform—recur regularly in later years when clerk-hire proposals were debated. In this instance, clerk-hire was overtly tied to committee reform. Congressman Newton Blanchard (D-La.) stated he had been opposed to clerk-hire authorization in the past, but supported the present measure. Not only would it bring about increased efficiency, but ". . .I (also) believe if we adopt this proposition . . . it will result in a great reform in bringing about later the abolition of from 15 to 20 useless Committees of this House that are now maintained simply because of the pressure upon the Speaker for committee chairmanships, which means a clerk to each of the chairmen."[10]

Opponents of the 1893 measure argued that it was an indirect addition to the members' salary and that the work of the office could be handled easily by the Congressman himself. Representative Samuel Peel (D-Ark.) stated that his office received forty to fifty letters per day and that he answered them himself, often in longhand. Some claimed that casework and correspondence had increased only because of the "bad seed and worthless documents" sent out by Congress, and the fact that people had been taught to "look to the government for everything."[11] Those supporting the measure cited the increasing workload and the equity of using public funds for work which needs to be done. They argued that staff would bring increased efficiency. During the debate one member rose, to appreciative laughter, with a partially written letter and pen in hand to say he couldn't manage to participate in the debate, as he was too busy.

The wording of J. Res. 21 is unclear as to whether the members or their clerks were to be paid the clerk-hire monies, although in the debate most members assumed the payment would be made to them.[12] In 1894, without Floor debate, the wording which was standard for the next sixteen years authorizing payment "to members and delegates" was adopted[13] and was included in that year's legislative appropriations bill.[14]

In 1896, clerk-hire was authorized year-round for Congressmen who were not committee chairmen (the total salary allotment thus became $1,200 per annum).[15] In 1898, a provision of an appropriations measure provided clerk-hire monies to committee chairmen "during vacation"—that is, when Congress was not in session,[16] and in 1902, an Accounts Committee Resolution was approved authorizing personal staff for committee chairmen during the session as well.[17]

Changes were incremental, and personal staffing continued to be controversial.[18] An 1896 amendment which limited clerk-hire to representatives who were not committee chairmen was offered and approved by a close vote (104 to 83) during debate. On final passage the entire Resolution was approved by 130 to 109. The 1898 clerk-hire provisions for chairmen took two tries, was amended to meet one objection, and finally slipped through when no point of order was raised against it in time.

In 1918, the appropriations bill for clerk-hire included provision that the clerks be "put on the rolls" and "paid directly by the Clerk of the House through the Disbursing Office."[19] This was a painful and divisive provision, raising issues of the prerogatives of legislative committees versus those of appropriations committees and of relationships with the press, with its innuendoes that clerk-hire allowances were being pocketed by members. Fully as disturbing, it called to mind past—and still rankling—injustices committed by the Senate, which the previous year had *added* a clause putting House clerks on the rolls for direct salary payment and had thus violated the long tradition that one house does not interfere in the internal affairs of the other. The Senate provision had been immediately knocked out by the House. For many, the payment proposal simply meant upsetting established ways. The provision failed when a point of order against it was sustained.

In 1919, similar clerk-hire provisions contained in the FY 1920 appropriations bill, H.R. 14078, were subject to complicated and time-consuming debate, with a number of Congressmen taking an active part. Eventually an amendment stating that no part of the clerk-hire allowance could be paid to a Member, delegate, or resident commissioner was approved, with the effect that clerks would be paid directly. This is one of the last times when prolonged debate on staffing took place on the Floor. Subsequent discussion has taken place in committee or has been subject to more automatic decision-making procedures.

Passage of this measure (P.L. 65-314) effected a major change in clerk-hire procedures. It was a further step in institutionalization of the House: procedures became less personalized, more bureaucratized; decision making became somewhat more automatic—henceforth allowances and staff numbers would be changed, but within the new general procedural processes in effect for clerk-hire. In addition, the process of professionalization which has accelerated in recent years may be said to have begun. The establishment of a procedure which regulates staffing by subjecting it to the processes of an administrative bureaucracy, even if only for payment of salary, implicitly recognizes the need for professional assistance in handling the congressional function.

Shortly thereafter, in July 1919, the new 66th Congress debated and passed H.J. Res. (House Joint Resolution) 104[20] which confirmed the staffing provisions of the appropriation measure, and added two further constraints which have continued ever since: a limitation on staff numbers (two in 1919) and a statement that clerks were "subject to removal at any time . . . with or without cause"—thus emphasizing the personal nature of staffing provisions.

In 1924, H.R. 8262 (P.L. 68-136) raised allowances for clerk-hire to $4,000 per year. A new regulation setting a maximum salary of $3,300 per year for House staff was added without debate.[21] Congressman James Byrnes (D-S.C.), later Justice of the Supreme Court and Secretary of State, had been the only member of the committee to file a minority report: he opposed *any* raises. In the House, a number opposed the bill on similar grounds and stated opposition to increasing government expenditures. Some members—not of the economy bloc—opposed the bill because it "discriminated" against the House, allowing fewer clerks and smaller clerk-hire allowances than for the Senate.

> Mr. Blanton (D-Tex.): And, as a matter of fact, they (the Senate) do not have a bit more work to do than a Congressman.
>
> Mr. Madden (R-Ill.): Well, they say they have, and of course we cannot deny that.
>
> Mr. Blanton: I can.[22]

Tension between the two Chambers and a desire for equality, at least on the part of the House, are themes which run throughout clerk-hire proceedings. A recent House example is the way computerizing of information and data retrieval has been handled, with the prerogatives of the Committee on House Administration carefully guarded.[23]

By 1924, the seventy Senators who were not committee chairmen were entitled to four personal staff assistants: one clerk at $3,300 per annum, one at $1,940 per annum, one at $1,830 per annum, and one at $1,520. Approximately 90 percent of the Representatives had two clerks.[24] The House office allotment of $3,200 per year was, by FY 1924, actually a *basic* pay allotment; the $240 bonus for each clerk in effect gave Representatives who employed two clerks a gross allotment of $3,680.

The concept of "basic" pay—as set by law—plus percentage or dollar increases continued in use in the Senate until 1968[25] and in the House until the 1970 Reorganization Act. By 1970 the allotment quoted as "basic pay" was far removed from the actual dollar figure. Initially, the "basic pay" concept resulted, apparently, from the practice of adding incremental percentage increases to salaries. Actual pay was figured by adding several different percentages (reflecting different government pay raises) to the basic pay. In fact, it may be that the system was established as a logical consequence of pay legislation being written to grant a percentage of salary increase; during the Depression, when Federal salaries were lowered, a percentage system was also used.

Subsequently, the basic pay device was apparently supported by many as a means of understating the actual cost of Congressional activities. With a perception on the part of Congressmen that constituents may view office expenditures as unreasonable, a consequence is to make it difficult to obtain precise data on costs. It reflects a general uneasiness about Congressional support expenses and perhaps an ambivalence about the Congressional role in an increasingly complex technological society.

By 1970, when the House finally adopted an actual pay system (1968 in the Senate), there were approximately ten percentage increases to the basic salary, pay tables had to be sent to each office interpreting the salary structure, and the major justification seems to have been obfuscation.

During the Depression years the steady trend toward increased staffing halted, and between July 1, 1932, and March 31, 1935, reduced clerk-hire allotments were authorized.[26] The House was virtually unanimous that there was need for reduced allotments, but the legislation was clearly meant to be temporary.

With restoration of the pre-1932 clerk-hire authorizations in April 1935 pressure began to build for increased staffing. In 1935, proposals for additional clerks were rejected, but by 1939 the Chairman of the Committee on Accounts, Congressman Frank Boykin (D-Ala.), introduced the necessary authorizing legislation, H.R. 6205. As reported by his Committee on Accounts and approved by the House, H.R. 6205 raised the basic clerk-hire allowance and authorized employment of an additional clerk for the first time since 1893, increasing the office staff to three.[27]

Proponents of the 1939 increase, echoing those who in 1893 argued for a government allowance for clerk-hire, pointed to the large number of Congressmen paying clerk-hire expenses from their own personal funds. The need was apparently evident to a number of House members, and the enabling legislation removed a burden, as for many the additional employee was already on the personal payroll.[28]

In 1944, after acrimonious and complicated maneuvering, the clerk-hire allotment for each Representative was raised $3,000, to $9,500 per year, and the maximum salary payable was increased by $1,100 to $5,000 per year (basic).[29] The Committee on Accounts (and later, the Committee on House Administration) fixed the number of staff at five, as this was not covered by the bill.[30]

During debate, points which are by now familiar, appear. Staff increases were considered too expensive, or were opposed on procedural grounds (a typical strategy) such as, it was authorization legislation in an appropriations measure or there had been no hearing by the Rules Committee.

Those supporting the legislation cited ever-increasing workload, particularly noting heavy mail and casework (especially veterans casework) increases. Congressman Sabath, Chairman of the Rules Committee, argued strongly that his committee reported a rule so promptly because it recognized that "the majority wanted *action*" and added that he strongly supported additional clerk-hire. He had been thirty-eight years in the House, longer than any other member. When he came, three to six letters and sometimes a telegram came daily; now there were hundreds of letters daily.[31]

"...It is most difficult for Members to obtain clerks for salaries that we...can pay them. We were able formerly to get a stenographer for $125 or $150, but today you cannot get help for that salary. You cannot get a man who knows anything at all for less than $200, or $250 or $300 a month and a good man with legislative experience or college education commands from $400–$800 a month...."[32]

Representative John Cochran (D-Mo.) added,

"... The matter has been before the Committee on Accounts for two years. (It has been) under study by the Special Sub-committee chaired by (Alfred) Elliott (D) of California. (It) recommended more clerk-hire and Committee staff pay raises. (We) went to the Appropriations Committee and asked that it be included there...."[33]

Two amendments introduced but defeated provided that the member must swear an oath that the additional help was needed, and no relatives could be employed by the member on his payroll.

STAFFING: 1946 AND AFTER

In 1946, personal staffs, although the numbers had increased since 1893, were nevertheless relatively small—a maximum of five employees authorized in the House and an average of six employees in each Senate office. Committee staffs were attached to committee chairmen, and usually moved between committees as the chairman moved. Committee staff numbers had not increased perceptibly since World War I—in 1943 there were 190 Senate committee aides and 114 in the House.[34] There was agreement that few committees had expert staff. According to one estimate, only 4 of 76 committees had appointed experts.[35] Yet casework was increasing and legislation becoming more complex, as debates on the Floor of the House and Senate make clear. And Congressmen were well aware of heavy workloads carried by staff. A major effort had been building for some time to effect a number of Congressional reforms. The movement culminated in the appointment of the Joint Committee on the Organization of Congress in 1945 (79th Congress) and ultimately in the 1946 Legislative Reorganization Act.

The Hearings held by the Joint Committee and the debates on the passage of the 1946 Legislative Reorganization Act reflect concerns and staffing needs of Congressmen and Congressional observers. Congress had responded to centralized budget procedures and increased Bureau of the Budget staff in the executive branch, by permitting the Appropriations Committee to obtain an increased number of expert assistants for aid in analyzing budget requests.[36] There was a general feeling by 1946 that the executive branch had increased tremendously, and that the imbalance needed to be corrected. The committee staffing discussion focused on the need for technical competence, an information analysis capability independent of the executive branch, and a continuing permanent staff which was nonpartisan and impartial. The premises of the discussion (and of the subsequent evaluations of the Act's implementation) appear to have been influenced by both executive branch staffing arrangements and public administration views.[37]

The provisions in the reported bill, S. 2177, for a Director of Personnel to "certify" and "recommend" staff to the committees for appointment reflects this although the provision was struck by the Senate during debate. A Floor amendment, later defeated, provided that no professional committee aide could be employed by the executive branch for five years after leaving Congress.[38]

Discussion about personal staff focused on an increasing workload and again, the lack of expert assistants. Congressmen particularly wanted help with casework, although some were dubious that the responsibility of accompanying constituents to agencies could be delegated. Others wanted more legislative assistance.

The issues were whether to *increase* staff; what activities could be delegated; and how best to provide expert professionals who would bring technical competence to legislative decision making.

The role of staff and the place of minority staffing, although less prominent, were discussed. A number of precedents were set by the 1946 legislation, but present Congresses continue to be concerned with these issues. The flavor of the discussion can be caught from several statements. Senator Owen Brewster (R-Me.) told the Joint Committee,

> "I assume from what I read that there is no controversy as to the utterly inadequate staffing of the committees, about which I could testify at great length, both from experience in the House and also in the Senate."[39]

Representative Mike Monroney (D-Okla.), Vice Chairman of the Committee, agreed:

> "The fact that we have struggled along for 10, 15, or 20 years with incompetent committee assistants, that is, insufficient committee assistants, to say the least, would lead to the conclusion that the membership of Congress recognizes the crying need for this technical assistance."[40]

Congressman Robert Ramspeck (D-Ga.) added,

> "None of these committees has been adequately staffed. . . . The members of the staff (of the Agriculture Committee) are helpful, and attentive, and sincere, but they have no special training for what they are doing, they have no special knowledge of the problems of agriculture, they are merely a clerical staff."[41]

Problems of obtaining and analyzing information, particularly vis-à-vis the executive branch, were described. Congressman Thomas Lane (D-Mass.) argued,

"...As regularly as the clock strikes the hour, and enforced by that striking, every Member is reminded every day of two facts, as closely allied as the hands of the clock. The first is that the demands on his time are incessant and even oppressive, and that his sources of information and assistance inadequate....We must rely on the very representatives of the Federal agencies for information when we are trying to exercise our supervision of their carrying out of the policy we have prescribed...."[42]

Office needs also received attention, often with colorful description of problems.

Representative Ramspeck also told the Joint Committee:

"...My observation of Congress goes back to 1911—I was a clerk, and secretary to a member for a year....The member I was with did not attempt to maintain any office in his district. As I recall my experiences with him, the mail we received dealt largely with free seed, rural routes, Spanish War pensions and occasionally a letter about legislation....Of course, at that time, the government affected people directly in only a minor way....It was entirely a different job."[43]

During Floor debate, Congressman W. R. Poage (D-Tex.) made a particular plea for an adequate office staff:

"...But, important as Committee work is, it falls far short of covering all of a member's work. Unless a Congressman has an adequate and efficient office staff, it becomes impossible to do any work satisfactorily....In short, the work in our own offices is basic. This bill falls far short in caring for the ever-increasing load of individual office work—yet this work, particularly veterans' work—is sure to rapidly increase."[44]

Shortly after the passage of the 1946 Legislative Reorganization Act both academic[45] and congressional[46] assessments were carried out. One observer categorized committees in the 80th (1947–1948) Congress: twenty-two were "well staffed," there were eight "committees with weakness," and three committees were poorly staffed. This assessment included staff training, tenure, nonpartisan appointment, and responsiveness. Many committee staff remained after changes in a party control in 1947 and 1949, but majority staff often became minority aides. Professional expertise, as measured by education and previous experience of aides, had increased.[47]

Congressmen themselves were not so sanguine. Although a majority thought that there was a great improvement in staffing, there was uneasiness about staff increases, some distrust of expertise, and a recognition that truly nonpartisan staffs was a difficult—and perhaps illusory—provision. By 1948, ninety-three Senators had appointed AA's, but some Senators complained that unqualified personal secretaries had been promoted to that job. There was concern that some committee experts weren't well-trained and some committees weren't using the staffing authority. Congressman Monroney complained that some members didn't know how to manage staff: "The difficulty Congress had found is that, never having worked with well-trained staff members, they did not know how to use them for maximum benefit.''[48]

A survey conducted by Senator Homer Ferguson's (D-Mich.) AA indicated that many Senators and Representatives thought the reforms were successful. Of the twenty-two Senators responding, 32 percent considered the reforms successful, 54 percent felt them moderately successful, and 14 percent said they were unsuccessful; of fifty-eight Representatives, 46 percent said the reforms were successful, 41 percent considered them moderately successful, and 13 percent felt they were unsuccessful.[49] However, Congressmen wanted further change: more staff assistance for Members, better committee staff, minority staff, and attention to pay and benefits so that Congress could compete for highly qualified people.

By 1965, when another joint committee on the organization of the Congress was established, many of these issues were of central concern. During hearings both members and academics discussed more adequate minority committee staffing (proposing a variety of percentage allotment), appointment of committee staff (sole responsibility should not rest with the chairman), and the need for scientific and technical aides. Members asked for increased and more expert personal staff, proposing various remedies such as pool arrangements for handling work. The 1970 Legislative Reorganization Act, with a provision increasing the number of committee professionals to six (from four), eventually grew out of these efforts.

As reported by the House Rules Committee, the Legislative Reorganization Act contained a section (Title IV, Sec. 451) which authorized administrative assistants for Congressmen and raised the permissible salary to one equivalent to that paid Senate administrative assistants.[51] The section was opposed on economy and procedural grounds and was deleted during Floor debate. After lengthy discussion and parliamentary maneuvering, a Floor amendment to put all House employees on a gross per annum salary was accepted.

In fact, staffing provisions were a minor part of the Act, and the changes made were incremental, although many of the points are familiar. Some aspects of staff—the role of the minority, tensions resulting from increasing size and greater specialization—are recurrent themes over the years, because there is no procedure which satisfies all members and because there are honest disagreements over need for staff and differences as to staff role and activities.

Committee staffs have come of age since the 1946 Legislative Reorganization Act. Of particular note has been the creating and staffing of special purpose subcommittees by the Senate Rules and Administration, Post Office, Interstate and Foreign Commerce, and Government Operations Committees in the late 1940's and early 1950's. Often these subcommittees were abolished within one to four years of their creation. But by the late 1950's a trend began to emerge, especially on the Senate Judiciary Committee, whereby subcommittees with staffs were functioning on a permanent basis.

By 1975, the so-called investigative or temporary committee staff chiefly used to staff subcommittees was well entrenched. The growth of staffs continued as the new Senate and House Budget Committees became operational and other committees continued to increase their requests for more staff. Additional investigative staff members were requested by committees in each year's budgets.

A relationship appears to exist between the rapid growth in committee staffs, especially in the last twenty years, and increased constituent demands and more complex legislative agendas. In the House, committees employed 193 aides in 1947. Staffs had nearly doubled, to 375, ten years later, and by July, 1976 had increased about 700 percent, to 1,548. The major increase took place in the investigative staff (from 33 to 936 since 1947), which both houses, until recently, preferred to increase rather than permit the number of permanent staff positions on the committees to grow. In 1947 there were 290 Senate committee staff members. By 1965 this number had nearly doubled, and by 1976 there were over 1,500, about evenly distributed between professionals and clerks. Between 1960 and 1975 the number of permanent staff of Senate committees increased from 200 to 325; investigative staff rose from 297 to 1124. In the House, permanent staff increased from 244 to 634, investigative staff from 194 to 910. The proportion of professional to clerical staff on Senate committees has remained relatively stable: in 1960, 42 percent, and in 1975, 49 percent, of the permanent staff were professionals; in 1960, 59 percent, and in 1975, 54 percent, of the investigative staff were professionals. In contrast, in the House during the same period, the proportion of professionals on the permanent staff nearly doubled, from 37 percent to 63 percent.[52] (See Table 2, Appendix, for further detail on Senate and House committee staff changes.)

In Congresses subsequent to 1946, momentum built for personal staff increases, and in the House for recognition of the AA position. A number of bills relating to both were introduced and clerk-hire allowances were increased frequently.[53] But it was not until 1970, in the Legislative Reorganization Act of that year (P.L. 91–510; 84 Stat. 1140), that the professionalization of House personal aides received specific statutory recognition. Table 3 (Appendix) indicates increases in personal and committee staffs.

Which groups of staff have increased? It is difficult to pinpoint precisely the number of jobs in each category over the years. Congress has no formal personnel system and little specific data on job changes over time. And there are no published longitudinal surveys by scholars.[54]

Our figures show that much of the staff increase has occurred in the following areas:

- in the Senate, there has been a major increase in legislative aides on personal staffs;
- on both sides of the Hill, other professionals (particularly press aides) on personal staffs have also increased;
- on committees, an increase in investigative staff has occurred because

committees have been constrained by various statutes from adding to their permanent professional staff. In 1970, both houses, and in 1974, the House of Representatives, raised the allotted number of permanent professionals on committees. (See Table 3 for minority staff figures.)
- support agencies have increased numbers of professionals also;
- in the Senate, the new group of legislative aides, the personal committee staff, appointed since July, 1975 (pursuant to S. Res. 60) numbered 291 almost a year later.

There has been a large increase in the number of aides performing legislative work in Senate personal offices; some offices report an increase of as much as several hundred percent in the last few years. This increase in legislative aides accounts for 34 percent of the total increase in personal staff aides between 1960 and 1975. The number of press aides has increased: from 17 in 1960 to 123 by December, 1975. Other types of staff have increased also, both to assist legislative and press aides and to handle the routine work of the office.

Neither the Senate nor House personal offices generally keep data on casework, Federal projects work, or mail load. But from the records available, casework does not appear to have increased dramatically in recent years; rather, it seems to have peaked during the later years of the Vietnam war. Additional caseworkers who were apparently appointed earlier have been retained and their numbers have remained high. And there are now a number of office managers in Senate personal offices.

Legislative aides in House personal offices also increased, although not as precipitously as in the Senate. It is now more common to find several legislative aides in each office than was the case ten to fifteen years ago. If freshman offices are any measure (and we think they are) press aides and assistants are also far more prevalent.[55]

A number of the committee investigative aides, a group which has increased, have responsibilities which relate to the decision-making and policy function of the Congress.

Another group of aides active in legislative work are the S. Res. 60 staff in the Senate, the personal staff aides appointed by a Senator to assist on committee work. In March, 1976, there were 291, with most Senators taking advantage of this means to increase legislative staff. Committee chairmen and ranking minority members appoint them for assistance on their other committee assignments. Of those on the rolls on December 31, 1975, 43 percent were professionals.

STAFFING ALLOWANCES

The present allowances for staff assistance offer both opportunities and constraints. All Senators and Representatives may appoint personal office staff to assist them. In the Senate, the allotment is based on state population and in March, 1977, ranged from $449,063 for states with less than 2 million population, to $902,301 for states with over 21 million or more population (California). Any number of staff may be appointed, subject to salary limitations of $49,933 for the top employee, five employees at no more than $46,927 and the rest at no more than $27,221. These figures reflect the average 5 percent salary increase granted to Federal government employees in October, 1976 and the pay increases in early 1977 for Congressmen and presidential appointees, which resulted in higher pay ceilings for top executive and legislative branch employees. Senators and Representatives may increase their employees' salary if they wish, when government salary increases are granted, but it is not required. As in the House, each Senator's total salary allotment increases when government-wide increases occur (allotments increased in October 1976 but not in March 1977.) The limitations on pay to individual aides also increase whether or not aides actually receive a higher salary.

House districts are approximately equal in population, and every Representative receives $225,144 for clerk-hire. Representatives may appoint a maximum of eighteen employees. Only one personal staff aide may receive the maximum salary of $47,500. (Ceilings on both personal and committee staff salaries are tied to the pay of Senators and Representatives, currently $57,500, and to pay levels in the executive branch.)

In the House one-twelfth of the yearly allotment for clerk-hire must be used each month or it is lost; in the Senate unused monies may be carried over until the end of the year.

Congressmen also receive allowances for office operations; the allowances differ for each Chamber, but the basic format is similar.

In the Senate the average office staff was thirty-one in 1976, with a range from fourteen to seventy. Not all Senators use their full staff-salary allotment. In 1974, forty-one Senators turned back $30,000 of their allotment and thirty-four turned back more than 10 percent; nineteen of the thirty-four were committee chairmen or ranking minority members. One Senator, William Scott of Virginia, turned back $189,000, 42.5 percent of his clerk-hire allowance.[56] For some members of Congress, it is a matter of ideology that they do not use their full clerk-hire allowance.[57] For others, a portion is turned back because it is difficult to budget the allowance exactly. A number of Representatives and staff argue that it is impossible to employ the maximum number of staff authorized if salaries are high enough to attract competent people.

In the House, in December, 1975, the average staff size was 15.5 and 102 members hired the maximum number of employees, 18; 104 members (22 percent) used nearly all their clerk-hire allowance, and 93 percent had requested the additional monies (then provided) for a research assistant. The average salary on personal staffs was $13,731, with 50 offices employing an aide earning the pay ceiling. Figures are comparable for December, 1976, with an average of 15.7 employees per office, and average pay of $14,849.[58]

Committees are funded in two ways: Permanent staff are authorized by law, and inquiries and investigative staff are funded yearly through resolutions approved by the administration committees of each House. This latter category of staff is considered "temporary," but in fact, many of the aides have been on the committees for some time. Appropriations, and more recently, the Budget Committees have authorization for staff under separate measures; they are not required to use the yearly resolution procedure.

Minority staffing on committees has been a recurring issue. Although the 1946 Legislative Reorganization Act provided nonpartisan professional staff, committees, in fact, vary in their organizational structure; some committees regularly appoint minority staff. Many staffs are more responsive to a chairman than to junior or minority members. The 1970 Legislative Reorganization Act provisions for a minority staff "on request" recognized these variations.[59] The lack of adequate minority staff is one issue. The equitable treatment of minority staff is another; in some instances, lower salary ceilings are in effect for minority staff.[60] Minority Senators and Representatives often must wait longer than members of the majority to appoint staff. In February, 1977, the Senate approved a provision that one-third of non-administrative staff on each committee be assigned to the minority.[61]

Minority members want minority staff to develop policy alternatives, to gather information independently, and to work on strategy. To outside groups, minority staff often serve as a point of access to committee decision making. The minority draft questions for witnesses and design amendments. Majority staff often view themselves as the major "legislation writers," with minority staff included in decision making primarily when votes are needed or for reasons of legislative strategy. There *is* agreement that minority staff play an important informational role for Senators and Representatives of the minority party.

Minority party committee staffs in both houses supplement the work of committee and personal staffs and are somewhat larger than party staffs of the majority party. Although a number of observers have followed the public administration approach urging nonpartisan staffing, in fact, most Congressmen seem to agree that there is rarely a truly nonpartisan staff. We would expect party designation of staff to continue. Occasionally, staffing arrangements similar to those of the Budget Committees may be used: a core staff for all committee work, and a group of aides appointed by individual members.

Congressional staffs have grown for a number of reasons: more complicated and complex policy needs, a greater congressional workload, and, we believe, a greater interest on the part of Senators and Representatives in using the assistance of skilled experts. In our increasingly complex world, problems are perceived as interdependent, and legislative approval of governmental programs requires knowledge of the issues and an analytic capability with increased need for expert staff. Congress has emphasized oversight more (1946 and 1970 Legislative Reorganization Acts and the Congressional Budget and Impoundment Control Act of 1974); this too requires staff assistance. Although the number of bills passed has not increased, the complexity of the legislation has.[62]

On office workload, data are sketchy. Senators and Representatives report that the workload has increased and cite more telephone calls, letters, and requests for speeches and visits. A larger population, better educated, and more sophisticated, contacts Congressmen more frequently.

Finally, there appears to be more willingness on the part of Congressmen to appoint and ask assistance of experts. The increase in complex issues and complicated legislation has occurred in conjunction with the election of new Congressmen, who have used and expect to continue to use expert assistance. Our research indicates that high seniority Representatives, with long tenure, increase personal staffs only incrementally, and usually appoint fewer than the maximum allowed. Most of any additional staff increase is clerical support staff. In the House this may be related to control of committee staff, but it also appears to be a result of a role orientation and a view of staff which has not changed much during the Congressmen's years in Congress. On the other hand, less senior and more recently elected Representatives have added professionals as well when increasing staff.

These changes bring Congress both opportunities and problems. The distribution of staffing resources continues to be important; problems result from increased size and specialization. In the following chapters we turn to analysis of staff attributes and activities, as we begin to assess the staff role in the legislative process.

NOTES

1. Nelson W. Polsby, "The Institutionalization of the House of Representatives," *American Political Science Review* (62), 1968, 144–168, discusses institutionalization of the House.
2. Between 1971 and 1976 the Committee on House Administration set the amounts allowed for clerk-hire (i.e., employment of personal staff). In July 1976 this procedure was modified in the aftermath of Congressman Hays's resignation; the committee may only approve cost-of-living increases in the clerk-hire allowance pursuant to any such increases granted under the 1971 Federal Pay Comparability Act; any other changes must be approved by the full House (H. Res. [House Resolution] 1372, approved July 1, 1976).
3. See *Congressional Record,* May 21, 1975, debate on H.R. 6950, Legislative Branch Appropriations, FY 1976, H4488-H4507.
4. Debate on H.R. 6205, May 16, 1939. "...no one is compelled to use the authorization." *Congressional Record,* May 16, 1939, p. 5608.
5. See yearly appropriation measure, 1885 (FY 1886)–1946.
6. See House of Representatives *Hearings* on legislative appropriations and the appropriations laws. The Senate more usually appropriates monies for "administrative and clerical assistance" (see, for example, the Legislative Appropriations Bill, FY 1977

[P.L. 94–440]) but as recently as 1966 increased "clerk-hire" (Legislative Appropriations Act, 1967, 80 Stat. 357).

7. Legislative Appropriations Act, FY 1931 and FY 1942, for example.

8. 23 Stat. 390.

9. J. Res. No. 21, March 3, 1893. "...on or after April 1, 1893, each member and delegate of the House of Representatives of the United States may, on the first day of every month during the sessions of Congress, certify to the Clerk of the House of Representatives the amount which he has paid or agreed to pay for clerk-hire necessarily employed by him in the discharge of his official and representative duties during the previous month, and the amount so certified shall be paid by the Clerk out of the contingent fund of the House of Representatives on the 4th day of each month to the person or persons named in each of the said certificates so filed: provided . . . further . . . (the amount) does not apply to members who are Committee Chairmen entitled to a clerk under the rules. . . ."

10. *Congressional Record,* 52nd Congress, March 3, 1893, p. 2478.

11. Congressman George Tillman (D-S.C.), *Congressional Record,* 52nd Congress, p. 2477.

12. Similar uncertainty continues to surface occasionally regarding use of various office allowances, such as stationery. In 1976 House "cash-outs," the payment of some unused allowances in cash, were eliminated.

13. Pub. Res. (Public Resolution) No. 32, 53rd Congress, 1894.

14. 53rd Congress, 2nd Session, 1894. Legislative, Executive and Judicial Appropriations Bill, FY 1895. Passed July 31, 1894, 28 Stat. 167 (1894).

15. 54th Congress (1896) H. Res. 248. The flavor of the debate in these early years of clerk-hire is evident in the statement of Representative Joseph Wheeler (D-Ala.): "Mr. Speaker, I tremble for my country. (Cries of 'Oh!,' laughter, and loud and prolonged applause.) The impatient cries of 'vote,' 'vote' from the Republican side of this Chamber, which we have heard at every pause in this debate are suggestive of the frantic appeals for 'Votes,' 'Votes,' 'Votes' which we will hear from the Republican party next November.

"A vote for this Resolution is a flagrant violation of your pledges to the people, and a grave violation of your duty as their representatives.

"Mr. Speaker, if this is consummated, honest men from lake to Gulf, and from ocean to ocean will in thunder tones rebuke this atrocity. . . ." *(Congressional Record,* May 8, 1896, p. 4997.)

16. 55th Congress (1898), H.R. 10691: Deficiency Appropriations Bill. (55 Chap. 571, *U.S. Statutes at Large* (30 Stat. 652).

17. 57th Congress (1902), H. Res. 90.

18. By 1907 it was customary to have one staff member in Washington and one in the District. The House provided staff for committees as follows: two clerks at $3,000; thirty-two clerks at $2,000; ten clerks at $6 per day during the session.

19. H.R. 12633. The bill, as finally passed, did not contain this provision. Debated March 1, 1918, *Congressional Record.*

20. Pub. Res. No. 2 (41 Stat. 162).

21. The bill was part of the general post-war adjustment of salaries and pay scales. The

1923 Classification Act had covered only the executive branch. In March, 1928 a special joint committee had been established to consider the legislative branch. The bill, H.R. 8262, was a product of the recommendations of this committee. In the House, it was referred to the Special Committee on the Readjustment of Salaries of Officers and Employees of Congress. The bill attempted to adjust salaries on the Hill so that they were comparable to those in the executive branch. H.R. 8262 passed the House under suspension of the rules procedure.

22. *Congressional Record,* 68th Congress, 1st Session (Dec., 1923–June, 1924), p. 5755.

23. See the House debates on the Legislative Reorganization Act of 1970. In 1975 the House Administration Committee established an Ad Hoc Computer Sub-Committee reorganized in 1977 as the Policy Group on Information and Computers, under Representative Charles Rose (D-N.C.).

24. *Congressional Record,* April 7, 1924, p. 5752.

25. Legislative Appropriations Act, FY 1968 (P.L. 90–57; 81 Stat. 127).

26. July 1, 1932: 8-1/3 percent reduction to $4,583 per year; April 1, 1933: 15 percent reduction to $4,250 per year; February 1, 1934: 10 percent reduction to $4,500 per year; and July 1, 1934: 5 percent reduction to $4,750 per year.

27. P.L. 76–216, 76th Congress, 1st Session.

28. Congressman Adolph Sabath (D-Ill.) argued for passage by saying "When I was first elected, each member did all of his clerical work here on the Floor of the House, where he had his desk. We did not have an office building then, and if our work was unfinished at the day's end, we took it to our homes or hotels. . . . It is not exaggerating to say that today each Member's office handles twenty times the amount of mail that reached Members 30 years ago. . . ." (*Congressional Record,* p. 5608.)

29. H.R. 5590, P.L. 78–512, December 20, 1944, effective January 1, 1945.

30. Records of Disbursing Office, House of Representatives.

31. *Congressional Record,* p. 9000, Dec. 7, 1944.

32. *Congressional Record,* p. 9000, Dec. 7, 1944. According to Lewis A. Dexter, *The Sociology and Politics of Congress* (Chicago: Rand McNally, 1969), Sabath was not very powerful. Nevertheless, it is instructive he enters a strong plea.

33. *Congressional Record,* Dec. 7, 1944, p. 9003.

34. WOL Radio address by Representative Mike Monroney, April, 1943, in *The Organization of Congress, Symposium on Congress* by Members of Congress and Others, Committee Print of the Special Joint Committee on the Organization of Congress, 79th Congress, 1st Session, 1945, p. 148.

35. *Ibid.,* p. 90.

36. H. Res. 69, 78th Congress, passed February 11, 1943. Discussed in "The Legal Basis for the Increased Activities of the Budget Bureau" by Horace W. Wilkie, *The George Washington University Law Review,* April 1943, Vol. II, #3, pp. 282–285.

37. See *Symposium,* 1945; Joint Committee on the Organization of Congress, *Hearings,* 1945 and *Report,* March 4, 1946 (S. Rept. [Senate Report] 1011); Senate and House Debates on S. 2177, *Congressional Record,* 6344–6578 (portions) and 10039–10104.

38. *Congressional Record,* June 7, 1946, p. 6448 and June 10, 1946, p. 6564.

39. *Hearings,* Joint Committee, 1945, p. 228.

40. *Ibid.,* p. 231.

41. *Ibid.,* p. 306.

42. *Congressional Record,* July 1946, p. 10054.

43. *Hearings,* p. 295.

44. *Congressional Record,* July 1946, p. 10082.

45. Gladys Kammerer, *The Staffing of the Committees of Congress* (Lexington, Ky.: University of Kentucky Press, 1949); "The Record of Congress in Committee Staffing," *American Political Science Review,* XLV (1951), pp. 1126–1136; and Kenneth Kofmehl, *The Professional Staffs of Congress* (West Lafayette, Indiana: Purdue University Press, 1962).

46. Committee on Expenditures in the Executive Departments, U.S. Senate, *Hearings* on Evaluation of the Legislative Reorganization Act of 1946, 80th Congress, 2d Session, February, 1948, and *Hearings* on Evaluation of the Effects of Laws Enacted to Reorganize the Legislative Branch of the Government, 82nd Congress, 1st Session, June, 1951.

47. Kammerer, *Staffing of the Committees,* and "The Record of Congress."

48. *Hearings,* 1948, p. 84.

49. *Hearings,* 1951.

51. Relationship between Senate and House on the matter of staff salaries has a long history of unevenness and, in some cases, bitterness. The Senate, of course, adopted clerk-hire officially eight years before the House; indeed, the fact that the Senate had clerk-hire was an important argument in 1893 for the House doing the same. Over the years, House debate often refers to Senate emoluments, including staff allowances.

  Occasional efforts had been made to effect standardization between the two Houses. But clerk-hire changes have been made (1) incrementally and (2) piecemeal (in the House, often for only one particular incumbent of a staff job). It is probably this situation as much as anything (and certainly not maximizing decision making) which was responsible for the 1970 situation of salary hierarchy. Ranking maximum salary ceilings for employees from most to least: aides on House committees had the highest salary ceilings, followed by, in order, aides on Senate Committees, aides on Senators' personal staffs, and aides on Representatives' personal staffs. The Rules Committee Report stated bluntly that ". . .many a Representative's chief aide has been lured to a Senator's office . . ." due to the higher Senate salary limit, and called ". . .committee and personal staff differentials both inequitable and obnoxious." (H.Rept. 91–1215, p. 29.)

  After the percentage pay raise in October, 1976, applicable to all government employees, Senate aides' salary ceiling was again higher than House aides'; in July, 1977, some differences in pay ceilings between these four groups continued after the pay raise for high-level government employees in March, 1977.

52. The number of professional (4) and clerical (6) staff was established for all standing committees (except Appropriations) of both Senate and House by the Legislative Reorganization Act of 1946. The number of professional staff for these committees was increased to six by provisions of the Legislative Reorganization Act of 1970. The House increased the authorized number of staff to eighteen professional and twelve clerical employees, effective at the start of the 94th Congress (1975). Investigative staff for standing committees, and staff of special and select committees, are autho-

rized for a congressional session by committee funding resolutions passed by each House annually; the number of staff so authorized is not specified, and there is flexibility on numbers permitted within the budgeted amounts for salaries and expenses.

53. In the House, eight by 1955, ten by 1965, eighteen in March, 1975.

54. Data in the Legislative Appropriations Subcommittees' hearings report aggregate staff numbers only. Outside sources of information on staff, such as the *Congressional Staff Directory,* are incomplete. We have drawn primarily on records of the Senate and House Disbursing Offices for our analysis.

55. Burdette Loomis, "The Congressional Office as a Small (?) Business: Members of the Class of 1974 Set Up Shop." Paper presented at the American Political Science Association Annual Meeting, 1976.

56. Hearings Before the Legislative Appropriations Subcommittee on the Legislative Branch Appropriations, FY 1976, p. 1227; *Congressional Record,* June 9, 1975, S. 10121.

57. See Susan Webb Hammond, "Personal Staffs of Members of the U.S. House of Representatives," unpublished Ph.D. dissertation, The Johns Hopkins University, 1973, Chapter V.

58. Hearings on the Legislative Branch Appropriations, FY 1977, Legislative Appropriations Subcommittee, U.S. House of Representatives, February and March, 1976, p. 664, and Testimony (mimeo), Clerk of the House, in Hearings on the Legislative Branch Appropriations, FY 1978, March, 1977.

59. The provision was rescinded in the House in January, 1971, at the start of the 91st Congress. Subsequently, provisions were adopted allocating one-third of statutory staff to the minority (Rule XI[6]).

60. See, for example, *Congressional Record,* June 9, 1975, S. 10126. See also James C. Cleveland, "The Need for Increased Minority Staffing," in *We Propose: A Modern Congress,* Selected Proposals by the House Republican Task Force on Congressional Reform and Minority Staffing, Mary McInnis, ed. (New York: McGraw-Hill, 1966). However, in at least one case in the House in 1976, the highest paid staff aide was minority staff.

61. S. Res. 4, adopted February.

62. The number of pages per bill has increased (see Allan Schick, "Complex Policymaking in the U.S. Senate," in *Policy Analysis on Major Issues,* Commission on the Operation of the Senate, Committee Print, 1976); a measure using the number of titles per bill would probably show an increase also.

3. *Personal Attributes of Staff*

State legislatures, or, indeed, the parliaments of other countries, do not have legislative staffs similar in magnitude to those of the U.S. Congress, which is both unique and more organizationally developed (in degree of organizational specialization, for example) than other legislative bodies in staffing arrangements. Examination of the background of staff in the U.S. Senate and House of Representatives assists analysis of staff roles, functions, and impact. It appears that the recent changes in the size and professionalism of staffs in the Congress have contributed to an increased congressional capability for analysis, informed decision making, and response to constituent requests.

In this chapter an overview of staff characteristics is presented. This will enable us to delineate salient attributes and to sketch a "profile" of staff aides. The congressional community is made up of Members and a large number of their employees. As with congressional organization, communication patterns, and other factors including attributes of staff presumably affect congressional operations.

SENATE PERSONAL STAFF CHARACTERISTICS

The average Senate personal office professional staff member maintains his legal residence in his Senator's home state; earns over $24,000 a year; is male, 38.5 years old; and has a college degree with some graduate work. This characterization of the average staff member gives little indication, however, of the varied backgrounds of those working for Senators. A former administrative assistant notes that there is "no set formula of what a staff member should be. It depends on the Senator."

Table 4 (App.) indicates that nearly two-thirds of professional staff members whose legal residence could be determined maintained legal residence in their Senator's home state. It is not mandatory that a staff member be from the Senator's home state and maintain his legal residence there. "I am increasingly coming to the conclusion that they should not be from (home state)," notes an administrative assistant. "It is great to have a receptionist who is from (home state), but beyond her and three or four others it is not necessary to have (home state) people. In fact it is sometimes a detriment, in that they may sometimes have their own constituency." He goes on to point out the problems that home state staff members can cause him, the Senator, and the total office operation. (We discuss the pros and cons of home state staff recruitment in more detail in the next chapter.) Home state staff, who know local people and concerns, facilitate the representative function and constituent service activity. Ties to state interests are important, particularly when re-election is a consideration (as it is). On the other hand, home state staff may be harder to fire, may not know the ways of the Hill nor the substantive and technical aspects of legislative decision making (or may use valuable time in learning). And, home state aides may become potential opponents in a later campaign—although this is more usual in the House than in the Senate.

Another administrative assistant stated that a staff member should generally be from the home state. "Although I am beginning to question this practice; we have hired two staff members recently not from (home state) who have worked out very well."

Most of the professionals who work for Senators are under fifty years of age (Table 5) and nearly 50 percent are under thirty-five. Later in this chapter we present data on the age of House personal staff and committee professionals. Although there are some variations among the groups (committee aides are somewhat older, and House personal staff in top positions are slightly older than their Senate counterparts), the *average* aide in all groups is fairly young without extensive previous experience. We think this may be due to a number of factors. Among them are the lack of clearly defined career patterns, and particularly of tenure, on the Hill. The flat organizational structure of each Chamber and of the within-Chamber subgroups means that lines of responsibility and authority are often not clearly defined; fluidity of structure rewards initiative, but can often be confusing and demands continuous energy to define a place in the office organization. One Senate AA described the results of trying to divide responsibilities for legislative work among several legislative assistants. He found that no matter how even the workload was initially, aggressive and active LA's eventually carried heavier responsibilities: They actively sought new work, saw the Senator more, and handled more legislation, more briefings, and were involved in more strategy sessions. In another office, LA's gather around the desk of the Senator, each asking for some of his time; we are not sure about this, but presumably there is somewhat more attention paid to the more energetic (and perhaps louder) aides. These factors may be more easily handled when young, and for a brief tenure, than during a long career.

Other factors affecting age relate, we think, to role orientations of aides. Many aides look forward to having their achievements acknowledged by professionals beyond Capitol Hill. But the work of aides is, in general, anonymous. Aides' names are not on amendments or bills; aides usually do not ask questions in hearings, sign their own names to letters, or acknowledge co-authorship of speeches. For some aides, this role is congenial for several years, but not as a career. But do Congressmen want to hire very young aides? The answer is a qualified "yes." For some positions, Congressmen look for bright young aides with new ideas, but an expectation for short tenure; continuity and stability are achieved by longer tenure of top-level senior aides. Younger aides can be paid less, and staff allowances can be stretched further. We would also speculate that Congressmen recognize the somewhat frenetic schedule of Hill life and accept a relatively high turnover in some jobs as a quid pro quo for continuity and experience in others, but require competence throughout.

Professional staff members were asked to respond to a question asking about their expectations of the age of the individual who would replace them. Those responding to this series of questions tended to prefer people under thirty-five, although they did not exclude those under fifty. How well do the staff expectations for attributes of professionals compare with the population of professionals now working in the Senate? In the responding population, five of ten staff members felt that the person replacing them should be between twenty and thirty-five years old. Over 45 percent of the responding total population are in this age group. Almost one-quarter of the staff members responding had a preference for someone between thirty-six and fifty to replace them; and in this same population, 38.4 percent are between thirty-six and fifty. Finally, 12.2 percent of the respondents were between fifty-one and sixty-five, but only one respondent expected that his replacement would be in this same age category. The younger a staff member, the more likely he is to prefer a replacement within his own age category. Among respondents, eight of ten of which are male, one-fifth felt that their replacement should be male, and 4.3 percent suggested a female replacement.

Over three-quarters of the population studied (Table 6) are male.[1] Further analysis reveals that of those staff members earning over $20,000 per year, males are represented in a greater proportion than would be expected if the sex of the staff member were of no significance. Only nine of eighty-seven of all staff earning over $30,000 per year are female. Of those earning between $16,000 and $20,000, over half are female. In the high-status occupational positions, such as administrative assistant, only three are female, and among the legislative assistants, eighty-two of ninety-two are male. Females are found most often in the following positions: executive secretary, eighteen of twenty-four; secretary, twelve of thirteen; personal secretary, twenty-three of twenty-four; and assistant clerk, seven of ten.

Where education level could be determined among the staff population, 289 of 470 have either a Bachelor of Science or a Bachelor of Arts degree (see Table 8, Appendix). Nearly all males, 221 of 235, and just under half of the females, 20 of 54, had obtained a B.A. or B.S. Only fourteen of the staff population have no college experience, and another twenty-seven have had college experience but did not receive a degree. Of all those not attending college, twelve of fourteen were female staff members. Nearly half, fifteen of thirty-four, of those having only some college were females. Nearly 15 percent of the staff population studied have law degrees and fourteen staff have doctorates. Only four of seventy-one lawyers were female, nearly all those having Master's degrees were male sixty-four of sixty-eight, and no female had a Ph.D. Thus, we can conclude that in proportion to their numbers, the female professional staff members hold fewer college degrees, earn less, and are found in positions of lower status than males.

These staffing patterns are similar to those in the House. Politics has been by and large dominated by men, and Capitol Hill is no exception. In September, 1976, the Senate approved a resolution (S. Res. 534) which encouraged the hiring of women and minorities and prohibited discrimination. Some offices are establishing a pay structure and position classification system based on job content and employee qualifications. We think the staffing patterns will change as women acquire specialized training and as society's expectations change.

Professional staff members on personal staffs are well paid. During the 92nd Congress, the upper limit on what staff members can be paid was over $36,000. Within the staff professional population, sixty-four (13.6 per cent) individuals received over $30,000 per year and ninety-six (20.4 percent) received between $24,000 and $29,999.[2]

Job titles[3] are not the best description of staff members' activities, but they do give a general indication of the type of jobs being performed. Within the total population of 470, forty-nine different job titles are used. "Legislative assistant" is the most common job title, closely followed by "administrative assistant." Other commonly used titles are: executive assistant, press secretary, press assistant, executive secretary, personal secretary, and special assistant.

Democrats within the staff population (Table 7) tend to hold a slightly more intense party preference than Republicans. Staff members responding to the question, "What is your political party preference?" generally tended to specify a strong preference for a particular party. Nearly 90 percent of the Democrats and 80 percent of Republicans specified that they were at least strong partisans.

Most Senate staff members identify with the same party as their Senator, although there is no absolute norm or rule that a staff member has to be a member of the same party as the Senator. Conflicting views were held by two administrative assistants who were interviewed about party affiliation of staff members. One felt it was important that a staff member be of the Senator's party, and the other noted that if a staff member is comfortable with the Senator's views it makes no difference which party he identifies with. (This is similar to the view expressed by a committee aide, who said, "It's *ideology* that's important.") But nearly five of ten staff members responding felt their replacement should be of the same political party as the Senator. And party affiliation is by far the most intensely held expectation of all attributes.

A subsample of the responding population (see Appendix) noted that their parents were fairly strongly identified with party. Their fathers were perceived as being attached slightly more to party than their mothers, although it should be noted that Republican mothers are perceived as being more intensely identified with party than the fathers of either party.

In comparing the strength of party preference of the parents of staff against the Senate staff members themselves (see Table 7), it was found that staff members express a stronger party preference.

Senate staff belong to both partisan and nonpartisan Capitol Hill organizations. Three types of organization were identified. Partisan organizations such as the Burro Club (male House Democrats), the Bull Elephants (male Republicans), RAMS, and the Monday Morning Meeting serve their members through political objectives. Nonpartisan clubs—the Association of Administrative Assistants and Secretaries and the Senate Staff Club (to which any staff aide may belong)— serve social and maintenance functions. State societies serve both social and political functions. Nonpartisan clubs are by far the most popular among staff professionals on Capitol Hill (membership mentioned by 111 respondents). Partisan and state organizational memberships were mentioned only by a small percentage of the staff population.

What are the political orientations of Senate professional staff members? A two-dimensional model was used to describe the political orientations of a subpopulation of forty-seven staff members.[4] Each staff member was asked to rank seven terminal values in order from most to least important to them.[5] Two of these terminal values, freedom and equality, represented their political orientation or ideology.[6]

To conceptualize the dimensions of political ideology, picture a square set on one of its sides. The examples of typical groups and individuals are taken from Rokeach's study of political values. The upper-left corner represents those staff members rating both freedom and equality highly, such as liberal Democrats, socialists, and humanists; the upper-right corner represents those ranking freedom low and equality high, such as Lenin, "Stalinist or Mao-type Communism";[7] the bottom right represents those ranking freedom and equality low, such as Hitler, fascists, and members of the Ku Klux Klan; and the bottom left represents those ranking freedom high and equality low such as Barry Goldwater and followers of Ayn Rand.[8]

The staff population tended to cluster on the capitalist–liberal Democrat side of the square. The three immediate clusters around the capitalist corner were made up of professional staff members working for conservative Republican Senators. The clusters surrounding the liberal Democrat corner were not as clearly delineated, but they tended to be made up of staff from the generally recognized liberal Senate offices. Thus, professional staff members tend to have political ideologies not too different from the Senators for whom they work.

A staff member's role behavior and experience over the long term in a Senate office has effects on his attitudes. Staff apparently become what they do and in a sense "unbecome" what they do not do.[8] Although evidence was not gathered in detail for this process, a few observations can be made.

The subpopulation was asked to note changes in their attitudes toward political party, democracy, and the effectiveness of Congress since they had been a Senate or congressional staff member. Their political party preference changed very little. But well over half of the subpopulation (83 percent) noted at least some change in their understanding of the effectiveness of Congress.

"My perceptions and attitudes have changed since I have been on the Hill. I came here thinking that all Democratic Senators got together and decided what they wanted. They don't do that," states a senior staff professional. He goes on to point out that, "I am [both] more and less partisan since arriving. I feel that the party is very important . . . but there are guys with you on an issue that you despise and against you are really nice individuals."

Personality characteristics of Senate staffers are important indicators of their behavior and enduring attributes. In an effort to determine the personality and group-role types of Senate staff professionals, the Bales "Interpersonal Ratings Form" was self-administered by a subpopulation of Senate personal professional staff members.[9]

The Bales "Interpersonal Rating Form" allows inferences to be made about group role and personality from behavior. Bales's assumptions about group process, upon which his model is based, are particularly applicable to Senate office organizations. Bales assumes that the group or office "spends some significant part of its time in trying to accomplish some task conformity with expectations of an external authority,"[10] and it "has some authority-oriented task as a part of its regular activity."[11]

The various types of group roles and their value-directions are represented by a three-dimensional spatial model of the population's position in the evaluative space. The three dimensions are upward–downward; positive–negative; and forward–backward.

The clustering of staff members in or near one quadrant on all three plottings is somewhat surprising. This is especially noticeable in the upward–downward by positive–negative space. Also when the listing of group roles and value-directions is inspected, a predominance of the upward–positive–forward (UPF) type is found. Only nine of the possible twenty-six personality types are found in the Senate staff population, and all these are positively correlated with UPF except one.[12] When the polarities of the positive–negative dimension are compared, positive is strongly associated with each staff member; no negatives are found in the population. Thus, a "General positive" characterizes the staff population. Along the upward–downward dimension, upward is also very strong among staff members. There is no significant number of downwards. Forward (F), also, is a fairly common dimension among the population. Only five backwards, F's polar opposite, are found and of these three are significant. A description of a pure UPF will be presented below, but it should be remembered that UPF types have been found to vary from the following description.

Bales has found that the UPF, the typical Senate professional staffer, is a conservative task leader[13] and "seems to identify himself with a good image of authority."[14] He sees himself as showing a high interest in group tasks and is valuable for logical tasks. "Of all the directional types, the UPF member is the most generally prone to say that he likes others, and to deny disliking them."[15] The typical staff person rates high on leadership and on total interaction initiated. The UPF person identifies with the "source of authority or legitimacy" in a group.[17]

> The UPF type is an inspirational leader, but on behalf of existing authority. This apparently is what most people mean by "leadership," and many people look for it. The "great white father" and the "great good mother" are UPF sterotypes.[18]

Finally, the typical staff person may test high on the additional traits of persistence, activeness, dominance, sophistication, high social status, and social participation—traits associated with the UPF personality.

And many of these traits do characterize professional staff members. They have a rich educational background and are paid fairly well. Both of these facts reflect high social status. Also, professional staff are members of a broad range of organizations on and off Capitol Hill, and the nature of their job demands active interchange with many policy groups.[19]

"It is most important that a staff member show initiative. He must be able to initiate legislation, handle problems. . ." states a professional staff member. The basic ingredients of the traits of leadership and high initiation of interaction are noted in this characterization. Another staff member, in a description of staff attributes, identifies group authority and legitimacy as important: "But loyalty is very important—if you don't like your boss and aren't content working with the rest of the staff you should leave, unless—if you don't like your boss—you don't mind prostituting yourself."

Thus, Senate professional personal staff members can be said to have a "core" personality type: conservative task leader. We would expect that this would typically describe House personal staff and congressional committee aides also.

HOUSE PERSONAL STAFF CHARACTERISTICS

House personal staff attributes are similar to those identified for the Senate. Although there are differences, the similarities are striking.

Most House offices, 84 percent of the sample, are headed by an administrative assistant (AA). In all offices, no matter how loosely organized, the AA's were regarded as the staff director. The AA continues to be a generalist, whether measured by job activity or by education and training.

Of all 92nd Congress AA's listed in the biographical section of the *Congressional Staff Directory, 1972,*[20] 9.8 percent had never attended college; 13.6 percent had some college; 41.1 percent held Bachelor's degrees; 14.7 percent had Master's degrees; 18.5 percent had law degrees; and 2.3 percent had Ph.D.

degrees. (See Table 8, Appendix.) The median age of the House AA is forty-one years, although they may be as young as twenty-seven or nearing retirement at sixty-five; 59 percent are forty or more. Twenty-three percent of the AA's are lawyers, 23 percent trained as political scientists, and 18 percent are journalists.

Older AA's are less likely to have formal educational training than the younger AA's. All AA's thirty years old or less had college degrees and 50 percent held Master's or law degrees. All of the AA's in the sample who had not finished college were over forty-five. Of the AA's over 40, 36 percent held a college degree; 36 percent held Master's or law degrees. Older staff may not have attended or finished college due to the Depression or World War II; this appears to be the pattern for both the sample and for others whose biographies are listed in the *Congressional Staff Directory*.

Administrative assistants tend to be older than legislative assistants. Legislative assistants are, in turn, older than other staff professionals, although, as with other professionals, a large majority are thirty or younger (see Table 5, Appendix).

One explanation for age differences in staff positions is that Congressmen often recruit close campaign workers as AA's. They are somewhat older than other staff professionals when appointed. And, once in Washington, the AA's may stay on with their bosses, although Congressmen with many years seniority sometimes need to recruit a replacement.

A majority of the staff members, 55 percent, in the survey had been active in politics prior to coming to the Hill. For some this meant working in recent Presidential campaigns. A large minority, 40 percent including a majority of the AA's, were directly involved in some aspect of the Congressman's most recent congressional campaign. A growing number of younger staff people have been recruited after college study of political science—with perhaps some direct involvement in political activity as part of their study. Another minority, not necessarily exclusive of those involved in campaigning, have been active in local party matters or college political clubs.

Because AA's generally have the closest district ties and the closest personal ties to the Congressmen, it is interesting to look at their involvement in their district's politics. Of the AA's, 59 percent had worked in district or state politics prior to Hill employment; indeed, in many cases, it was because of this involvement that the AA was invited to Washington as an employee. Most AA's are involved in district politics; they may spend several months in the district at congressional election time, often on the campaign staff.

Like their bosses, professional staff assistants do not often have executive branch experience. In 29 percent of the offices surveyed, no staff member had had any experience in any branch of the Federal government. Of the aides, 12 percent had served in positions in state government, one having served on a state legislature staff; 25 percent had held jobs in the executive branch of the Federal government, 33 percent of these positions having been in legislative liaison; 8 percent had worked on staffs in other congressional offices. It would appear that staff jobs are filled primarily by men and women with a legislative and local orientation, reflecting to a great degree the experiences of their bosses.

Staff backgrounds vary considerably, and Congressmen view staff positions as requiring different kinds of training, experience, and expertise. Many expect differing lengths of tenure also.

Typically, the administrative assistant has worked with the Congressman he serves in a first campaign, and joined the staff upon the member's election. Of the AA's in the sample, 73 percent came to the Hill with the Congressman at the time of his first term.[21] Although there is, of course, some turnover in staff among Representatives who have been in Congress for some time, nevertheless, a large proportion of the AA's have remained with their bosses.

When Congressmen replace administrative assistants, they may promote a staff aide who has already served on the staff over a period of years, or in some cases, a personal friend or professional acquaintance is hired. Of AA's who were replacements, six, or 33 percent, had previously been legislative assistants in the office; 50 percent had come to know the Congressman in the course of his congressional duty, either in his work with the executive branch or through local politics. The remainder were appointed after a typical recruitment search.

As recently as 1960, few members of the House had LA's, although staff aides performed some of the duties now assigned to LA's. Ten years later, in 1971–1972, a majority of House offices, 64 percent of the offices surveyed, employed LA's. For the 95th Congress (1977) the percentage would be even higher. There also appears to be a trend to divide the legislative workload among two, or even more, legislative assistants, as Senators do. This reflects the growing specialization of House staff, the increasing workload, and what appears to be an emphasis on legislative activities by more Congressmen. Legislative assistants are recruited on the basis of skill, training, and background. In some instances, they are recruited from within the staff, but they have generally had job experience or educational training which gives them competence in the subject matter and expertise in the legislative process. They tend to be issue-oriented, often concerned about national priorities, and are, quite naturally, also oriented toward finding legislative solutions to problems.

As might be expected, the LA position, which has recently come into its own as a result of increased specialization, requires more training, and LA's are trained more specifically for a legislative function. Of the LA's in the sample, 92 percent (eleven of twelve) of those under thirty held B.A. degrees; 33 percent held law degrees; one LA was still attending college but was a senior in his final semester. Of the LA's over forty, one held an M.A. in political science; one held a B.A. degree but had no further formal educational training; and one had some college. All of the remaining LA's, aged thirty to forty, had some graduate work, and two of the three held a graduate degree (M.A. or law).

A large majority of legislative assistants, 73 percent, hold degrees in law or political science. Although they are younger than AA's, their training is more directly related to law and/or the congressional function. Of those surveyed, 39 percent were trained in political science (25 percent of these held graduate political science degrees); 28 percent held law degrees; 11 percent (two) were trained as journalists; 22 percent (three) were trained in other fields. Training increasingly appears to have a political science or legal orientation, either from formal education or previous work experience. When the prior jobs of legislative assistants trained in fields other than law or political science are considered, 90 percent of all legislative assistants bring knowledge of congressional processes and function to their jobs.

A number of staff professionals have a journalism background. Many AA's, especially, have majored in journalism. These professionals may perform some press duties, but are not designated "press assistant" and hence are not included in the press group analysis. Aides designated as "press assistants" often have specific expertise in media work, with journalism training and prior experience in radio, TV, or newspaper work. Of the four press assistants in the offices surveyed, two were journalism majors and one majored in English. All had worked in journalism prior to their present positions. In one other office, a lower-level staffer who assisted the AA in press work also majored in journalism in college and had worked in radio and TV.

Four offices, 16 percent of the sample, hired research assistants who perform a variety of research duties, such as collecting material for a speech or working on issues which may eventually result in legislation. All the research assistants held college degrees. Several were engaged in graduate training or expected to attend graduate school in the future. During the 92nd Congress, research assistants were lower-level professionals often appointed to a first job at relatively low salaries. This changed somewhat in the 93rd Congress when a specific provision was approved providing for appointment of research assistants at a salary considerably higher than that of a number of LA's.

For professional aides other than the AA or the LA, the B.A. is ordinarily the only professional degree necessary. Of the staff members surveyed, only one professional did not hold a college degree, although most did not hold degrees beyond the Bachelor's. In addition to degrees completed, a number of staff assistants in the House are currently attending law or graduate school.

In some congressional offices, an office manager shares supervisory responsibility with the AA. The office manager hires and supervises secretarial personnel, overseeing daily workloads and taking responsibility for much of the mail and the everyday work flow. In 23 percent of the House offices with AA's, there is an "office manager" or "executive secretary" performing these activities. Occasionally, the Congressman's personal secretary acts in this capacity. Office managers are usually women with a number of years' experience on the Hill in a variety of positions.[22] Often she has worked for several different Representatives. She has begun as a secretary, usually has handled casework, and has wide contacts among staff in both the executive and legislative branches. She brings continuity, judgment, and often good political sense to the office staff. Because she has handled a variety of assignments, she is particularly helpful in supervising younger secretarial staff. A staff organized this way is similar to committee staffs where a distinction is made between clerical and professional staff. Professional staffs are headed by a professional supervisor and clerical staff aides are headed by a clerical supervisor, and much of the coordination occurs at the supervisory level.

The percentage of women on House personal staffs has remained fairly constant, 65 to 70 percent, in recent years. As staffs have increased, the number of women and men employed has increased at a constant ratio (see Table 6, footnote d). The proportion of women on staffs does not appear to vary significantly by party; in 1971 in the offices surveyed, women comprised 72% of the staff of Republican Representatives and 70% of the staff of Democratic Representatives.

The significant factor, however, in assessing the role and function of the professional staff is the position Hill women in both House and Senate occupy. The number of women in professional positions drop sharply. And a woman professional may be expected to handle typing and routine office chores which would not be expected of a man holding the same position. For instance, Trevor Armbrister, Senator Donald Riegle's (D-Mich.) assistant in writing *O Congress*, inadvertently alludes to this dual role when, in his Foreword, he graciously thanks the then-Representative's female legislative and Federal projects assistants for devoting "evenings and weekends to typing the final manuscript."[23] Both are mentioned later in the text in connection with their professional duties.

Of the AA's in the sample, five, 23 percent of the total, were women. Once women attain AA rank, a majority have pay and duties similar to those of their male colleagues. However, the route to the AA position generally differs: The secretarial route was used by four of the five women AA's.

The situation is somewhat different at lower professional levels. Of the eighteen LA's, four were women. They had duties generally comparable to those of men LA's. They were paid less, but they were also younger and had fewer graduate degrees. They did, however, have more pertinent prior work experience than men LA's. All the professional office managers and executive secretaries in the offices surveyed had started as staff secretaries.[24]

COMMITTEE STAFFS

A survey of committee staff professionals enables us to draw a profile of these aides. Many are young. A number expect to move off the Hill to pursue careers elsewhere. However, most bring specific skills and training to their Hill jobs. A great many aides have an extensive, and often impressive, background in executive departments or in related groups of a policy subsystem.

Although Hill contacts with prospective employees are often haphazard, hiring is in most instances based quite specifically on training and skill—more so, it appears, than in the often more generalist personal staff jobs. This does vary by committee, and not all aides view their staffs as competent and well-trained professionals. One Senate aide told us, ". . . try and present a true picture of the legislation in review. Pie in the sky? [We] need a new hiring system . . . less patronage, less nepotism."

It is not always possible to trace overlapping staff jobs. For example, aides on a committee staff may actually serve as legislative aides to one Senator and work on both committee and noncommittee matters. Spontaneous responses indicated a number of instances where this occurs. The situation is more frequent in the Senate (from which all of the spontaneous responses came) and seems to result from earlier Senatorial control of committee staff and more flexible staffing arrangements. (We discuss this more fully later.)

In general, committee staff aides are relatively young, with specific training either by education or previous jobs, and less "local" than their counterparts on personal staffs.

Although the modal age of committee professionals is thirty-one, age of individual aides varies considerably. Five aides responding were twenty-three, the minimum age reported. One aide was sixty-eight, the maximum age reported. An occasional older aide can be identified in staff biographies found in the *Congressional Staff Directory*. Average committee staff age is forty. Table 5 explicates these data more fully, and also compares House and Senate standing committees. The major difference evident is that House staffs are somewhat older (average age, 42.9 years) than Senate staffs (average age, 37.8 years), with far fewer professional aides under thirty or even under forty.

Most committee aides are legal residents of Maryland, Virginia, or the District of Columbia—jurisdictions "local" to Capitol Hill. Although a number of aides have initially been recruited from the home states of appointing Senators and Representatives, they apparently do not continue home state ties, at least for purposes of legal residence. This is in contrast to personal staff aides, many of whom keep local ties, including legal residence, in their home states.

The difference may be an indication of committee aides' careers and professional interests. It also may reflect differing recruitment patterns. Committee aides are more often recruited from other government jobs in Washington; personal staff are somewhat more likely to be recruited through home state ties. House committee staff are somewhat more "local" than aides in the Senate (see Table 4).

Committee aides are highly trained specialists. Law is the predominant field, and nearly half of all committee professionals hold legal degrees. Most committee professionals completed college; although some aides do not hold college degrees, the percentage is lower than for either Senate or House personal staff.

Some interesting variations in educational training of House and Senate committee aides are evident from the data in Table 8. Eight percent more Senate aides are lawyers; 5.5 percent more House aides hold doctorates. Overall, more staff of Senate committees than of House committees hold ad-

vanced degrees. Fewer Senate aides have no degrees. Staff of the joint committees are the most highly trained: 50 percent are lawyers; 62.6 hold degrees
beyond the Master's level; all aides have at least a Bachelor's degree.

These data confirm what a number of Capitol Hill aides and observers have
long claimed: that Senate committee staff are somewhat more highly trained than
their House counterparts. The impact of these differences on legislative outputs is
not clear. Senate aides are also younger, and it may be that expertise through
training is balanced by experience gained on the job. Certainly young Senate
aides, both committee and personal, are heavily involved in policy work. It may
be that they spend more time on legislative work which requires some technical
background and that House aides proportionately spend more time on other types
of legislative work, or on nonlegislative work such as Federal projects assistance
and political advising.

At the professional level, men hold most committee staff jobs (see Table 6).
The House committees employ fewer women in professional positions than do
Senate committees; and there are fewer women professionals on committees than
on either House (31 percent) or Senate (23 percent) personal staffs. We suspect
this may be changing slowly.

The data on party preference, and its intensity, confirm that the Hill climate is
indeed a partisan one, where aides indeed hold a party preference, and where most
aides hold that preference strongly. And not surprisingly, that partisan milieu is
weighted toward the Democrats, the majority party (see Table 7). Senate committee staff are somewhat more partisan (in the sense of party preference) than
the House, and both are more partisan than joint committee staff. The Senate also
is the most Democratic, and more Senate aides hold their party preference "very
strongly." The party preference responses differ from the way staff view their
partisanship as aides: 59.8 percent report that they serve on a majority staff, 17
percent report serving in minority staff positions, and 23.2 percent serve on
nonpartisan staffs. Nonpartisan staffs have, apparently, a majority of Democratic
identifiers, a not unexpected finding. One aide pointed out something we observed in some personal staffs as well, that "party is not as important as political
philosophy."

A far greater proportion of committee aides, as compared to personal staff,
have held executive branch jobs prior to their Hill appointment. Some aides
move back and forth between the executive and legislative branches; others move
among various jobs on the Hill. Both types of career patterns are more usual for
committee than for personal staff (see Table 9).

Of the committee aides responding, 35 percent had moved to their present
committee job directly from the executive branch, and executive branch work is
the most usual path to committee appointment. Committee aides report working
as attorneys in executive branch agencies, as investigative agents, foreign service
officers, economists, and budget officers. A few have worked in executive–
legislative liaison positions. A typical career pattern was reported by a committee
aide who had worked in research and development in a defense-related corpora-

tion, moved to a civilian position in the Defense Department, and then worked for two different congressional committees. Another staffer worked first for a Federal agency, then for a committee, moved back to the Federal agency in a higher position, and subsequently went to a different committee. Of all committee aides responding, 44 percent have worked in the executive branch at some point in their careers.

The second job most frequently held prior to appointment to a committee position is on the personal staff of a Senator or Representative. Some aides also move between committees and some between the two Houses. One aide noted needed staff characteristics: "This is no place to indulge in an ego trip. Everything is done in the Member's name and the most effective staff personnel are those who generally do not make headlines."

The career patterns, as well as the training and expertise reflected in the data, may be a result of the specialized and often technical needs of committees. The recruitment patterns (see Chapter 4, below) are similar to those for personal aides. "Who knows whom" is very often important, as is the impact of chairmen and ranking members.

CONCLUSION

Staffing has become more institutionalized, and the increase in allowances has contributed to the attractiveness of top slots as a career post. Aides are young, with Senate aides younger than House aides and with some patterned variations for different jobs. Aides generally have had specialized training; this is particularly evident for staff in specific legislative jobs. Aides are partisan, and often hold their party preferences strongly. However, in the world of Capitol Hill, with bargaining, negotiation, and compromise important decision-making processes, party preference is balanced by typical personality characteristics of social participation and conservative task orientation. And much of the work of policy formulation is nonpartisan or bipartisan, with cooperation across party lines apparently increasing. Other findings indicate that:

- aides tend to share the liberal or conservative attitudes of their bosses;
- personal staff are often from the home state of the members they work for;
- young persons occupy many staff positions;
- females are underrepresented in professional positions;
- staffers have strong party preferences;
- staff have a "general" personality type; and
- staffers are highly educated.

Knowing the attributes of staff will help in determining the impact they make and the reasons they act as they do.

The comments of both Congressmen and staff indicate overwhelmingly that personalization of staffing continues on the Hill. Prized qualities include personal loyalty and ''ability to think along the same lines as the boss.'' Congressmen are demanding more expertise and technical skills, but the staff people reflect by and large their bosses' role behavior: on personal staffs, an expert generalist in a personalized job situation, and on committees, an expert, perhaps a technician, but also most usually in a personalized job situation.

NOTES

1. Males tended to respond to the general questionnaire at a slightly higher rate than would be expected. One reason for this may be the low number of secretaries, twenty-three of sixty-six, responding.

2. With pay increases and the executive pay raise, the ceiling as of July, 1977 was $49,933; one aide could be paid this amount. The ceiling in the House was $47,500.

3. Job titles are taken from U.S. Senate, *Report of the Secretary of the Senate,* 92nd Congress, 1st Session, August 6, 1971 (Washington, D.C.: Government Printing Office, 1971), pp. 25–82.

4. Milton Rokeach has hypothesized that the two terminal values, freedom and equality, are the two basic dimensions of political ideology. He partially validates these claims through a content analysis of writings from the four corners of political ideology. Milton Rokeach, *Beliefs, Attitudes, and Values* (San Francisco: Jossey-Bass, 1970), pp. 171–172. Also see his *The Nature of Human Values* (New York: Free Press, 1973).

5. The terminal values were selected from the eighteen-terminal-value section of the Rokeach Value Survey, distributed by Halgren Tests. A shorter, seven-value version of the Survey was used. The terminal values that the staff members ranked were: a sense of accomplishment, a world at peace, equality, freedom, national security, salvation, and wisdom. See Parrott, American Psychological Association Convention, *Proceedings,* 1970, pp. 447–448.

6. A partial test for internal validity of this conception of political ideology within the subpopulation was made. Freedom and equality loaded on different factors within a three-dimensional space after a factor analysis utilizing the Varimax method was performed.

7. Rokeach, *Beliefs,* p. 171.

8. Rokeach, *Beliefs,* p. 171.

8. Daniel Katz and Robert L. Kahn, *The Social Psychology of Organizations* (New York: Wiley, 1966), p. 188.

9. A slightly modified version of the Interpersonal Ratings, Form A, was used. All questions of Form A were used except in the case of question 16. Form B, question 16, was substituted for question 16 on Form A. Robert F. Bales, *Personality and Interpersonal Behavior* (New York: Holt, Rinehart and Winston, 1970), pp. 3–21. For a detailed discussion of the logic, mathematics, and framework upon which the Form is based, Bales's text should be consulted.

10. Bales, pp. 5–6.

11. *Ibid.*, p. 7. Bales's model is based on a factor analysis of 143 value-statements (p. 497). He replaces the "mathematical model of factor analysis with a verbal model consisting of a limited number of classes" (p. 458). His verbal model is bound by three dimensions: upward–downward; positive–negative; and forward–backward. To further clarify the dimensions, Bales compares them to other polarities: upward–downward with dominance–submissiveness; positive–negative with love–hate or good–bad; and forward–backward with conservative–radical.

    An appropriate degree of caution is urged in interpreting the personality and group-role types identified for the professional staff members. Since the ratings are self-generated, a staff member (in Bales's words) "might fail to recognize the negative elements in his personality in group role" (p. 15) that would appear in the ratings given to him by others in his office. Furthermore, the limited population from which the data were collected leaves additional room for caution.

12. *Ibid.*, p. 460.

13. *Ibid.*, p. 14.

14. *Ibid.*, p. 208.

15. *Ibid.*, p. 209.

16. *Ibid.*

17. *Ibid.*, p. 210.

18. *Ibid.*, p. 212.

19. Harrison W. Fox Jr., "Personal Professional Staffs of U.S. Senators," unpublished Ph.D. dissertation, The American University, 1972, pp. 159–172.

20. Charles L. Brownson, ed., *Congressional Staff Directory* (Washington, D.C.: Congressional Staff Directory, 1972).

21. Includes one Congressman with discontinuous service, whose present AA came at the time of the member's election to his most recent continuous service.

22. This contrasts to the Senate, where a number of office managers are young women with management training. The recruitment network appears to differ: In the House, older secretaries assume office-management duties with a primary focus on managing the work flow; in the Senate, personnel management and extensive record keeping are important components of the job.

23. Donald Riegle with Trevor Armbrister, *O Congress* (Garden City, N.Y.: Doubleday, 1972), p. ix.

24. For further data comparing men and women staff assistants see Hammond, "Personal Staffs," especially Chapters IV and V.

4. *Staff Recruitment and Tenure Patterns*

Recruitment of Congressional staff is important to decision making and policy formulation. Staff aides are information processors, conduits to members, policy advisors, and in some instances decision makers. Recruitment determines to some extent staff activities and roles and thus affects Congressional decisions and policy output. The focus of this chapter is on the various factors that make up the recruitment process and explain tenure patterns.

What factors determine who a Congressman hires? Two important ones are hiring procedures and Congressmen's perceptions of their staffing needs. Although employment offices run by the House and the Senate operate on both sides of the Capitol, recruitment and hiring, particularly of professional staff, continue to be based primarily on informal, non-routine contacts and "who knows whom."

In periods after an election there is a fluidity to hiring which does not occur at other times. New Congressmen are deluged by hundreds of applications for staff positions. For them, as for incumbent Congressmen, applicants recommended by contacts have been through at least a preliminary screening procedure which can save time. Other Congressmen send applicants. Constituents leave résumés. Acquaintances in the state or district call about positions. These contacts all serve as personnel sources. One Congressman, commenting on the recruitment process, said, "Recruitment is haphazard. People really choose you. In a way, the congressman and his staff are more or less driven together."

We think this is important. There are a variety of screening mechanisms which do lead applicants to one office rather than another. Office milieus vary. Some members pay more. Congressmen focus on particular issue areas. These characteristics are fairly widely known and discussed on Capitol Hill. In some offices and for some applicants, party, region, and ideology may be as much a factor in recruitment and hiring as training, skill, and expertise.

Congressmen weigh several factors in hiring personal staff. A major one is whether to hire only from the state or district. Many Senators and Representatives begin this way, and the majority of first-term Representatives do have staffs, both professional and secretarial, with district ties. At this stage in the congressional career, it appears to be both easier and more natural to hire state or district people. Contacts in the state are widespread, and there may not be many Washington contacts. Hiring nonconstituents requires screening procedures which involve either Washington trips or close Washington friends who can make hiring decisions. In addition, cultivating ties with the state or district is viewed as particularly important during the first term, and hiring state or district people is one way to do this. But one freshman Congressman, in discussing this balance, said: "(What we really need) are bright, young people who are willing to work hard. Hill experience isn't so necessary. It's important the first two to three months of a freshman's term, but after that, staff without experience can really get along O.K."

Hiring state or district people has dysfunctional consequences, however, which may make professionalization more difficult. One Congressman noted: "The problem of hiring is complicated by taking people from the district." And a staff member to a senior Representative commented on the "split" life of staff members from the district: "At first we tried to have everyone from the district. It didn't work for secretaries, though. They'd cut their hours to go out (to the district) to see their boyfriends, or they'd even live here and go back to see their husbands every weekend. Now we just look for competent people."

Nevertheless, most offices prefer staff with state or district ties, and many of the top-level professional staff do come from the district or state. Administrative assistants (AA's) often handle political chores in the state in addition to their Washington duties and generally have district or state ties. Senior Congressmen are somewhat less likely to have AA's from the district or state but many do. Legislative assistants (LA's) are less likely to be from the district or state. Press secretaries or the professional staff handling press often come from the state. Contacts with state and district TV, radio, and press persons are an important aspect of the communications function in the Washington office. Also, a press aide who is not from the district or state may, initially at least, be at a disadvantage in dealing with journalists representing local media.

HOUSE PERSONAL STAFF RECRUITMENT AND TENURE PATTERNS

Of the House offices surveyed, a minority insist that all employees, including secretarial personnel, be from the district. A very large majority, 80 percent, prefer that most personnel have district ties. A small minority, 20 percent, do not look for staff with district ties at all. This latter group uses the Select Committee on Congressional Operations' Office of Placement most extensively.[1] In offices where there is an effort to recruit staff from the district, 62 percent of the professional staff *are* constituents. Many offices look for people from the state if no one with district ties is available.[2]

Party is not a significant determinant of whether or not the aides are local; 64

percent (14 of 22) of aides in offices of Republican Representatives were local, 61 percent (17 of 28) in Democratic offices. Seniority also appears to make little difference, although the pattern is mixed, with the most senior and most freshman Congressmen employing the same proportion of local aides. When just AA's are considered, senior Congressmen appear to consider an AA with local ties less important than their more junior colleagues (see Table 10).

Policy attitudes, as measured by *Congressional Quarterly*'s conservative coalition scores, appear to affect staff localism. Congressmen with the lowest conservative coalition support hired the fewest local aides, and the strongest supporters of the conservative coalition hired the most local aides. However, other variables may converge with policy attitudes to bring about this result. For example, Southern Congressmen, many of whom are strong conservative coalition supporters, also hire a large number of local aides (80 percent). (See Table 10.)

Unexpectedly, Western Congressmen hire fewer local aides (50 percent) than their colleagues from other regions (Midwest: 69 percent; East, 80 percent, South, 80 percent), although most Western Congressmen *prefer* that their top staff be from the district. This may be an indication of the difficulty in persuading prospective staff from distant districts to move to Washington. AA's (73 percent in offices studied) and press aides (81 percent) are more likely to have local ties than LA's (59 percent) or other professionals (43 percent).

Another consideration in staffing is balancing the need for Hill experience with knowledge of the district (assuming that both cannot be found in one employee). Most Congressmen look for a staff with both types of experience. For first-term Congressmen the specific balance appears to be a particularly important decision. Certain jobs lend themselves to staff with Washington experience. For instance, a number of women have made the Federal casework slot a quasi-professional career. Since truly competent secretarial help is in short supply on the Hill, most Congressmen do not insist that their secretaries be from their district. Most offices, however, have a receptionist with district ties. If a secretary or clerk has district ties, she is often also the receptionist.

Most offices try to hire personnel of the same party and ideological inclination as the Congressman, although a small group very specifically state that party affiliation was never investigated and did not matter as long as the employee did the job well. In most recruiting, the political background of applicants is known, especially if the office relies on the "informal contact" recruitment system. Very often staff people feel they cannot work for someone whose ideas they do not support, and want to feel that they and "The Boss" are thinking along similar lines. Occasionally, an applicant will be asked how the Congressman views an issue and how this could be made clear, in a letter or a press release, to constituents. In a way, this is as much a skill test as a political test, as obviously one aspect of staff success is ability to interpret the Congressman's position correctly. Most generally, however, party similarity is the litmus test for compatibility.[3]

Very occasionally, Congressmen hire in order to have representation of a specific attitude, e.g., geographic, or of party groups in the constituency. One administrative assistant had been hired because he was acceptable to all elements of the party after a particularly hard fought and bitter primary. A number of applicants for the job had worked for primary opponents of the Congressman. Although the AA had been involved in the primary fracas, he had convinced the Congressman that he fully supported him and would be loyal. In another instance, a black AA had been initially hired twenty years earlier as a staff assistant by a white Congressman in order to represent the black groups in the district. The staffer had stayed on the Hill with several Congressmen representing the district. Representation of district groups is usually not a significant consideration in recruitment, however.

Congressmen did not agree on whether or not office organization and needs change as seniority increases. But many noted that the skills and expertise they required of staff members had changed during their tenure in office. It is difficult to separate the casual factor involved. Increasing seniority, changes in the overall Congressional workload, changes in committee assignment which forced changes in staffing, and the realization that the function of the staff was different from the Congressman's perception prior to actually taking his seat in the House, all appear to contribute to change within a Congressional office.

Recruiting and Hiring: Freshman Offices

Freshmen Congressmen have some particularly critical decisions to make and note strongly the lack of guidance on the role and function of their professional staff. Although the three freshmen in the sample staffed their first-term offices in quite different ways, a common thread which runs through their experience is the use of contacts; as previously noted these are significant in all hiring on the Hill. Other members of the state delegation, both Congressmen and Senators, were important in advising and also in assisting in the actual hiring of staff.

All the freshmen tried to weigh the need for district experience, for Hill expertise versus district ties, and for technical knowledge in staff hiring. All freshmen Congressmen surveyed had hired some aides with Hill experience but without district ties, and all felt this had proved useful. All also followed the pattern set by their state or city delegations in the division made between district and Washington offices, and all seemed to be satisfied that the system was working properly.

One Congressman hired several staff, an office manager and two lower-level secretaries, who had worked for his predecessor who was retiring. He and his predecessor were of the same party and similar policy persuasions. The Congressman feels strongly that he benefited from this arrangement as he was able to hire knowledgeable people with loyalty to the district and its concerns. He also felt that certain staff jobs should be filled by district young people, and he brought with him two key professionals who had been active in state and district politics. In addition, during an initial period he employed his predecessor's AA, who left shortly to join a committee staff. The AA was particularly helpful during the period when the two professionals new to the Hill were learning the ropes; after moving to the committee, he continued to be available to offer advice and assistance. However, when he left the Congressman decided not to fill that particular slot, but instead to distribute some of the workload differently. It was apparent that he was more comfortable with his own men in key slots.

This first-term Congressman felt keenly the frustrations of being a freshman. He had obtained appointment to a prestigious committee, and had hired what he felt was an extremely competent staff, capable of assisting him both on general legislation and on committee work. He articulated what he saw as the problems of being a freshman—of the House hierarchy and the norms and folkways which make a freshman feel like a "cog in a large machine." Although he had served in the legislature of his state, he was unprepared for the slow start on the legislative aspects of his job. He also was worried—and somewhat angry—at what he felt were dysfunctional aspects of being a member of the minority party in Congress: Not only as a freshman, but as a Republican, he was low man on the totem pole when it came to committee staff assistance, questioning, or any other of the myriad aspects of congressional life which are governed by seniority and party. "As a freshman minority member, the committee staff is just of no use," he noted. He expects to add possibly two additional members to his staff, a legislative aide who would assist primarily on committee matters and possibly another caseworker.

A colleague, a freshman Democrat, also felt the frustrations of being a freshman member and what he called the "make-believe" of the legislative process. He pointed to more senior members with "no legislation to their names," and felt that although there was a lot of co-sponsoring, and other motions of legislative action, there was in actuality little innovative policy making. Trained as a lawyer, he had previously served in the executive branch and also in his state legislature. "Legislation is a very minor part of the job," he said, and ticked off the priorities for a freshman legislator: individual constituents first, "group" constituents next—e.g., groups needing HUD grants, hospital funds, etc., to meet district needs. "I can perhaps have some influence in *this* area" (as opposed to the legislative area) he said. His perceptions may have been influenced by state redistricting, with consolidation of his district and the district of a very senior member of his own party expected. Hence, he devoted a good deal of his time, and his staff in Washington was very concerned with, the redistricting battle and their assistance to constituents. Nevertheless, he had hired two legislative aides, one for assistance on general legislation and legislative mail and the other for help on committee work.

In his initial hiring this Congressman had, as had his freshman colleagues, relied on the advice and contacts of other members of his delegation. He had been "inundated by résumés," and had largely hired people he knew or was told about. Two professional staffers moved from the offices of defeated members of

Congress (one a Senator and one a Congressman), both of the same party and policy attitude. These people, along with an executive secretary who came from the office of a defeated Senator of the other party (but of a similar policy attitude) gave him a basis of Hill expertise. His other professional staffer had worked with him in the state legislature, and been active in his campaign. "Staffing is a real problem," he said. "To some extent, it evolves as you go along—as to the type of staff and type of people." He had "proceeded on the theory that a chief of staff was bad," and that "the people were the most important aspect of staffing." But he also noted that he really had not had anyone who could be a "chief of staff" anyway, as his high-level campaign volunteers had been "doctors, lawyers . . . people who wouldn't leave their jobs to be AA."

The Congressman was diffident about not only his own ability to affect policy, but also about his status as a freshman member—and his staff appeared to reflect this. It was younger, less professional, more temporary, and much less organized than any other office surveyed. The Congressman was concerned about the claims which men active in his campaign felt they had on him for employment and felt that obligations deriving from the campaign were ever-present in an initial staffing situation; on the other hand, he had "operated on the assumption that if someone was already on the Hill, and good, he wouldn't want to work for a freshman Congressman—or maybe he's angling for something better, like the Senate, and this would be just temporary." The reasons for his particular staff setup are probably varied: his redistricting battle, and hence a primary emphasis on the district office, which handled the heavy casework load; frustration at (1) being a legislator ("the problem is that there are not many places for people in elected politics on a full-time basis—a legislator has minimal influence, . . .but the alternatives are limited, and in our system of government we need to have good legislators too") and (2) being a freshman. Because so much time was of necessity devoted to his district, he had not apparently begun to make the contacts in the House which are so important to functioning in that body. This office may be atypical in that the Congressman was forced to devote so much time to matters somewhat extraneous to his job as Congressman (a redistricting fight, in particular), but his reliance on the experience and advice of other members of the delegation, on the use of contacts in hiring, and on staffing to handle an extended legislative and policy function are typical of other freshmen members.

The third freshman office surveyed also exhibits the typical pattern of assistance from state colleagues and the importance of contacts in hiring. The Congressman and his campaign manager—who became his AA—organized a systematic screening procedure for applicants, and with the assistance of others in the state delegation already on the Hill, hired a staff with a blend of Hill expertise and district ties. By the middle of the member's first congressional session, his office appeared to be a smoothly functioning operation, with wide staff contacts on the Hill and in the executive branch.

This newly elected Congressman had the support of Senators and several

House members from his state who had seniority and wide Washington contacts. As with other recently elected members, there were many applications for staff jobs—"at least 300 to 400 letters." The Congressman-elect asked the senior members of the delegation in the House and one of the Senators to look around the Hill for people who might be interested in coming to work on the staff. These incumbents screened interested applicants. In early December when the Congressman-elect and his AA-to-be came to Washington they interviewed fifteen applicants, and hired four. These four had had House and Senate, as well as executive branch, experience. Some were secretaries (one of whom became a Federal projects aide because of her expertise); one held a top-level professional position in the office. The other staff members were brought from the district, and had been active in the campaign. All blended into what appeared to be a smoothly functioning operation. One aide said, "I'm more and more impressed with the importance of choosing the right staff, and the method (member) used. There is a blend of experience and inexperience on the Hill, of district or not. The talents are diverse, the styles differ but are complementary. I look at other new offices, and see so many holes there."

The implication clearly was that, in spite of some difficulties—apparently endemic to many offices—of keeping the diverse talents and different styles happy, nevertheless in this office things really did go pretty well, and all the staff (including over-qualified lower-level personnel) felt they were doing important work and seeing some accomplishment. This office was already involved in major legislation important to the district and in executive department negotiations. In this, as in matters of staffing, it may be significant that both Senators were of the same party as the freshman and had some Senate seniority. There had been no staff changes or office reorganization since the start of the session.

The factors important in a smoothly operating staff organization for freshmen Congressmen appear to be wide advice and assistance from knowledgeable incumbents and a fairly clear idea on the part of the Congressman-elect as to his staffing needs. The two freshmen Congressmen who had served in their state legislatures were perhaps ill-served by their experience when they moved on to the Hill: they were less clear about their staffing needs, and appeared to be more tied to a pattern of local politics. Both had had staff turnover since the start of the session and had made or expected to make at least minor reorganization of staff duties. The Congressman with previous experience in the executive branch had the most clearly organized procedure and philosophy in staffing his office. It appears that previous experience may have been a factor in initial organization of offices.

Constituency factors may be at work here also. The Congressman with previous executive experience also came from a state with a close-knit and powerful party; in his previous work, he had developed an expertise which made him valuable to the district at a national level (and perhaps less vulnerable to *all* constituent demands). The freshman Congressman with district politics a part of his daily workload had of necessity de-emphasized his Washington staff.

Several conclusions emerge. Initial staffing for freshman Congressmen is similar in many respects to the replacement hiring of incumbents. The same factors are weighed; "contacts" and who knows whom are also significant. But in many cases, staffing a freshman's office is haphazard. It is clear that more help—organized, and institutionalized (as one Congressman put it)—is needed by newly elected members. Contacts will undoubtedly continue to be important but Congressmen-elect need some general body of information about staff duties, available applications, and information sources which is not now presently available.

Tenure

The pattern of turnover in the professional jobs varies. In the AA positions, the most prestigious and probably the most diversified, there is not a great deal of turnover. In several instances, when turnover occurred the new appointee had several years experience on the staff of the Congressman. There is also less movement from one Congressional office to another at the AA level.[4] Even among Congressmen in the most senior quartile, 50 percent of the Republicans and 33 percent of the Democrats had employed the same AA since their first election.

Of the Congressmen employing AA's 66 percent had hired the present AA upon first entering the House. The average tenure of employment is nine years; median is eight. Two AA's have served twenty years in the same office; five have served ten to fourteen years. In offices where there has been AA turnover, the average length of tenure is 5 years; the median 4.5. In a system where contacts and precedents are important, experienced staff assistance can increase the effectiveness and output of the Congressman. Although several Congressmen noted they preferred some professional staff turnover as they valued creativity and fresh ideas, one added, "But an exception is probably the AA...."

Legislative aides have shorter tenures. The average is 2.3 years, with 6 years the longest any of the sample had stayed with the same Congressman. LA's are promoted to AA (two in the sample); move to another office (three had worked for other Congressmen); or move to committee staff jobs or the Senate. Many LA's, however, look forward to moving to jobs outside of the Congress after several years and a number of Congressmen seem to encourage this. "It's probably good not to have people stay on the staff too long," one Representative said. LA's who are lawyers may move to private law firms or to legal positions in the executive branch; the others often join research organizations or do other government-related work. Because LA's hold a higher proportion of law degrees, there may be greater ease of movement to non-Hill jobs.

Turnover is also greater for press personnel, as well as for lower-level backup staff. In part, this is due to their youth. Several staff members were holding one of their first jobs; predecessors had left to pursue careers in law outside Congress, to return to graduate school or, in the case of women, had dropped out of the job market to marry. More staff members in these jobs than in AA positions had had previous experience in other congressional offices or in other areas of endeavor such as teaching or as an executive secretary. Their recruitment was not tied so directly to the election of the Congressman. Except in the case of first-term Congressmen, they had not worked on the campaign.

The pattern for staff who are office managers or handle individual casework is different. Many caseworkers have had long experience in congressional casework, and have developed expertise in the field. Although occasionally caseworkers move to an LA or other staff slot, more likely they have moved up from secretarial duties and will continue to perform jobs with secretarial content. Most caseworkers are women. Many can move with ease from one office to another on the Hill. Office managers show a similar pattern: usually starting on the Hill in a secretarial job, they develop an administrative expertise which enables them to move between offices with ease. They are more likely to be involved in policy matters than caseworkers and may occasionally change party when changing positions.

Staff tenure is affected by a number of factors. A significant one is the amount of responsibility the staff assistant has. This is measured both by the actual job content (does he draft the newsletter, the press releases, or does he rework the Congressman's draft; does he work on independent legislative projects, developing his own information sources and having his own suggestions accepted) and his place in the office hierarchy. If, for example, a young staffer has a fair degree of substantive legislative and research content in his job, he may find it dissatisfying if he spends most of his time justifying his work and ideas to the AA rather than directly to the Congressman. Most offices make an effort to overcome problems of this sort: having lower-level staff give presentations of their research to the entire staff and to neighboring staffs, or assuring that the staffer accompanies the Congressman to the Floor for a Floor speech or to a committee for testimony. Salary and age are also important. Young staff are expected to leave after awhile—often for graduate school, or perhaps for a higher-level job on another staff. Low salaries, even when offset by responsibility and substantive job content, do not compensate staffers sufficiently over a long period of time. Work in a "glamour office" at low salaries may leave staffers feeling vaguely disgruntled, and a consequence is frequent turnover.

SENATE PERSONAL STAFF RECRUITMENT AND TENURE PATTERNS

Recruitment and tenure patterns for Senate personal staff are similar to those in the House. Most staff members get their jobs because they happen to be in the right place at the right time. "It is who the Senator notices, and who we know," summarizes a staff assistant. He goes on to point out that "the Senator may work with a guy on an issue, and then at some later time hire him." Another staff member commented that his office hires "people in a haphazard fashion."

Recruitment patterns of Senate professionals are not systematic, but they adhere to a general opportunity structure. Staff incumbents have rich educational backgrounds, but educational attainment alone does not assure a prospective employee a job opportunity. A staff member notes: "You asked me about (the) matter of educational attainment, and you will notice I downrate it . . . I hold two M.A.'s and still downrate it." The opportunity to be a staff member depends to a large extent on a sponsor. The sponsor may be the Senator or another staff member. Remembering it is "who you know" rather than "what you know" is important to prospective Senate staff members. For example, among those staff members responding to the questionnaire fully six out of ten knew the Senator in some capacity before they were hired. They knew him in forty-six different capacities such as newsmen, friends, office interns, college classmates, and through business dealings (see Table 11).

The opportunity structure is fairly well defined for prospective Senate staff professionals. They must be well educated, be in the right place at the right time, know the Senator or a member of the staff, usually be sponsored, and then hired. In the Senate, as in the House, personal office and committee staffs serve as recruitment sources. If a Senator retires or is defeated, a number of his aides may look for jobs on the Hill. One staff member told of the "full-time job of the AA" of a defeated Senator after the election—to "get new jobs for all those staff people." The AA succeeded remarkably well, placing them in both Senate and House offices and on the campaign staffs of unannounced but aspiring candidates for the Presidency. He also got himself a job.

There may be some effort to hire someone whose work is "known" to either the Senator or his AA personally. One AA detailed the problems resulting from hiring several legislative aides who came highly recommended but whose work was not known personally; that office now hires *only* those who have previously worked with the office in some way. Few offices seem to operate such a closed opportunity structure; indeed, few may have such a luxury. But this does highlight the difficulty of congressional recruitment in a loosely structured system.

Professional staff members have come from many different social backgrounds. Their fathers' main occupations range from janitor to Congressman, with over 100 separate occupations being mentioned by the respondents.

Senate staff occupational mobility is again quite varied. Professional or quasi-professional training is the rule for those moving into professional staff positions. Before joining Senate staffs, they have been lawyers, businessmen, engineers, and teachers, for example.

"It is not that unusual for personal staff to go to committee staff and the reverse," notes a staff member. Many respondents cited particular examples of personal staff movement from the Senate office to committee staff. Of the fifty-seven cases noted, all but fifteen of those leaving the Senate office for a committee position were legislative assistants. The substantive concern of the LA makes him a much more likely candidate for movement to committee than the AA, press secretary, or other staff professionals.

"After Kennedy was elected," notes an AA to a Democratic Senator:

> "Many of the people (on the Hill) went over to the Executive. Some served on the White House staff. Others moved to very responsible positions—such as assistant secretaries, college presidents, and FCC chairmen. There are literally hundreds of guys who have moved to responsible positions."

He goes on to point out that "many staffers move on, but others, I guess I am one, stay on for years. All staffers are not competent—some have been around here for years and don't do anything."

STAFFING REQUIREMENTS

What do Congressmen look for in hiring staff assistants? The tangible and measurable qualifications of expertise: law; journalism—increasingly, with experience in TV news; secretarial skills; and research and writing experience. Many seem to look, also, for staff with communications and interpersonal relations skills. For example, a political scientist with experience in community organization, a journalist with public relations experience, a lawyer who has handled legislative liaison work, or a media and engineering expert with experience running a division in a Federal government agency program. Several Congressmen and aides mentioned the critical need for having staff who write well for mail, newspaper columns, testimony and statements, and so on. One Congressman said, "I constantly underestimated the need for writers (before I was sworn in). There is enough communicating with the district to keep one person busy. . . .My LA and the interns are rapidly becoming writers." Another Congressman noted, ". . .the critical shortage of people who can draft letters, statements, testimony, well."

Congressmen also look for qualities which are not easily measured. Someone who "enjoys government and doesn't mind the long hours. . . ." Another Congressman said, "I look for staff who are highly motivated, with a desire to serve. Flexible people. A deep sense of idealistic responsibility." This Congressman has "made an effort" to hire young people and is proud of the number of alumni of his office in government service. He views staff employment as a time to instill a sense of public service, and as training in the functioning of government.

A senior Republican looks for employees who will be conscientious, "not la-de-da," and have compassion. He tries to assess how well applicants will work together, as "it's really got to be a coordinated team. I also must have people who will say 'wait'—the staff *must* bring both the pros and cons of an issue to me."

It seems to add up to loyalty, long hours, conscientious application to the work, willingness to learn, and an ability to apply native intelligence to one's work.

One staffer said, "The most important thing is to think along the boss's lines," and this was echoed by others. What seems important here is that there be certain basic assumptions which are shared. And similarity of political values of aides and Senators does exist, as reported in the previous chapter. But after this baseline position, aides are valued for professional judgment and expertise. "Thinking along the boss's lines" means knowing his interests, his political values, and matters (such as constituency concerns) which are important to him. It may mean assessing specific factors (group support, impact on the constituency, cost effectiveness) when advising on legislation; or it may mean knowing when he would be ready to compromise on legislative strategy. But the value of staff, in the judgment of a number of Congressmen, is that knowing all these factors, staff can say "It's time to compromise *now*," or, "discount that factor this time." Most, but not all, would agree with a senior Congressman who said, "the staff philosophy must reflect the members' philosophy."

There is no agreement on whether a Congressman is best served by bright, young staff who do not stay very long or by older, more experienced staff, who are knowledgeable in the ways of the Hill. Frequent turnover puts greater demands on Congressmen and staff aides, and may prove dysfunctional during the learning process. But longevity may be dysfunctional also, as staff settle into routines which are rarely jolted. In fact, there is fairly frequent turnover of lower-level professionals and among secretarial staff as well, but continuity in staffing is achieved with the longer tenure of the AA. Most Congressmen would probably agree that this is a pretty good mix.

COMMITTEE STAFF RECRUITMENT AND TENURE PATTERNS

Recruitment and tenure patterns of committee staff are characteristic of Congress. Recruitment depends heavily on contacts. Although hiring is based on expertise, knowledge of an opening is usually dependent on who knows whom. Most committee staff are appointed by the committee or subcommittee chairman (75.2 percent) or the ranking minority member (14 percent), although the full committee often concurs. Nearly half of the committee staff responding reported previous acquaintance with the person making the appointment. Acquaintance ranged from being a colleague to professional contact, often as a former employee (49.2 percent), to casual acquaintance. What may be of primary importance, particularly in the personalized world of Capitol Hill, is that a number of staffers did not know the appointing agent previously.[5]

Senate committee aides are slightly less likely than House aides to know the person who appoints them. More Senate (15 percent) than House (6.5 percent) aides have moved from personal staff to committee staff, and many more in the

Senate (13.3 percent compared to 3.3 percent) have had previous political contacts. In contrast, House committee aides report acquaintance primarily through previous professional employment contacts. The apparent contrast may be an artifact of reporting; further research would shed light on whether there are in fact somewhat different recruitment network operations. It should also be noted that somewhat more than half of those reporting acquaintance did not respond when asked the circumstances of that acquaintance.

Of the committee aides, 35 percent were recruited directly from the executive branch. The next most frequent recruitment source was other Congressional offices—most often, the personal staff of a member. There is recruitment within a subsystem: Appropriations Committee staff have worked as executive agency budget officers, and staff on authorizing committees have experience within that subject-matter subsystem.

Tenure of committee staffers varies slightly between the two Houses. Senate aides report somewhat briefer tenure on committees: 56.3 percent had served less than four years, in contrast to 44.5 percent in the House. This same pattern is evident for other tenure periods: slightly more House aides are in each of the longer tenure categories. (See Table 13)

Staff aides were asked whether various characteristics would be important in hiring a replacement. A slight majority (51.5 percent) felt that being of the same party was not an important consideration; 76.1 percent would recommend that a new staffer be well informed on Congressional practices; and 70.1 percent felt that skill in public relations would be important. Very large majorities indicated that age and sex should not be considerations. Nearly a third, and more in the House than in the Senate, would recommend promotion from within the committee.

There is some ambivalence, and occasional bitterness about recruitment practices. But the more frequent comments are reflected by one staffer, who said:

> "Committee staffing fluctuates less than that of [Senate or House] offices. Competent, knowledgeable staff tend to remain in place, or move laterally or upward in the Senate. Incompetents don't last long on committee staffs with the mortality rate among young male staffers particularly high."

And another specified,

> "The most important consideration would be to find someone with 5–10 years experience with industries and/or agencies which are affected by the types of legislation the committee deals with. In other words someone who has advanced beyond the theoretical to an understanding of how the real world operates."

There is a good deal of movement on the Hill between Congressional offices, and our impression is that this movement is increasing as a Hill career becomes more attractive. This kind of job movement appears more prevalent in the Senate, where Senators control committee staff earlier in their Senate careers, and where the larger number of legislative assistants on personal staffs serves as a ready pool for committee personnel. Some Senate observers maintain that there is indeed an emerging career pattern and that legislative assistants on personal staffs are regularly promoted to committee staff. The movement results partially from scarce clerk-hire resources for personal staff and somewhat more generous committee staff budgets. Although this may be true in some instances, in general the movement is not all in one direction, but rather back and forth between personal and committee staffs.

Some Senators have organized offices so that salaries, vacation policies, and other administrative matters are structured similarly for both personal office staff and committee staff under their control. The arrangement is in part an effort to treat all personnel equitably and in part a management tool, as clear organizational lines of authority and accountability are set up for all legislative aides. As a result, staff movement between the two Senate subgroups is facilitated.

S. RES. 60 STAFF

The personal committee aides which Senators have been permitted to appoint since July, 1975, have been recruited extensively from personal staff aides, especially from legislative aides. Committee staffs have also been sources for S. Res. 60 personal committee legislative aides. S. Res. 60 clerks have been drawn from both personal and committee staff. This recruitment pattern may shift over time, but we would expect that Senators will continue to maintain flexibility of appointment and to move aides between committee, personal staff, and S. Res. 60 positions. This flexibility was facilitated by an early change in the salary allowance procedures under S. Res. 60. Each senator was originally allowed a net dollar allowance per committee membership if he had no staff on the committee. The Senate Appropriations Committee acted to allow Senators aggregation and accumulation of salaries among committees. This action had the effect of establishing legislative clerk-hire accounts which conformed to personal office clerk-hire accounts already in effect.

LEGISLATIVE STAFF: A CAREER?

As congressional staffs have become larger and more specialized, several trends are evident. First, a career of being a Hill aide has developed. The most salient example may be in the field of Federal casework. In addition, congressional secretaries move between offices and across the Capitol fairly frequently. One AA, in listing turnover in secretarial personnel during the past year, noted that nearly all had left for better paying jobs in other offices.

At the professional-staff level too, a Hill career is possible. One Senate AA interviewed had moved from a job as AA to a Congressman to being LA to a Senator and then AA to the Senator. Another staff man, with legal training and experience, had moved from a House committee staff to a Senator's personal staff, and back to the staff of a different House committee. Presumably because of the closer local ties of Representatives, there is a somewhat lower frequency of movement among their top staff.

A few staff members interviewed previously worked for Congressmen of the other party. But the more usual move is within a party, from one Representative or Senator to another of the same party; and even more usual (and circumscribed) are moves among Congressmen of the same general political persuasion—as between members of the DSG or the Wednesday Group in the House.

There is also movement between the legislative and executive branches, especially in those positions where the same expertise is useful. Lawyers move between committee and executive branch staff jobs, as do some foreign affairs and other issue experts. Persons holding legislative liaison positions in the executive and LA or AA positions on the Hill may be interchangeable. This often occurs following a change in administrations. Hence, Hill experience is valuable to a staffer who spends different stages of his career in other government jobs.

In the flat organizational structure which characterizes Congress, with multiple subunits and centers of power, there are few clearly defined lines of promotion and career movement upward. Within specified subunits, a personal office or a committee, some job changes are clearly characterized as promotions—moving from LA to Chief LA, or from LA to AA. Some movement between offices is similar: from LA in one office to AA in another. But other moves—from legislative assistant on a personal staff to a similar position on a committee, or from one AA or committee staff director job to another, can more readily be perceived as lateral moves. Yet the career patterns of many Hill aides are characterized by just such moves.

Several consequences flow from this, in our view. First, there is a fluidity to congressional positions which is not present in more hierarchical organizations. The system permits rapid reassignment of scarce resources (in this case, funds for staff salaries) when needed, and a restructuring of staff positions. It also results in some bargaining and negotiation on both status and salary, less attractive consequences in our view if occurring in a completely unstructured environment.

A number of offices, both personal and committee, now set salary structures and organizational lines of authority, in an effort to reduce the uncertainty which has often characterized congressional staff jobs. As this occurs, and as positions become somewhat comparable between offices, the consequences of job changes may become clearer and career patterns more discernable.

One AA reflected on changes in congressional staffing: "A congressional staff aide is really a whole new career field. There's a healthy tendency to get people who are more qualified. People are much more interested in the content of the work—it's more than just a job. Actually, they are much more idealistic too." Two House staff aides felt that both specialization and professionalism had increased, but one commented: "Yes, House aides are more professional, but in function, not necessarily in training." Another aide felt that the generalist nature of the House staff jobs, although more specialized than previously, detracted from the professionalization, and noted, "We're not all lawyers—the Senate is more professionalized." He also mused on his future—what type of training was his LA position giving him for a non-Hill job?

Several Congressmen commented on the increasing expertise required of staff. Some Representatives and Senators stressed the importance of having lawyers as legislative assistants. Congress operates in a complex world; legislative decision making involves a complexity of sophisticated issues, and staff is being hired to meet these needs.

At present, we do not know enough about career patterns of Hill aides. There has been no systematic collection of data, over time, by either Senate and House personnel records offices, or by outside observers. Such longitudinal data would facilitate analysis of linkage between staff career patterns and Congressional decision making.

It would seem a reasonable hypothesis that staff oriented toward certain types of career patterns may have different types of impact on the policy formation process, and analysis of career patterns will be useful in various ways. In later chapters, we present some analysis which suggests that previous experience shapes not only subject-matter expertise, but also communication and information contacts, and, finally, a framework for participation in policy subsystem and policy impact. Previous experience contributes, also, to role orientation. Our data, as well as our experiences as Hill aides lead us to the view that different groups of aides have different role orientations.

A typology of career orientations may be helpful in clarifying the differences. The categories are closely linked to role orientation, that is, to how the staffer views the job as well as the types of skills used in the job. Career orientations of professional staff are based on the following role types: Hill Professional, Hill Specialist, Professional Specialist, and Impermanent Careerist.

Those who are Hill Professionals use typical congressional skills such as compromise and negotiation to facilitate the functioning of the office and the member in his job. The supplementary aspect of staff jobs is emphasized. Professional Hill people tend to emphasize Congress first and a profession second. The staffer uses skills more specific to Congress, and as time goes on, less specific to the practice of his profession. Hill Professionals tend also to be Hill careerists; they see their new careers as serving on Hill staffs (personal or committee) and expect to stay on the Hill if their present boss is defeated or retires.

The Hill Specialist also uses typically congressional skills, often in an administrative capacity. However, in contrast to the Hill Professional, the Hill Specialist's skills are easily transferable to an area outside Congress if he wishes. As with the Hill Professional, his primary orientation is not generally to a specific profession, but because of his particular expertise and the job he fills, he moves to jobs off the Hill more easily and more often.

In contrast to these two categories, the Professional Specialist is more oriented toward a profession. He uses his professional training on the Hill. His skills are transferable, and his own career is not necessarily submerged in that of his boss. These staff aides tend to have somewhat temporary Hill careers. Although this type of staff person may remain on a committee staff for an extended period, they often move from the Hill in order to pursue their own profession less tied to a personal staff role.

A number of younger staff are what might be called Impermanent Careerists. The aide has professional training, but is not entirely clear where or how, over time, that training should be used. The staffer does not consider the job in Congress as permanent, but does not have any specific plan for a next move. A number of these staff aides are college-trained women in lower-level professional positions who may not continue to work full time, or who may shift to volunteer work. These staffers appear to combine a professional role with strong personal ties to the particular Congressman for whom they work.

The presence of different career orientations raises interesting questions as to the possible differential impact on the decision-making process. For example, do aides who tend to emphasize Hill rather than professional contacts have narrower communications networks than aides who put a profession first and place practicing that profession (the Hill) second? Or, alternatively, do aides emphasizing very broad professional contacts miss significant political inputs from the Hill which may be crucial to passage of legislation? Do aides with a career Hill orientation get "locked into" certain approaches, with a consequent possibly dysfunctional impact on policy formation? Or are aides who see their Hill work as a stepping stone to something else more interested in looking for the next position than in the negotiation and attention to detail which may accompany passage of obscure legislation? Are they too flexible? Identification of career patterns can yield further insights into the congressional process.

CONCLUSION

Staff recruitment and tenure patterns vary slightly with different staff subgroups, but there is a basic underlying similarity of pattern. The variations should not, however, be ignored. The differences, for instance, in the tenure of senior aides and lower-level professional staffers on House personal staff are important in bringing about a balance of stability and continuity and an infusion of fresh ideas. Although we do not have complete comparative historical data, it appears that a consequence of increasing institutionalization of the staffing function is a more easily definable opportunity structure on the Hill.

Staff recruitment is generally nonsystematic, based on personal contact, recommendation, knowledge of an opening, and often is facilitated by a congressional sponsor.

Training, skill, and expertise are important base-line factors in hiring. But party and ideology are as significant for many applicants. Other factors, such as Hill experience or ties with a home state or district, often figure into the recruitment equation.

Our data enable us to identify somewhat different tenure patterns for groups of staff (Senate personal, House personal, Committee) and for specific jobs (AA, LA, and so forth).

The consequences of recruitment patterns are not entirely clear. If indeed, applicants choose offices more than offices recruit applicants, we suspect that the pool from which Senators and Representatives select staff is more limited than might be desired. On the other hand, the attitudinal data on staff which we discuss in Chapter 3 indicate that staff share a political mind set with their bosses; one consequence is that however wide the recruitment process, some degree of self-selection occurs.

The consequences of the tenure patterns are clearer. With relatively short tenure in lower-level professional jobs, there is a fluidity to congressional staffing which permits rapid advancement and a good deal of responsibility early in a career; there is also an infusion of new ideas, and enthusiasm. Rapid turnover at lower levels also, however, results in time lost to replacement and training. Senior aides, with longer tenure, bring stability and continuity.

Several Congressmen and staff reflected on their view of staff tenure. One Congressman makes a policy of changing legislative assistants every year or two. He likes the "fresh, new ideas" and the enthusiasm which young LAs bring to their jobs: "The problem is that someone gets on the Hill and doesn't like to leave it. Hill people—maybe with the AA excepted—ought to leave after some time. It's a vicarious experience, and the youthful enthusiasm goes. Then the job isn't as much fun, and the aide doesn't deliver as much. A Hill career ought to be about a five year stint." A senior colleague agreed: "I think it's probably good not to have people stay on the staff too long—I'm not sure this applies to the top slots—but there are only so many top slots; people get trained, and they'll want to move on."

The permanent professional (committee) staff, appointed on merit, which the 1946 congressional reformers envisioned, has gradually (and partially) been implemented. Thus training and experience (tempered by political acceptability) are the essential elements in virtually all professional staff appointments.

As careers for congressional aides become more usual, continuity and stability can be expected to increase without loss, we hope, of new ideas and youthful enthusiasm. Congress may need to recognize—and even institutionalize—this balance by building in career changes for aides, perhaps through such devices as staff training opportunities and fellowship programs in both Federal and state government.

Many congressional staff are joining the ranks of the free professionals. Congressmen will still retain courtiers,[6] but we think their ranks are being supplanted by careerists.

NOTES

1. The discussion applies to Washington staff. Field office staff are necessarily from the district or state. Also see John D. Macartney, "Political Staffing: A View from the District," unpublished PH.D. dissertation, University of California at Los Angeles, 1975.

2. "Local" and "localism" here are defined as "having district and/or state ties."

3. Many Congressmen distinguish between professional staff and secretarial staff in looking for compatible attitudes. In general, when the office works as a team including secretaries, who take part in a certain amount of participatory democracy in this office, the entire staff shares similar policy attitudes. But because secretarial work is a skill which, strictly speaking, does not often involve policy, secretaries transfer to other offices readily. One Republican, generally regarded as conservative, had recently hired a secretary from a "liberal" Democrat. Other offices would regard this kind of transfer as difficult to make.

4. The Senate would seem to present a different pattern, with more movement of high-level aides from one office to another—this, perhaps, because Senators have longer terms and do not always need to maintain local ties to the same extent. There is also more movement between AA and subcommittee and committee staff, perhaps because Senators control committee staff much earlier in their careers than do Representatives.

5. Comparison over time is not possible, as detailed surveys have not previously been conducted. But based on interview comments and other data, "cronyism" and patronage appointments appear to be decreasing.

6. Lewis A. Dexter, "Court Politics: Presidential Staff Relations as a Special Case of a General Phenomenon," paper presented at the Annual Meeting of the American Political Science Association, Chicago, September, 1976.

5. The Organizational Milieu

Many members and their aides are convinced that no two offices are alike, and it is true that since expertise, personality, and job and role perceptions often differ, Congressional offices do indeed vary. But every Congressional office handles casework, answers legislative mail, communicates with constituents, performs committee and other legislative work, and engages in research and legislative oversight.[1] This similarity of workload is undoubtedly responsible for the underlying organizational patterns evident in both Senate and House personal offices.

Scholars have found that in some instances variables such as seniority, party, region, and policy attitude are important determinants of congressional behavior. Our data indicate that these also play a role in office organization. Very senior Congressmen in the House, for example, have "hierarchical" offices: the office is organized so that there are clear lines of authority which run to the top professional (usually the administrative assistant); the work of other professionals in the office is reviewed by the AA and sent on to the Congressman, rather than sent to him directly by the professional who did the work.

Does committee or office organization affect the legislative and policy-making process in a systematic way? If, for example, interoffice communications networks vary with office organization patterns, information sources may differ, perhaps impacting in turn on the type of substantive analysis performed by aides. Or, it may be that hierarchical offices offer a different type of staff support than those in which all professionals have direct and frequent access to the Senator or Representative. Some tentative conclusions can be reached.

HOUSE OF REPRESENTATIVES

Patterns of Staff Organization

The parameters of Washington staff operations are defined by the member's decision about the establishment and functions of a district office (or offices).

Some district offices are primarily "intake" offices, sending requests and complaints to Washington for action. Some handle casework in the district. Occasionally, district offices take on press work, newsletters, scheduling, and other duties. Most Senators and Representatives now have at least one state or district office, and many have several; the size of the state or of the Congressional district appears to be the primary determinant of the number and location of district offices—the larger the district or state, the more offices.

Although a very few atypical House offices have virtually no Washington office, the majority of Congressmen base most of their staff on Capitol Hill. And, even though there may be a highly paid field representative or a district office staff handling casework, the Washington office is charged with coordination of the overall workload.

In many Capitol Hill offices the professionals work quite closely with the Congressman on matters specific to their job. In some offices, this type of contact is relatively infrequent; in others, it is almost constant. In virtually all offices, whether or not job content is clearly defined, there is built-in flexibility to enable some shifting of boundaries when the office workload necessitates it. Professionals in two offices specifically mentioned that on a big mailing, for example, *everyone*—Congressman included—works on getting it out.

Almost all the lower-level professionals agreed that coordination and cooperation with other staff members was useful, often necessary, and ultimately depended on individual initiative. In a group as small as a House congressional staff, there are rarely built-in coordinating mechanisms, few middle-level personnel to review and coordinate work, and an overall office function which is uniquely personal.

Three patterns of staff organization, from most to least structured are present. This is also the case in the Senate (see Table 14).[2] The "Hierarchical" (Type I) has one senior staff aide, usually titled administrative assistant, coordinating the work of the office, both in terms of workload and content. Virtually everything crosses his desk on its way to and from the Congressman. In addition, he may have responsibilities for some aspects of the substantive work of the office—legislative, or press, or Federal programs, for example.

In some hierarchical offices, every effort is made to provide lower-level professional staff with interesting projects and responsible and satisfying job content. Opportunities also exist for each professional to work with the Congressman on some specific matters. However, final responsibility for the office rests with a top-level staff person, who has authority and responsibility for supervising other professionals.

Another method of organization is the "individualistic" (Type III). Here, professionals with certain loosely defined functions operate independently, working directly with the Congressman on matters within their purview, coordinating among themselves—primarily for information and to avoid overlap—and clearing certain things with the AA when tasks for which they are responsible fall in the areas which he oversees.

In some individualistic offices, a number of professionals have responsibility for their work in a final form. In others, the Congressman really acts as his own AA, making decisions as to material needed and supervising several staff members directly; he is the coordinative, advisory staff man as well as boss.

A middle pattern is that of a loosely organized hierarchy, a "coordinative" (Type II) office. An administrative assistant clearly coordinates the work of the office, but operates more as an advisor than a "clearance person" for most professionals on the staff; the professionals have independent, and sometimes very frequent, access to the Congressman.

Within the coordinative pattern, there are two major variations:[3] most typical is the office where the AA and the LA work as a team, dividing responsibility according to expertise, but at least apprised of, if not involved in, each other's work (Subtype IIa). The AA is technically the senior member of the team, and he is top man in terms of ultimate responsibility. But for most matters, where the professional staff are concerned, the office is similar to an "individualistic" office, with each professional working with the Congressman in areas which are his speciality. This arrangement is most prevalent when there are only two professionals in the office; in offices with more than two, more overt coordination apparently becomes necessary, formal coordination, if not clearance procedures, being put into effect. Less usual is the other variation: the AA as a coordinator and advisor for the work of other professionals in the office, who nevertheless may have direct access to the Congressman themselves (Subtype IIb).

Schematically, the organization plans in the House vary as seen in Table 14.[4] One office in the sample fits none of these patterns easily, and may be taken as representative of some few atypical offices. The Congressman acts as his own AA, directing all senior staff closely. Technically, it can be classified as an "individualistic" office, as staff have direct access to the Congressman, working with him on their own work. There is a subtle difference in the operation of the senior staffers, however, for in actual fact they do not act independently but work under close and continuous supervision of the Congressman. They are not "professionals" with specialized training and expertise and a certain loyalty to their profession. Most staffers in this office are senior-level secretaries with competence in locating information and a good deal of clout, which they are not afraid to use in the Congressman's name. The office is heavily oriented toward service to constituents; the Congressman concentrates legislatively on committee work, for which he relies on committee staff. For these reasons, the office is not included in some of the detailed analyses of individualistic offices which follow.

There is no clear preponderance of any one organizational pattern in the House. But a majority of Congressmen do favor an organizational arrangement which is at least a loose hierarchy: hierarchical and coordinative A (Subtype II A) comprise 56 percent of the sample. The advantage of this type of arrangement is that someone is clearly in charge when the Congressman must be away, and the Congressman need not become involved in matters such as division of workload unless he wants to do so. One dysfunctional consequence is the importance of the personality and operational style of the AA: in one hierarchical office, the Congressman complained that a lower-level semi-professional staffer had recently left because of a personality conflict with the AA. Presumably, in a more individualistic office, it would be possible for two disparate personalities to coexist, although, given the close working conditions which are part of a Representative's office, it may be only a matter of time before one would leave.

A strong minority of Congressman have organized or do lean toward an individualistic office. In a few cases, all staff of these offices, both professional and secretarial, participate in staff meetings and have input into both office and policy decisions. The individualistic office may be the most difficult operationally, particularly if staff increases bring more professionals. An extraordinary amount of close cooperation, communication, and trust at the senior staff level is required for this type of office structure. In addition, it appears that the Congressman must devote more time to working with his staff, particularly as some staffs in this group tend to have more professionals than other offices have (three or four, as compared with one or two in an hierarchical office, two or three in a coordinative).

It may be that as staffs, and numbers of professionals, increase, the coordinative office will be found more frequently. It allows latitude for professionals, yet structures needed coordination.

A clearer pattern of organization emerges when party alone is considered. The Democrats divide evenly among the three organizational patterns, and between more hierarchical (I and IIA) and less hierarchical (IIB and III). A definite minority (33 percent) favors a completely hierarchical arrangement; and a minority (33 percent) favors a completely individualistic office. Among Republicans, there is again an evenly divided distribution among several types of organization. Republicans are evenly balanced between a hierarchical (I) and nonhierarchical arrangement (II and III) and fairly evenly between more hierarchical (I and IIA) and less hierarchical (IIB and III) (see Table 15).

The major difference between Republicans and Democrats is that no Republicans have "individualistic" offices; they prefer some lines of authority, even if only loosely delineated. Although this is a clear difference, party is most likely not the primary causal factor here; rather, other factors, which may have contributed to choice of party, are more important. These would include professional training and experience of both the Congressman and his staff, as well as advice from their congressional delegation. Complete statistical data on all House Republicans and Democrats would no doubt shed fuller light on the causal factors involved.

Seniority

Seniority does have a bearing on the organization of House offices. As Table 16 shows, all the Congressmen in the top seniority quartile have hierarchical

(Type I) offices. Conversely, none of the least senior Congressmen has an hierarchical office, and the percentage of Congressmen with individualistic offices is greatest in the least-senior group.[5] The pattern of office organization may change over time if more junior Congressmen, as they gain seniority, keep coordinative and/or individualistic patterns.

Several conclusions as to why this pattern prevails can be drawn from interview data and observations. First, senior Congressmen appear to be influenced by (1) past staffing arrangements and (2) a focus on committee work. Congressmen in the most senior quartile came to the House when staffs were much smaller and professional work could be handled by one employee. In most instances, as staffs have grown, the Congressman has added secretarial rather than professional staff. This inclination not to "diversify" was reinforced by the Representative's increasing specialization and focus on committee work, with greater access to and reliance on committee staff; in turn, this meant less pressure to hire additional professionals and some tendency for the personal office to emphasize constituent service. Other factors, such as personal predilection and background may also contribute to this type of organization. A further factor, nebulous but possibly significant, is future ambition. Staff members in different offices of senior Congressmen stressed that "the Congressman isn't running for anything else." Several senior Congressmen with hierarchical office organizations have one professional assistant who combines AA, press, and LA functions. In addition, senior Congressmen who are Democrats are generally older and would not be expected to run for other offices. Senior Republicans, while younger, are ranking minority members of committees and subcommittees and can reasonably be expected to continue in these positions.

The most junior Congressmen, while contributing disproportionately to the "individualistic" offices, actually are distributed throughout all types except the hierarchical. Indeed, a majority prefer a coordinative office. Again, drawing on interview data and observation, it appears that while hierarchical organization is not as congenial to least senior members as it is to most senior members, some loosely defined lines of authority and some coordination are present. This may be due to the increasing use of several professionals on the part of least senior members. Almost without exception, the Congressmen in the least senior quartiles expressed a wish to be involved in legislation and policy analysis, and had hired staffs and were drawing on outside information resources which would enable them to do so. It is presumably more difficult to keep professionals happy if access to the Congressman is limited and one top-level staff man supervises and reviews closely all work.[6]

The two middle seniority quartiles are distributed in similar frequencies across the three types of offices.

In the future the inclination of the more junior members to hire more professionals may result in fewer hierarchical offices on Capitol Hill. If changes in committee staffing continue to be made (with staff resources more evenly dis-

tributed) and if, as seems to be likely, younger members continue to hold a view of their legislative function which includes concern for broadly based national issues and an ability and willingness to abstract to the national level specifics of constituent service complaints and concerns, the coordinative office will become more important.

Within each party, a generally similar pattern of office organization is evident for each seniority group (see Table 17). Freshman Democrats have somewhat more individualistic offices, whereas freshman Republicans have organized coordinative offices. Republicans of middle seniority split between hierarchical and coordinative offices while Democrats with the same seniority slightly prefer the coordinative types.

Policy Attitude

Policy attitude does not appear to affect type of office organization greatly (see Table 18). The offices of the least conservative Congressmen are distributed with equal frequency over the three types of organization. Congressmen in the middle on policy attitude find an hierarchical office more congenial, and none has an individualistic office. The most conservative Congressmen again are fairly evenly divided on their office organization. There is no clear pattern which would serve as evidence that a certain policy predilection "causes" or even is related in any way to a certain type of office organization.

Region

Region appears to affect type of office organization in a curious way. No region is identified with any particular type of office organization (see Table 19). However, there is some clustering, and the reason for this seems primarily related to communication patterns (see Chapter 7). These in turn are derived in large part, and particularly in early years in the House, from state and regional contacts. For example, 60 percent of the individualistic (Type II) offices in the sample are run by Congressmen from the Midwest. Interviewees in these offices described unexpectedly close contacts between both staff and Congressmen, based initially on shared regional concerns. There was also repeated contact with their Senators, who were good friends and tended also to run individualistic offices. "Senator X has lots of legislative assistants running around—it's a madhouse," noted a House staff member.

Region is also important to office organization in the focus of casework; in this instance, it is not so much region of the country as relation to the decentralized regional offices of the Federal government's departments and agencies. Thus, casework is handled by the district offices of urban-based Congressmen from the East, Midwest, and West where regional offices are easily accessible *and* where others in the delegation handle casework this way. Our data suggest it is possible there may be similar clustering among some Southern Congressmen.

Previous Background

Background (defined here as a combination of formal education, training, and work experience) should also be considered as a possibly important variable relevant to staffing. Matthews' work on the Senate posits a typology of Senate staff organization, the bureaucratic or the individualistic, related to a Senator's previous executive experience. He quotes one staff member as noting that, "Lawyers by definition, are lousy administrators."[7] It does not seem to be quite that simple in the House, but background does appear to have some influence on the kind of organization a Congressman finds most congenial.

Sixteen (64 percent) of the Congressmen surveyed had previous experience in state legislatures; two (8 percent) had significant administrative experience in the executive branch of Federal or state government. None had served in the President's cabinet or as governor of a state—hence, type of previous governmental experience differs significantly from that of the Senators as described by Matthews.[8] Seven of the sixteen with previous state legislative experience also have some executive experience, either in business or government.

The amount of time the sixteen Congressmen served in state legislatures varied from two to twenty-eight years. Presumably, longer service would be more likely to affect office organization, yet both Congressmen with long state legislative careers have hierarchical offices. Two other Congressmen have had experience in local politics, ward, city, or small town. Both have hierarchical offices.

Of those with hierarchical offices 70 percent have had executive experience; but 60 percent of those with individualistic offices also have had some executive experience. Of the twelve Congressmen with previous executive experience, 58 percent, a majority, do have hierarchical offices. However, a substantial minority, 25 percent, have individualistic offices. Among Congressmen who have had no previous executive experience, a large majority (67 percent) have nonhierarchical offices.

Lawyers prefer a middle-range office organization (67 percent have coordinative offices); few have either hierarchical or individualistic offices. Of the individualistic offices, lawyers preside over 40 percent and previous executives over 60 percent. Businessmen appear slightly to prefer an hierarchical office: of thirteen Representatives, 54 percent have hierarchical offices, compared to twenty-three percent each with coordinative and individualistic offices.

Matthews suggests that "Senators who have had long political careers in local politics, in state legislatures, or in the House of Representatives generally have rather individualistic offices."[9] Of the Congressmen surveyed, eighteen had held state or local political office prior to election to the House. Of those eighteen, 44 percent had hierarchical offices, 33 percent ran coordinative offices, and 22 percent ran individualistic offices. Of those with hierarchical offices, 88 percent have also had executive experience. Of those with coordinative or individualistic offices, 20 percent have had executive experience.

Thus, it appears that executive experience rather than involvement in local politics, with its concomitant lack of reliance on staff and "great faith in the personal touch,"[10] may be the more important factor in determining office organization.

Of those who have had previous political experience, 55 percent are lawyers, and 21 percent have hierarchical offices. Of those with previous political experience who are not lawyers, 75 percent have hierarchical offices.

Matthews points out that often several influences converge in the same direction. This is substantiated in the case of lawyers in the House: 82 percent have previous political experience; of these, 89 percent have nonhierarchical offices. Lawyers with no previous political experience divide evenly between hierarchical and nonhierarchical offices.

Background, then, appears to influence staff organization within fairly wide limits. Those Congressmen with executive experience tend to have more centrally organized staffs. Lawyers with previous political experience tend to have less bureaucratic staffs. But previous political experience does not mean a nonbureaucratic staff. For instance, one Congressman interviewed had served in a state legislature which provided staff assistants. He noted that when he first came to the House he organized his personal staff as it had been in the state legislature. This initial organizational pattern had not changed substantially during his years in the House, although numbers had increased. As it happens, he has an hierarchical staff.

Division of Workload

The workload in congressional offices can be divided by subject area or by function. In offices organized according to subject area, staff handle mail, legislation, background work for speeches, and even schedule engagements, coordinated by the appointments secretary, for an issue area. The most common division is between domestic and international issue areas. Occasionally, within domestic issue areas staffers will handle separate subjects. Less frequently the division will be between the Member's committee and noncommittee work; approximately 17 percent of the sample organize the professional work this way.

The functional distribution of work is somewhat more common. Within this pattern, there is usually an administrative assistant, a press aide, one or more legislative aides, a caseworker and possibly lower-level, backup personnel. Most offices do not have a professional to handle each function; generally one aide combines the work of several functions. The AA, for example, will handle administrative work and press relations. Whether an office is hierarchical, coordinative, or individualistic does not seem to be relevant to the functional or area-specialty division of work.

SENATE

Patterns of Staff Organization

Three major types of Senate office staff organizational patterns have been identified by professional staff members. These patterns are similar to those found in the House.

Nearly half of all Senate staff members perceive their office as lacking any organizational pattern at the professional staff level. This is an individualistic or Type III office. An aide describes this type of office: "Organization doesn't make any difference in this office. The Senator talks to each of us. There are twelve or so individuals that the Senator can talk to. Whom he talks to depends on the issue." In this type of office, "each staff member may go directly to the Senator." Also, there is a feeling in this type of loosely organized office that, "we must protect the Senator from being overwhelmed. Sometimes we must act in his name."

In hierarchical or Type I offices the administrative assistant is seen as being the "most directly related to the Senator on a line basis." Many of the large staff operations by necessity have this type of line organization. "We are one of the biggest staffs on the Hill. Maybe we are too large—85 people, 27 professional (including personal and committee staff)." A former administrative assistant in an office similar to the one above noted that he was replaced by an individual who was a known "organization man." He felt that his former office had grown too big for him to handle, and that after the new administrative assistant arrived the office seemed to be better organized. Large offices tend to have expertise in many areas, but there may be drawbacks to this type of office. A staff professional notes: "We have expertise in many areas. We have known the trees but have not seen the forest."

The third type of office, Type II, is coordinative. There are two staff members through whom direct access to the Senator is funneled. In this type of Senate office, the two staff leaders would tend to be the administrative assistant or executive assistant and the legislative assistant or press secretary. Nearly one-fifth of the responding population felt that their office was organized along these lines.

A recent trend noted in a number of Senate offices is the decentralization of staff members. "We are trying to get all our non-legislative work back to our home state. We have moved (staff members) back recently and (staff member) spends half his time there. I will be going back in a few months." An administrative assistant notes that: "We have the largest contingent of staff outside our office of any Senator . . . 16 staff members operate out of our five major (urban) centers in our state. Seventeen staff members are in this office [Washington]."

A number of offices, both Senate and House, are moving staff back to the state or district to handle a major proportion of the office workload. Two factors accelerating this move are the decentralization of Federal agencies and the lack of office space on Capitol Hill. A number of Federal agencies with which Senators' and Representatives' staffs deal on casework or Federal project matters have well-staffed regional offices in major cities throughout the country. Casework originating within the districts is often handled by the regional agency office— hence, it makes a lot of sense for a Congressman to have state or district casework staff. A recent study of Senate offices indicates that most freshmen Senators handle casework in their states, whereas the most senior Senators continue to have caseworkers primarily in Washington.[11]

For both Senate and House, the number of district and state offices has increased in recent years. Fifteen years ago there were fewer. We suspect that this is a result both of greater citizen demand and of increasing populations. Not so long ago, Senators and Representatives often knew many of their constituents personally. They had held various elective offices prior to election to the U.S. Congress; with this background and trips back to the state, and vacations spent there, Congressmen could keep in close touch. This has become more difficult in states with large populations: elections tend to be media-based as in California, and/or a large portion of the population transient. Today, it is more difficult to keep in touch with the constituency without a district or state office staff.

Few Representatives or Senators work as Congressman Barrett (D-Pa.) of Philadelphia did for many years; he went home to Philadelphia every evening after the House adjourned and held office hours, meeting personally with constituents who had waited for him. Senator Joseph Biden (D-Del.) commuted daily to Wilmington; he was reported to hold informal office hours with constituents during the train trip. When Senator George Aiken of Vermont retired in 1974, his successor promptly established a state office, something Aiken had never felt was necessary.

Some Senators share state office space and their staff handle casework together. For others—whether of the same or different parties—cooperation of this sort does not seem practical. Senators may not want to share credit, or may in fact feel in competition with the other Senator from the state. They, and their staffs, cooperate only when necessary. The House, with more clearly delineated districts and no overlap with another Representative, unless redistricted together, has less of this competition.

In many cases, pay scales are lower away from Washington, and allotments for office staff salaries can be stretched further. Finally, space on Capitol Hill, which is at a premium, can be freed if staff are moved to the state. Crowded working conditions, particularly in the Washington personal offices, can be alleviated. We expect to find that personal office decentralization will continue.

A consequence of decentralization is that intraoffice coordination is more necessary than ever, putting additional demands on office procedures and routines for coorperation and communication.

Party

In the Senate there is no significant relationship between a Senator's office organization and party affiliation. For respondents whose office could be identified, Democratic and Republican Senators are about equal in terms of coordinative office patterns. However, offices of Democratic Senators tend, more often than Republican ones, to be organized as individualistic offices. Fully half of the Democratic offices are individualistic as compared with 38 percent of Republican offices. Republican offices tend to be slightly more hierarchical than individualistic, 43 percent versus 38 percent.

Seniority

Seniority is not an important factor in determining Senate office organization. A majority of Democratic Senators regardless of seniority utilize the individualistic organization. Both senior and nonranking Republican Senators favor an hierarchical office organization. Offices of nonranking Senators (both parties) and of chairmen (Democrats) are most often individualistic; those of ranking minority members (Republicans) more often are hierarchical. Nonranking Senators more often have coordinative offices than senior Republicans and Democrats. These findings are mixed, and no clear patterns emerge.

Region

Senate office organization does vary by region. These regional differences may be a function of office budget, Senator's personality, or decentralization of the personal office (that is, a smaller in-Washington staff). For instance, many Eastern Senators have coordinative offices, whereas the majority of Midwestern and Southern Senators have individualistic offices. Western Senators tend to favor the hierarchical office organization, but there are a high percentage of individualistic offices among Western Senators which can be directly related to staff size. Many Western offices receive the minimum office dollar allotment, which is based on population, and thus have fewer staff members.

In the Midwest staff size must be considered less a factor in determining office organization, since these states are among the top ten in population and thus are provided funds for moderate to large staffs. Personal styles seem to be more important determinants of office organization. For example one Midwest Senator likes to deal directly with the members of his professional staff and not through an LA or AA.

Some Southern Senators have begun to decentralize their office structure by dispersing staff among three to six state offices. We think this explains in part their tendency to choose the individualistic office organization.

Interpersonal Relations

Professional staff members expect that fellow Senate staff members will have a good working relationship with other professionals, both those in the legislative branch and outside it: newspapermen, executive agency personnel, members of the President's personal staff, and interest group leaders. Fully three-quarters of the staff members in our study consider a good working relationship with outsiders important.

Staff members generally perceive their interpersonal relations with persons within their offices as being positive. Almost all staff members say that they have a very high-quality working relationship with their Senator. The quality of the working relationship of staff members with both their fellow staff members and outsiders is also generally positive. Therefore, most staff members expect to face relatively conflict-free work situations (see Table 20).

Conflict-free work situations are necessary because of the heavy workload and the need for "team" cooperation among office staff professionals. Long working hours and the initiative and ability to perform tasks rapidly are prerequisites for many professional Senate staff positions. An administrative assistant noted that he would not hire a staff member who had worked in the Federal bureaucracy because his initiative would have been killed by the relatively small bureaucratic workload!

Cooperation among Senate office staff provides means by which complex and varied activities can be performed. For instance, a national issue may arise, such as environmental protection, that generates tremendous constituent interest as exemplified in letters and telegrams. These letters must be answered and in some cases legislation will be drafted. In time, projects may result that require the individual attention of staff and members. And finally, individual cases will develop out of the imediate effect of the project(s). All of the above may require coordination of effort and shared expertise among the Senate office staffs.

Of special interest is the staff member's view of his relationship with his Senator. Over 96 percent of the staff respondents say they have a good or very good working relationship with their Senator. To further amplify this relationship a subpopulation of nearly fifty Senate professional staff members were asked to characterize their relationship with their Senator on an authority, power, and influence scale.[12] This scale was constructed to measure the "power" relationship between the Senator and the responding staff member.

The relationship, Table 21, was designated as being either symmetrical, each having equal influence or power over the other, or asymmetrical, with the Senator perceived as having more power, influence, or authority than the staff member. Also, the emotional overtone of the relationship was defined as being either positive, negative, ambivalent, or indifferent.

A number of observations, Table 21, may be made about the Senator–professional staff member relationship:

- Senator–staff relationships of influence may be symmetrical as well as asymmetrical;
- Little or no perceived negative emotional orientation or conflict is noted by staff in their relationship with their Senator;
- Authority relationships, as a type of influence and power, are based on the attraction of the Senator and pressure or urging from the Senator in addition to submission or obedience from the staff member;[13]
- The most commonly perceived relationship between a Senator and professional staff is that of pure influence, which is characterized in symmetrical relationships by mutuality, permissiveness, "allowing each member of the pair to be himself,"[14] and also by indifference; and in an asymmetrical or uneven-influence relationship, by popularity.[15]

In summary, staff most often see themselves as being a friend of their Senator. And staff in the subpopulation do not perceive any negative emotional relationship with their Senator. In addition some aides report that their Senator serves as an authority figure. This type of relationship can be characterized as being either charismatic or submissive-to-a-dominant figure orientation.

COMMITTEES

Patterns of Staff Organization

Just as the organization of staff in Senators' and Representatives' offices varies, so does the organization of professionals on committee staffs. Patterson[16] identified three types of committee staff organization: Type I, in which the staff director supervises all clerical and professional staff members; Type II, in which the staff director supervises clerical personnel but professionals deal directly with the chairman; and Type III, with two lines of authority (one for clerical staff and one for professionals), running through a chief clerk and a staff director.

Data presented here focus particularly on the line of authority between the professional staff member and the committee chairman. With increasing numbers of professional staff, do "individualistic" offices continue to exist? Is there any preference for organization with clearly delineated lines of authority, or for some coordinative organization—as we find in the larger personal staffs of the House and the Senate? A peripheral question but, we feel, important and related, is the relationship of the professional aide to the various members of the committee. Is the aide responsible only to the chairman? Or does he work for all members of the committee, or for the majority (or minority) only? Both Congressmen and their personal aides often view committee staff as primarily loyal to the committee or subcommittee chairman or ranking minority member. Our interview data, as well as Floor debates on staffing, such as the 1975 Senate argument and debate on S. Res. 60, support this view.

Of the committee professionals, 75 percent report a direct responsibility to one Senator or Representative; of those, 44 percent report a direct responsibility to the committee chairman, and 11 percent report that they are responsible to the ranking minority member of the committee. Another 33 percent are responsible to a subcommittee chairman, with 3 percent responsible to the ranking minority member on a subcommittee. Only four staff aides reported responsibility to the committee as a whole, although several more made a point of stating their dual responsibility—first to an individual Senator or Representative and *then* to the committee. The picture of responsibility which emerges supplements the views of personal aides. It is not difficult to understand why nonranking members say they "don't trust committee staff for much beyond technical work," or why junior Senators argued so vigorously for additional legislative aides to assist with committee work.

A majority of committee professionals view their committees as hierarchically organized (see Table 14). Although some 10 percent of the committee aides drew their own organization charts, 56 percent of all aides report an hierarchical authority structure, with professionals supervised by a staff director. When the 10 percent who drew their own organization charts are omitted from the calculation, 62 percent of the aides perceive an hierarchically structured working environment; 25 percent view their committees as "coordinative," with two chief aides coordinating the work of committee staff. Slightly more than 13 percent of the professionals report an "individualistic" office, in which all professionals have open access to work directly with committee chairmen. The organization of House and Senate committees is similar: 65 percent of House professionals and 57 percent of Senate professionals perceive their committees as hierarchically organized; nearly 23 percent of House professionals and 29 percent of Senate professionals view their committee organization as "coordinative." Few—13 percent in the House and 14 percent in the Senate—view their committees as "individualistic."

The Senate–House differences may be due to the fact that more Senators "control" committee staff earlier in their Senate careers and to the consequent shifting of aides between committee and personal staff fairly frequently. This results in a milieu where there is more likely to be direct access to Senators by staff members; the Senate committees seem to have a less tightly organized environment than those in the House. However, the striking aspect of committee organization is the number of similarities. In addition, other factors, such as subject matter of the committee (e.g., appropriations versus legislation, banking versus foreign policy), do not affect committee organization.

We would hypothesize that some of the factors—such as span of control—identified in the literature as important to complex organizations affect House and Senate personal staffs as they increase in size and complexity and also affect the organization of committee staffs. Although still small and personal as organizations go, and generalized in spite of increasing specialization and complexity, nevertheless in comparison with personal staffs, committee staffs are larger and more bureaucratic and increasingly exhibit more of the characteristics associated with complex, specialized organizations.

WORK SPACE

In both the Senate and the House personal office space is allocated according to the rules of seniority. Each Senator, upon arriving from his home state for the first time, is given from five to seven adjoining rooms in the Russell or Dirksen Senate Office Building, the number of rooms being dependent on the population of the state. He may also place certain office machines in a room in a nearby building, which may be shared by other Senators. If a more senior Senator desires the office space of a retired or defeated Senator, he can exercise his prerogatives and move to this suite. Although a senior Senator may move quite easily, he has little to gain by a "better" location within the Senate office buildings. "One thing I have noticed is the sameness of all Senate offices," comments a senior staff member. "Senators from small states have five rooms, those from larger states six rooms. They are all connected together, have the same furniture, carpets; it is frightening. I think this has an effect on the organization or the running of an office."

House office space is assigned in a similar way. Because constituency size is approximately the same, the number of office rooms assigned to each Representative does not vary. Each Representative receives three rooms (room size may vary). Both Senators and Representatives move their offices so as to be near the principal offices of their major committee assignment, particularly if they are senior on the committee, but a number of factors may be taken into account in deciding where (and whether) to move: distance from the Capitol, arrangement of the office rooms (corner suites in the Longworth House Office Building are sought after), or facilities (Rayburn instead of Cannon on the House side).

In personal offices on both sides of the Capitol, and for committees as well, space is at a premium and many office staffs work in extremely crowded conditions: Desks are jammed in six or seven to a room, papers and books are piled on the floor, and the noise level is so high that it interferes with work. Aides find it difficult to hold conferences or to talk on the telephone in confidence. Some aides conduct interviews and meet constituents and lobbyists in the Senate and House cafeterias rather than impose on their co-workers. In most offices, the Congressman's office is regularly used for conferences when he is away. New aides take their "serious work" home in the evenings. The work conditions clearly interfere with productivity. New aides often report that getting used to the noise level of an office is a major problem. A new Senate office building, the Philip A. Hart Building (an extension to the Dirksen Building), is presently under construction; both Senate and House are currently examining ways that present space might be used more effectively.

One major consequence of the limited space available is that both committee and personal staff may be housed in widely separated offices. This puts additional stress on intraoffice communication and coordination, and, we think, puts a premium on good management practices. Some staff think office location affects relationships with the Senator or Representative, and that, at least for personal staff, being located in a contiguous office brings easier communication and perhaps a smoother relationship. One function of staff is as a sounding board, and wide-ranging discussions often take place late in the day after the Senate or House has adjourned. If a Senator or Representative has to seek out staff in an office annex this may result in less interaction.

CONCLUSION

Two factors have brought changes in office organization among present Congressmen. The first results from the changes in staffing allowances as well as legislation such as the 1970 Legislative Reorganization Act. Staff increases have made necessary somewhat more formal office organization. Many Congressmen have chosen to increase the number of secretaries and caseworkers, the non-professional and semiprofessional staffers. But there is a growing trend to add professional assistants (as our figures on the increase in legislative aides show).

Changes in seniority status affect office organization in a substantial number of House offices. The type of change varies. In some cases it may be gradual and not actually result from a conscious decision. As the member gains seniority, he becomes increasingly occupied by committee work; if his party has organized the Congress, he may control committee staff, particularly if he chairs a subcommittee, or the committee itself. He then begins to use his own personal staff less on legislative and policy matters, and their chief function will become constituent service. The legislative and policy roles of the staff will be generally limited to acting as a communications conduit, either for noncommittee legislative matters, or for committee-related matters which may be brought to the member's attention through a constituent complaint.

A change in committee assignment may also bring about a change in office organization. (The committee assignment results from increased seniority: A more preferred committee choice is granted.) Because the member ranks low in committee seniority, he may feel the need of increasing his personal staff—hiring a legislative aide or a researcher—to assist him in committee work.

Increasing seniority and change in rank on committee may also result in more, not less, focus by staff on legislative work. One Congressman interviewed had recently become ranking minority member on an important subcommittee; he became entitled to a committee aide to assist him in his committee work. The aide was hired and based in the Congressman's personal office. Within a fairly short time the Congressman made a conscious decision to emphasize legislative work more strongly; the aide joined his staff, and not only handled his committee work but assisted the Congressman in a variety of legislative and policy matters which were not committee-related. The decision to emphasize legislative matters is an interesting example of a possibly unanticipated consequence of attaining high seniority; it appears to be the opposite of the generally accepted notion, supported by some political science literature, of the effects of increased seniority.

A somewhat similar situation can result, apparently, after four or five terms in the House: two Congressmen were reported reorganizing their professional staffs to obtain more assistance in legislative and policy-related work. In both instances, recent legislation allowing Congressmen to hire additional staff had been important in the restructuring. However, other considerations also entered into the changes; in one instance, it was quite specifically stated that "the Congressman wants more visibility." It may be that after a certain number of terms some Congressmen reassess their own function as a representative and vis-á-vis national politics, with consequent staff changes related to opening options for the future.

A Representative in the second-highest seniority quartile, who serves on one of the exclusive committees, thought that staffs do change over the years. "At first, there are a lot of political overtones—you hire people who have been your political supporters or have worked with you in your campaign," he noted. This is borne out, for example, by the large number of administrative assistants who come from the district to Washington with their bosses, having served, often as campaign manager, in that first campaign. This Congressman went on to say:

> "Over the years, I rely more and more on expertise. I've been able to work more responsively with the legislative function. There is a problem though in having more security, and that is that you specialize more, not only on general committee work, but within the committee. But you need a personal staff because the committee (staff) is the property of the chairman. You *must* have a personal staff to offset the advantage of the chairman."

Another senior Representative, a Republican, felt much the same way. He, too, serves on an exclusive committee, and is ranking minority member on an important subcommittee. He reflected:

"As my seniority has increased, there have been more committee assignments. The work of my staff has certainly become more complex—both in assisting on committee work, and in handling much more of the constituent (service) load. My strong feeling is that the workload is far heavier, and that my staff must perform more. It's really a function of my subcommittee assignment."

He went on to describe district-related matters which had been brought to him because of his subcommittee assignment; his personal staff had worked closely with committee staff on legislative changes which would alleviate the problem in the district but also nationwide. This is not an atypical example. A number of fairly senior Congressmen had sought legislative solutions to a national concern which had initially been brought to their attention by a district individual or group because of their particular committee assignment. Dexter has written of the selectivity with which matters are brought to a Congressman's attention, geared to perception of the Congressman's interest (or bias).[17] In this case it would appear to have unanticipated consequences.

Such "abstracting" of a district problem to a higher level may be partially a function of a specific seniority level. Representatives in the highest seniority quartile did not appear to do this regularly, for which there may be several reasons, among them concerns and responsibilities of chairing a committee or subcommittee and lack of easy adaptation to what is apparently a changing and less parochial House, with which they are not so comfortable as their lesser-ranked colleagues. But both Senators and Representatives with high but not highest seniority have attained important committee assignments with some measure of responsibility. They are sufficiently secure so that it is not necessary for them to devote most of their time and their staff's time to constituent work (and the concerns of reelection). But because they are known as specialists, they may attract complaints which might not otherwise come to them. It may be that this group makes particularly important contributions in terms of legislative effectiveness, creativity, and oversight which would be worth further exploration.

For a small minority of Congressmen, changes take place in office organization when a key staff member leaves during the Congressman's first few terms on the Hill. Of the eight Representatives in the sample serving three terms or less on the Hill, three had made major changes in office organization when a key staff member left. Most had redistributed the workload among the professionals on a more clearly defined functional basis. In one office this meant that the AA left and was not replaced. His administrative work was divided between a legislative aide, a press aide, and an office manager; all felt that the new system worked very well. One Congressman noted it had taken him longer—about four terms—to structure and hire the kind of staff he needed.

With additional staff and increasing legislative and research capability in many offices, staffs are faced with coordination needs. In hierarchical offices, the senior staff aide (usually an AA) does this. But a few offices which are not hierarchical now hold regular staff meetings to coordinate work, and in some cases, to discuss issues. The entire staff may attend, or only the professional staff may meet. The Senator or Representative sits in as he is able; in his absence the senior staff aide runs the meeting. Many unscheduled staff meetings may occur after House and Senate adjournment and staff in the office start discussing the day's events, or when the Congressman informally polls his staff on a pending vote; but the formally scheduled staff meeting is an effort to deal with the increasing size and institutionalization which is occurring in the Congress and among staffs.

Although the same patterns of office organization are evident in the Senate and the House, there are some differences. A major factor is size: House personal staffs are limited to eighteen, and several of those aides will work in district offices; Senate staffs are far larger, an average of thirty-one but ranging to seventy or more, many of them based in Washington. Both seniority and party appear to affect office organization patterns in the House more than in the Senate.

Senate staffs are both larger and more specialized. A Senator may have a number of legislative aides, and, after S. Res. 60 was adopted, in 1975, several personal committee aides as well on his staff. Relatively few Representatives have a number of legislative aides. Another trend is noticeable in the Senate where a division of function is occurring in some offices with the appointment of both an administrative assistant and an executive assistant and with the appointment of office managers.

Committees in the two Chambers are more similar to each other than to individual Congressmen's offices, although in size and specialization committees resemble Senate, rather than House, offices.

Each type of organizational pattern carries with it opportunities and constraints. In an individualistic (Type III) office, staff initiative can be encouraged and a variety of issues covered, but time and energy must be spent in coordination and information exchange. In an hierarchical office, careful scrutiny of office output is possible, and the Congressman may be freed of extensive involvement in office work matters; it appears that the policy focus must be more limited than in offices where final responsibility is divided. Coordinative offices offer a good deal of flexibility while allowing some specialization; but a fairly clear division of responsibilities and activities seems necessary for friction-free operation.

The type of organization affects the activities and responsibilities of staff, including communications patterns (both intra- and interoffice) and the flow of information, ideas, and policy analysis. In the following Chapters we turn to these.

NOTES

1. The legislative oversight function of Congress is often more talked about than practiced. It is of central concern to some observers. Oversight appears to be more often relevant to committee staff work, although Congressmen have made reputations in areas which are technically legislative oversight and have depended largely on the

work of personal, not committee, staff. See below for a discussion of personal staff work on legislative amendments arising out of casework, a form of legislative oversight which appears to be used increasingly by national-issue oriented Congressmen who are beginning to attain middle- to upper-rank seniority on powerful and prestigious committees. Provisions of the Legislative Reorganization Act of 1970 and the Congressional Budget and Impoundment Control Act of 1974 strengthen Congress's oversight capability.

2. These patterns are based on the organization of the professional staff members and their relationship with the Congressman. In most offices, the work of secretarial staff is reviewed by one of the professionals; if it is not—as, for example, is the situation with some caseworkers—those staff were considered professional.

3. Subpatterns of the coordinative office are not as evident in the Senate, perhaps because of the larger number of middle-level professionals.

4. Classifying the offices is of necessity a somewhat subjective exercise. It is based on observation, and interview data on communications flow, staff access, and professionals' job descriptions.

5. A study presently under way by Jeff Fischel and Burdette Loomis finds that freshman Congressmen in the 94th Congress (1975–1976) often have coordinative offices or, in some instances, a more formally hierarchical office. For a preliminary report, see Loomis, "The Congressional Office as a Small (?) Business."

6. But one junior member has organized his office so that most professionals are supervised by a top-level aide. Young professionals work on projects independently under the supervision of senior staff men. An effort is made to have the young staffer present the finished product himself and to include him in any briefings. In this office the senior staff men are considerably older than the junior professionals and also share previous school and work experience with the Congressman. In addition, most of the junior professionals are women; the senior professionals are men—which does make some difference on Capitol Hill.

7. Donald R. Matthews, *U.S. Senators and Their World* (Chapel Hill, N.C.: University of North Carolina Press, 1960), p. 86.

8. Matthews, p. 86 ff.

9. *Ibid.,* p. 87.

10. *Ibid.,* p. 86.

11. Janet Ellen Breslin, "Constituent Services", study prepared for The Commission on the Operation of the Senate, in, *Senators: Offices, Ethics, and Pressures,* Committee Print, 94th Congress, 2d Session (82–053), 1977.

12. Modified from Richard A. Schermerhorn, *Society and Power* (New York: Random House, 1961).

13. *Ibid.,* pp. 5–6.

14. *Ibid.,* p. 2.

15. *Ibid.,* p. 4.

16. "The Professional Staffs of Congressional Committees" by Samuel C. Patterson, *Administrative Science Quarterly,* March, 1970, Vol. 15(1), 22.

17. Lewis Anthony Dexter, "The Representative and His District," in Robert L. Peabody and Nelson W. Polsby, (eds.) *New Perspectives on the House of Representatives* (Chicago: Rand McNally, 1963), pp. 3–29.

6. Activity and Jobs of Staff

Congressional staff perform a variety of activities to support the work of Congress. For instance, staff open the mail, read and answer it, often sign the member's name, and send responses to the concerned constituents. Members, due to great demands on their time, must rely on staff to assist them in much of their work. Most members now serve as guides to the proper course of action. Knowing the member's goals, staff perform the activities that help establish and maintain the member's position.

Increases in legislative workload and constituent demands in the last twenty years have been partially responsible for the growing reliance on staff. A Senator who came to Congress in 1962 as a Representative noted that his predecessor used to receive fifteen to twenty letters a week from his constituents and answered them all, himself, in longhand. Today, the Senator receives 2,000 to 3,000 letters a week, hundreds of phone calls, and may be invited to attend half a dozen events in a single evening. A consequence has been that he has had to involve staff in almost every activity that is a part of his position as Senator. In summary, the member is a generalist, performing and directing legislative, constituent-service, oversight, party, campaign, and press activities while depending on his support staff of specialists. It is important to note that a generalist member must act out numerous roles, many outside the Congressional arena, but his staff has the opportunity to specialize within the confines of the walls of Congress.

The two major types of congressional staffs, committee and personal, perform a wide range of activities. Major personal staff tasks are handling constituent problems: casework and projects, requests for information, correspondence, visits with constituents and special interest groups. Press and legislative work are also important activities. Senate offices with larger staffs tend to be more specialized than House offices. In both House and Senate personal offices, six major activity clusters are found: administration, legislative, research, press, correspondence, and oversight. Committee aides' activities include bill drafting, investigating, and dealing with lobbyists. Administrative, research, correspondence, oversight, and some press functions are also performed.

In personal offices, administrative work is generally handled by a Congressman's administrative assistant (AA) and in some Senate offices by an office manager or an executive assistant. A professional staff member who handles constituent problems often deals with both constituents and lobbyists, supervises office personnel, and reacts to political mail.

The legislative and research function of the office is typically handled by one or more legislative assistants (LA's) and, in an increasing number of offices on both sides of the Capitol, a researcher. Most House offices and all Senate offices have LA's. They may work with the member on committee matters, write Floor remarks, perform legislative research, draft bills, read and analyze other bills, and write articles. In the Senate, even the personal staff of committee chairmen and ranking minority members do a significant amount of committee work. In both houses, unless a member controls committee staff appointments, he often feels he must rely on his own personal staff for major assistance in committee work.

Press aides and assistants advertise their member's work through the media. Secretaries, clerks, AA's, LA's—everyone answers the mail, including the member himself. They provide an informational service to the constituent and produce the letter or telegram that treats a particular problem.

Finally, the personal staff aides' activities are guided by the Congressman's ideology, interests, personality, the quality and quantity of his relationships with other Congressmen, the congressional structure and atmosphere, and home state considerations. Other factors which are significant are the Congressman's perception of his role and of the type of district he serves, his training and experience, and his view of the Congressional mandate.

HOUSE PERSONAL STAFF

In House offices there are not enough staff for each type of activity to be performed by a different individual; hence, House personal staff jobs are more generalist than most Senate personal staff positions.

The AA supervises the personnel of the office, coordinates and assigns workload, oversees hiring, payroll, and use of office allowances, and also handles duties within a specific area of expertise—most generally press and Federal projects. In a minority of offices, 16 percent of those surveyed, there is no AA. In those offices routine administrative work—office supervision and ordering of supplies, for example—is generally handled by an experienced executive secretary. The more policy-oriented administrative duties are handled primarily by the Congressman himself, in some cases with assistance from a political aide in the district. Most typically, however, the AA functions as the Congressman's alter ego and surrogate, and often has long-time ties of his own with the district. He talks with constituents and lobbyists, attends meetings for the Congressman, tries to anticipate information needs and to filter communications through a perception attuned to the Representative's views. The AA is the most generalist staffer in an increasingly specialized environment.

Legislative functions of the office are typically handled by an LA. In a few offices, 28 percent of the sample, where there is no legislative assistant, Congressmen handle legislative matters themselves and obtain some fairly routine data from staff assistants working under close supervision of the member or devote their major attention to committee work and use committee staff exclusively for this. In most offices, however, one LA handles legislative matters in all issue areas: briefing, drafting Floor statements, researching data, and drafting amendments. He often also handles legislative mail, i.e., letters from constituents about pending legislation or current issues. Legislative assistants feel that they cannot do in-depth work which they would like to do, and often articulate dissatisfaction with the generalist nature of their jobs. House members are beginning to appoint more than one LA or are appointing legislative secretaries to handle legislative mail or research assistants to work with the LA. Among Congressmen with high activity in the legislative area (large number of bills introduced, co-sponsored, and/or staff engaged in extensive committee work) there appears to be a trend toward further specialization of legislative duties. Often this means that two or more legislative assistants who specialize in different areas are employed.

Fully 84 percent of the offices surveyed, all but four, use personal staff for fairly extensive committee work. It is clear that personal staffs are making a substantive input into the committee legislative process by doing initial research and data gathering on issues, briefing for hearings, drafting amendments and individual views for reports, and on occasion handling committee correspondence and drafting press releases. Unless a member controls committee staff appointments, he often feels he must rely on his own personal staff for major assistance in committee work. This is true whatever policy position the member may take. For instance, neither a member's score on the Congressional Quarterly Conservative Coalition Scale nor a nonpartisan committee staff makes a difference in this regard.

The major reason for using personal rather than committee staff is that the Congressman can be sure his own attitudes and interests will be reflected. Comments during interviews indicate Congressional thinking: a seventh-term Democrat who serves on two committees and chairs a subcommittee said, "Committee staff can be inside lobbyists for certain things. You have to watch this." A senior Republican said, "The key guys (on a committee staff) reflect the chairman. Therefore, I do my own work. You can't even use minority staff if you want to do something which is against the minority (ranking) member who controls it." Except for chairmen and ranking minority members, personal staffs of a large majority of Congressmen are deeply involved in substantive committee matters. We would expect, as in the Senate, that although there has recently been some dispersion of subcommittee staff resources, some personal staffs will continue to be deeply involved in legislative activities.

Staff also give major assistance on legislative work not related to their bosses' committees.[1] Depending on the Congressman's interest and the office organization, staff input may be a strong force in legislative policy making. If the office organization is rigidly structured, with specific guidelines for staff work, impact on issue priority as well as specifics of policy will be less than in those offices where staff are encouraged to give some attention to development of issues and can, on occasion, spark a member's interest in issues previously of little concern. Staff work ranges from a one-time but thorough briefing with opinion, to a comprehensive strategy involving initial concern, gathering and analyzing data, "selling" the Congressman (as one LA put it), and following through on legislative drafting, testimony, data gathering, and coordination with the appropriate committee. Some staffers seek out speaking invitations for the Congressmen from groups with a specific interest, calculating that the speech will serve as a vehicle to arouse both the Congressman's concern and his follow-through. One LA said, "It's really at the speech stage where I have the greatest impact. After that, when an issue is into the legislative process, it's almost too late."

Also important are the links made by some offices among individual casework, administrative oversight, and legislation. Some Congressmen use a constituent complaint regarding an individual problem with a Federal program as a method of agency oversight. While the Congressman and his staff are in the process of solving the individual situation, they will also examine agency administration of the law in general and on occasion will bring about change in agency procedures. Constituent casework may also lead to legislation. One Congressman, for example, was alerted by a constituent to problems in the payment of Medicare claims. After investigation, an amendment remedying the situation was drafted and subsequently approved by the Ways and Means Committee and passed by the Congress.

Evident from the data are the growth in recent years of staff involvement in planning and execution of strategy and the increase in bipartisan cooperation, both member and staff, around a specific issue. On the SST issue, for example, staff played a major role, devising Floor strategy, assigning jobs, and presenting a total plan to their bosses.

Press matters are, in many offices, handled by the AA, who also takes responsibilities for Federal project assistance and often is a close advisor on district matters. But the number of offices appointing press assistants is increasing: 16 percent of the sample in the 92nd Congress.[2] The press function includes regular news releases, newsletters, columns for local newspapers, and radio and TV tapes. In offices with a staffer titled "Press Assistant," all these activities are done frequently and with a certain planned professionalism. In addition, many press assistants double as writers: drafting speeches and Floor statements or testimony for the Congressman. Press assistants in the House reflect the increased utilization of specialized expertise.

Another example of increasing staff specialization is found among offices who have hired research assistants. These staff collect data for a speech or work on issues which eventually may result in legislation, not necessarily related to matters under the jurisdiction of the committee on which the Congressman serves. Very often research is related to district problems. In one office, a staff man hired to do special research developed legislation on gas pipeline safety after a pipeline explosion in the district. Even though the initial impetus for office concern was district oriented, the output was national legislation.

Most offices do very little original research, relying on data from a wide range of sources.[3] Staff gather and synthesize factual and analytical material. There is heavy reliance on the executive departments for data, as well as on lobby groups and, increasingly, on expert consultants and advisors. One office sent the legislative assistant out-of-state to examine historical data and to interview on an issue of concern to the district, but this type of basic research is extremely rare.

Federal project assistance now occupies a good deal of staff and often members' time. Although the major effort involves contacts with Washington agencies, a number of offices are prepared to assist district groups at all stages of a grant application, even giving advice on how to prepare the application. A top staff person, most often the AA, generally performs this function. In a very few offices, a Federal projects assistant helps the top staffer, performing an information function and making initial contact with both district and Federal agencies.

SENATE PERSONAL STAFF

Senate staff members perform a great number of activities for which a Senator receives credit, but they are under certain constraints. In their activities, staff members are guided by the Senator's political attitudes and ideology, the needs and concerns of his state, his role in the Senate, his interests, and the organizational realities of the office. In addition, it should be made clear that the activities of top assistants may vary widely. "Some assistants perform little more than routine responsibilities; others are in every sense advisors and assistants."[4]

The full Senate professional staff population was asked to identify what activities they were engaged in and the intensity of these activities.[5] Responses indicate that, for example, nearly nine of ten staff professionals handle at least once a week such constituent projects as sewage systems, urban renewal, water systems, dams, roads, airports, health grants, and educational assistance (see Table 22). These types of projects are important to the development of each Senator's state and thus, in most offices, receive a great deal of professional staff attention. Professional staff also handle some constituent casework, but casework is most often handled by other staff members who are not in the professional category. Thus, it is of much more active concern within each Senate office than the data indicate.

Other activities in which professional staff members are actively engaged are opinion and pressure mail, other forms of correspondence, and visits with constituents. Engaging in recurrent activities such as these leads to role behavior. Observers and participants of the staffs of Congress have noted various "types" of staff activity clusters. The data that follow empirically validate many of these observations and suggest new interpretations of staff role behavior.

The staff professionals' general role(s) is defined by one or more of the recurrent staff activities within the total set of interdependent Senate office activities. Five meaningful factors were empirically identified by taking the intercorrelations among the responses of staff members to the activity items and subjecting them to a factor analysis utilizing the Varimax method. These factors have been designated as general professional staff roles. In the following paragraphs each of the general staff role types is identified. A list of the activity items that identify each type is also included along with the factor loading of each item on the role type (factor).

Role I: Interactor

A staff member scoring high on this factor interacts with individuals who have political problems or issues to push. For those in this role category, a great deal of time is spent handling constituent problems, interacting with lobbyists, and reacting to political mail. More specifically, the staff member performs the following set of activities:

- Meeting with lobbyist and special interest groups (.63)
- Handling constituency problems: projects (.76)
- Handling constituency problems: casework (.70)
- Visiting with constituents in Washington (.69)
- Answering pressure and opinion mail (.48)

A staff member who assumes the Interactor role has been given considerable responsibility for one of the more important clusters of activities performed in a Senate office. Oftentimes the AA or other senior professional member is given responsibilities in this area.

Interacting with lobbyists and special interest groups is shared to some extent with the Investigator (Role V) who has a factor loading on this activity of .41. The Interactor may also be engaged in campaign activities on occasion as the factor loading is .35.

Role II: Supporter

Role II, the Supporter, provides legislative and journalistic support for the Senate office. The activities most often engaged in by this role type are:

- Accompanying Senator in committee (.54)
- Writing Floor remarks and speeches (.91)

- Working on legislative research, bill drafting and reading, and analyzing bills (.70)
- Writing magazine articles, books, and speeches other than those for Senate Floor use (.56)

It is the Supporter who is found writing the Senator's public statements. The activities identified load higher than any others within the set of role types, and it is likely that a staff member loading on this role type will very actively perform these activities.

The Supporter shares the activity, "Writing magazine articles, books, and speeches other than those for Senate Floor use," with Role IV, the Advertiser. This activity also loads moderately (.51) on the Advertiser role type.

Legislative assistants and staff assigned to cover substantive issue areas are the most likely staff members to be acting within this general role.

Role III: Corresponder

Secretaries, clerks, and those who spend much of their time in the Senate office sitting before a typewriter are identified with this role type. The Corresponder provides an informational service to the constituent and produces the letter or telegram as output. Activities on which this staff member scores high are:

- Writing letters of congratulations and condolence (.63)
- Writing correspondence other than described (.34)
- Answering requests for information (.68)
- Handling opinion ballots (.66)
- Mailing government publications (.57)

The activity, "writing correspondence other than described," is shared to some extent with most of the other role types but most especially, the Advertiser (.32). Corresponders may also be found helping out "on pressure and opinion mail" (.31). The person characterized by this role is often a senior secretary or office manager who is earning over $12,000 per year and may be considered a quasiprofessional; other staff are under his or her direction, and he or she has responsibility for producing a final product.

Role IV: Advertiser

Press aides and assistants advertise the Senator through the media—press, radio, and television. Staff members in this role are likely to engage in campaign activity also. The activities within this role include managing press work, radio, television (.64), and working on campaign (.58).

Advertisers also may "write magazine articles, books, and speeches other than those for Senate floor use" (.51) and work "on correspondence other than described" (.32).

Role V: Investigator

The Investigator oversees the activities of the executive or judicial branches of government. A staff member in this role scores high on keeping track of investigations and oversight (.59).

Two other activities may be performed on a regular basis by the Investigator: "working on legislative research, bill drafting, and reading and analyzing bills" (.41); and "meeting with lobbyists and special interest groups" (.41).

Very few staff members perform this role exclusively; usually another set of activities is performed in addition.

The position that staff members occupy in a Senate office is defined in terms of their role(s)[6] and the intensity of activity in which they are engaged.[7] Each staff member has been assigned role scores for each of the five role types. These scores denote the intensity of activity in which each staff member is engaged. For the purpose of this study, the population was broken into thirds based on the intensity of the activity level for each of the five roles: High (H); Middle (M); and Low (L). Staff members in the top 15 percent within each role type are designated as being highly active (VH) staff members.

In Table 23 (App.), staff members are grouped according to patterns of role types. These patterns are discernably different according to the intensity of activity across role types. How intensely developed are the repertoires of staff members in each category? This can be measured along a generalist–specialist dimension.

Staff members in Category I are exclusive generalists. They are very actively engaged in a very broad range of roles. Nonexclusive generalists (Category IV) are engaged in a broad range of roles but not at the same level of activity as the exclusive generalist. Staff members in these categories occupy many positions in their office organization. Exclusive specialists (Category III) and nonexclusive specialists (Category VI) are engaged in a narrow range of activities within the Senate office. Exclusive specialists perform a set of activities at a greater frequency than does the nonexclusive specialist. Only one role as well as one position in the Senate office organization is occupied by exclusive and nonexclusive specialists. The multispecialist (categories II and V) is midway between the generalist and the specialist in terms of role differentiation. A staff member in the multispecialist category may occupy more than one but not many (four or five) separate positions. Nonparticipants (VII) are not identified as being part of the population of Senate staff members.

The position(s) of staff members can be further described by looking at a table of role types, Table 24, within selected Senate offices. Person One within Senate office A is engaged mostly in activities that are characteristic of the Supporter and Advertiser role types. In terms of our previous discussion of staff specialization, Person One is an exclusive multispecialist with tendencies toward being a specialist. In the office organization space as defined by role scores, he is very close to Persons Three and Four in his Supporter role and Persons Two, Three, and Six in his role as Advertiser. Person One as a Supporter is more active than other professionals in his office. And he is not as active in his Advertiser role as Person Two. If all persons within the Senate offices were compared on a similar basis, then the spatial position(s) for each staff member would be identified. Table 24 gives the coordinate values for the spatial positions of each staff member.

In looking over Table 24, many persons are generally performing one role relatively more frequently than the others. This confirms that staff specialization, in one or two clusters of activities (role types), is relatively common throughout the Senate. In fact, with recent staff increases, especially the creation of personal committee staff, role differentiation seems to be increasing. In most organizations, and Senate and House offices are typical, as staff size increases, specialization of personnel is encouraged. For instance, four, five, or more legislative assistants in an office may divide up the "world" with one specializing on energy, another on transportation and urban affairs, and so on. Furthermore, the press section may now have both a speech writer and a press assistant.

It has been generally assumed by those studying or acquainted with the congressional staff system that as a Senator gains additional committee staff, his personal staff will tend to be less active in legislative matters. Within offices of senior Senators (as measured by years of continuous service) and of committee chairmen, however, personal staff members were found to engage in legislative activities at a fairly high level of intensity. For instance, in the office of a Senator who is a senior ranking minority member of a Senate committee with over eighty committee and personal staff members he can call his own, three of the five personal professional staff members responding to the questionnaire were actively engaged in legislative matters as designated by the Supporter role type.[8] The scores on this role type of responding staff members of committee chairmen show that many personal staff members are engaged in activities related to legislative matters.

Perceived Effects of Behavior

Each staff member of the Senate personal staff subpopulation (Table 25) was asked to evaluate the effects of his behavior on the individuals within his role set, including persons from within and outside the office. Most staff perceive that they have at least some positive relationships with persons they work with. No staff member noted that he had a mostly negative relationship with Senators or Senate staff. This finding tends to reinforce earlier comments that Senate staff professionals perceive little conflict among themselves and members of their role set. This is significant in that staff activity is performed in a low-conflict environment, leading us to observe that cooperation is a norm widely held by staff.

With heavy workload, staff has little time to waste on "bureaucratic battles" and must depend on the support and assistance of other aides. However, intrastaff and interstaff battles do exist on occasion, and take energy, of course.

Each staff member was asked to indicate how he felt about certain activities or organizational memberships of a staff member. Table 26 presents the range of intensity of staff role expectations for selected statements. Few staff members would limit memberships or activities. Joining organizations that try to influence public policy elicited the greatest number of proscriptive responses. In this instance, nearly one-fifth of the population felt that this particular type of behavior should be avoided. There is a general lack of intense feeling by staffers about the activities and memberships of their fellow professionals. It seemed to make little difference to the respondents if other staff members engaged in the enumerated activities or memberships except in the case of taking an active part in the Senator's campaign.

Staff members belong to a broad range of organizations on Capitol Hill[9] and are engaged in diverse activities. There tends to be a laissez-faire attitude about organizational memberships, although in some offices where a staff member is an officer of an organization, pressure is exerted on the other eligible staff in the office to join.

The most intensely held of all role expectations for staff activity measured in this study are those associated with the senatorial political campaign.[10] Two-thirds of all staff feel that this activity should be actively pursued. A distinction can be made between political and campaign activity. Most activities performed by staff are political in that they support the member. But only a few are campaign related. For instance, receiving contributions and working directly on re-election matters are generally considered campaign activities. As campaign laws continue to be tightened, we would expect that the distinction between political and campaign staff activity will receive a great deal of attention, and that both Congressmen and staff will separate the activities. At present, staff members who actively work on a campaign generally do so on their own time (after work or when on leave) or go onto the campaign staff payroll. Letters and inquiries to a Senate office which are campaign related may be sent to the campaign office for an answer; if a constituent is involved, however, the line between campaign and political activities may not always be clear.

In administering a second questionnaire to a subset of the original Senate population, additional questions relating to role expectations were asked. If "never" is defined as a proscriptive response, then only in the case of a staff member concerning himself with the personal life of a Senator do we find a significant role-behavior prohibition. The surprising responses to this question are at the other end of the scale. Nearly one-fifth of the staff subset feel that the personal life of the Senator deserves their attention on a regular basis. Their response to this question gives a general insight into staff involvement with the Senator's personal life. Occasionally, a Senator's personal staff may look after the children, pets, spouse, house, or car. Thus, staff may be courtiers,[11] serving in many capacities which, of course, vary a great deal with different offices.

Senate Legislative Personal Staff

In June, 1975, the Senate, after extended debate, created a new category of staff: S. Res. 60 positions for assistance on committee work for Senators on those committees who did not have committee staff.

The Legislative Appropriations for FY 1976 provided that each Senator would have a separate account up to $102,000, for the employment of legislative aides for committee business; the total Senate appropriation for FY 1976 was $3,500,000. (For FY 1977, a total of $5,500,000 was appropriated.) Those Senators with existing assistants on a committee were not given additional staff help. Proponents of this measure felt that the staff aides would allow more active participation of the"junior Senator" in legislative and oversight work of the Congress.

It is too early to assess the effects of this additional group of aides. A number of them have moved from legislative assistant positions, and we would expect that they would score high on the Supporter and Investigator roles.

COMMITTEE STAFF

Committee staff people are actively involved in drafting bills, investigating, providing information, and seeing lobbyists, activities that lead to the making of policy and the performance of oversight. In the course of such duties they are in contact with the bureaucracy on average almost daily. Contact may be made to discuss future legislation, the implementation of a public law, information about a particular program or project, or any number of topics associated with program authorization, appropriation, budgeting, or oversight.

Committee aides report that they work with Congressmen in hearings, on the average, about once a week and in mark-up, conference, and executive sessions about once a month. They work on legislation more frequently, "at least once a day," and write remarks approximately once a week (see Table 27). Committee aides and aides on personal staffs perform many of the same activities. But the frequency with which these activities are engaged in, and hence, by implication, the amount of time devoted to them, varies. As Table 28 indicates, activities of committee aides in both houses are more similar than activities of committee aides compared to personal staff aides.

In some instances, the activity of Senate personal aides is very similar to that of Senate committee aides, and both are different from the activity of House committee aides. For example, Senate staff meet slightly more frequently with lobbyists and special interest groups than do House committee staff.

Among committee aides, general roles are more difficult to identify. But two general roles seem to be of note: the Supervisor and the Companion. The Supervisor is engaged in working with other committees and supervising clerical and professional staff, whereas the Companion assists the Congressman in hearings, markup, conference, and executive session. Supervisors and Companions are found on both House and Senate committees.[12]

CONCLUSION

In this chapter, a variety of activities have been identified and described for personal staff and committee aides. In the House, the jobs of professional aides in each office have been summarized and data presented on the proportion of offices appointing administrative aides, legislative assistants, press secretaries, and other professionals. Several trends with regard to staff activities can be identified. For example, there are an increasing number of offices with press aides and several legislative assistants. Also, staff activity in planning legislative strategy seems to be on the increase. Senate and House personal staff are at work on legislative and policy matters relating to the Senator's or Representative's committee work, even in committee chairmen and ranking minority members' offices.

The activities of Senate personal staffs are summarized and described. Five roles are identified, using frequency of activity data.

Observations are made about the role specialization of Senate staff members. Reinforcing earlier conclusions about House aides, Senate staff is shown to be both multispecialist and specialist; in a few instances they are generalists within the office setting.

Additional data enables us to describe aides' expectations regarding staff activity and perceptions of the effects of that activity. Particularly significant is the high staff tolerance for organizational memberships and the expectation (65 percent) that most staff will take part in the Senator's campaign.

Also, we have compared activities and jobs for personal staffers with committee aides. Much of the work is similar but varies along interesting continua such as contact with lobbyists and special interest groups.

A prime factor leading to legislative accomplishment is the ability of a staff member to communicate with his fellow staff members and Congressmen. The intensity and quality of staff activity makes little difference if an idea, amendment, or bill cannot be brought to the attention of the people working in Congress.

NOTES

1. Staff work of this type should be viewed in the overall context of other cue-giving groups and individuals. See, for example, studies by David B. Truman, *The Congressional Party: A Case Study* (New York: Wiley, 1959); Alan Fiellin, "The

Functions of Informal Groups in Legislative Institutions: A Case Study," *Journal of Politics,* (24), 1962, pp. 72–91; Julius Turner, *Party and Constituency: Pressures on Congress* (Baltimore: Johns Hopkins Press, 1951); Warren E. Miller and Donald E. Stokes, "Constituency Influence in Congress," *American Political Science Review,* LVII, (1963), pp. 45–56; and Donald R. Matthews and James A. Stimson, "The Decision-making Approach to the Study of Legislative Behavior: The Example of the U.S. House of Representatives," a paper delivered at American Political Science Association Annual Meeting, New York, 1969.

2. A higher percent in the 94th for freshman offices. See Loomis, "The Congressional Office as a Small (?) Business."

3. Problems of data collection and reliance on outside sources have been of concern to Congressional scholars and commentators. See, for example, essays by Kenneth Janda and James A. Robinson in Alfred de Grazia, ed., *Congress: The First Branch of Government* (Washington, D.C.: American Enterprise Institute for Public Policy Research, 1965) and John S. Saloma, *Congress and the New Politics* (Boston: Little Brown, 1969). See also studies by the Commission on the Operation of the Senate, U.S. Senate.

4. Charles L. Clapp, *The Congressman: His Work as He Sees It* (Washington, D.C.: Brookings Institution, 1963), p. 71.

5. These activities were suggested by Saloma; Warren H. Butler, "Administering Congress: The Role of the Staff," *Public Administration Review,* XXVI (March, 1966); Norman Meller, "Legislative Staff Services: Toxic, Specific, or Placebo for the Legislator's Ills," *Western Political Quarterly,* XXX (June, 1967), pp. 381–389; Dexter, *The Sociology;* Robert Sherrill, "Who Runs Congress?" *New York Times Magazine,* November 22, 1970; Matthews, *U.S. Senators;* Malcolm Jewell and Samuel Patterson, *The Legislative Process in the United States* (New York: Random House, 1966 and 1977); and Haynes Johnson, "Congressional Staffs: The Third Branch of Congress," *The Washington Post,* January 18, 1970, pp. 1A and 17A.

6. Each of the five roles identified with professional staff members are general dimensions denoting a proclivity of the population to engage in particular activities. From this general information, individual staff members can be given a score for each role type. Five scores for each staff member were computed by standardizing the raw activity variables, giving each variable equal standard deviations and means. The standardized variables were multiplied by the factor-score coefficients. For each person the sum of this product was computed for the five factors or role types. Thus, staff members were assigned a score for each of the five role types. In calculating the scores for each role type, the complete-estimation method was used. This method, when used in constructing a factor matrix or score, sums the regression weights of each standardized variable (z score). See Norman Nie, Dale H. Bent, and C. Hadlai Hull, *SPSS Statistical Package for the Social Sciences* (New York: McGraw-Hill, 1970).

7. For a full discussion of specialization, consult Bruce J. Biddle and Edwin J. Thomas, eds., *Role Theory: Concepts and Research* (New York: Wiley, 1966), pp. 34–35.

8. The Supporter role type is defined by four activities: accompanying Senator in committee; writing Floor remarks and speeches; working on legislative research, bill drafting, and reading and analyzing bills; and writing magazine articles, books, and speeches other than those for Senate Floor use. The first and third of the above

activities are always related to legislation, and the second and fourth activities are many times related to legislative matters.

9. See Fox (1972), pp. 96–158.

10. Senate Rule 43 prohibits political fund-raising activities by Senate employees unless they are compensated at more than $10,000 per year and are designated in writing to the Secretary of the Senate by the Senator. U.S. Congress, Senate Committee on Rules and Administration, Senate Manual, 92nd Congress, 1st Session, (Washington D.C.: Government Printing Office, 1971), p. 64. (Modifications occurred in 1977.)

11. See Lewis A. Dexter, "Court Politics."

12. Based on factor analysis of committee staff responses.

7. Communications in the Congress

Personal and committee professional staff play a key role in establishing and maintaining communications networks vital to the functioning of congressional offices.[1] Staff aides gather, analyze, and evaluate information on substantive issues and on legislative strategy. They are links to other actors in the congressional system, as well as to those outside Congress.

In the executive branch, staff work, including staff data collection, is important to final decision making. Top level policymakers bring their own expertise and perceptions to consideration of a problem but also rely on staff work—generally through several hierarchical levels—to gather and analyze the data on a specific issue.

Staff input into congressional decision making is often more immediate and direct. Particularly in individualistic personal offices, where all professionals have frequent access to the Congressman without many intervening layers of hierarchy, staff sources of information can be crucially important to informed decision making.

Communication depends on both formal (e.g., committee-to-personal-office) and on informal, less institutionalized channels in which factors such as personal contacts and shared characteristics such as party, region, state, and attitude, provide a framework for communication. Congressional "class" (Congress of election) can also be a factor. Both the 94th Congress freshmen in the House and the "freshman" group in the Senate,[2] for instance, are important communications groups, and work together on a number of matters. An hindrance to communications is the powerful drive of Congressional groups and actors to guard information. Information is power, and at times there is little perceived payoff from information sharing. Coordinating mechanisms—the party leaders, regional caucuses, and ideological groups—seek to overcome the autonomy of the subunits and to share relevant information. However, both gaps in information and overlap and duplication of effort continue to occur.

Another factor in communications patterns is both the quality and quantity of information available to Congress. To many observers and analysts, information is plentiful, but the problem lies in obtaining timely, analytic, and topical information. Attempts to solve these problems have led in turn to staff growth.

INTERNAL COMMUNICATION CHANNELS

Intraoffice and Inter-Office Communication

Congress if a verbal culture: much of the information exchange occurs in the form of briefings, hearings, discussions, and meetings. As office staffs increase in size, particularly in the Senate, communications within an office become more important and more difficult.

In addition, intraoffice communication patterns tell us something about the management of the office. Some Senators consider it important to talk with staff, at least briefly, each day—at least to "walk through the office and say hello". Others view this as a time demand which should be unnecessary in a well-managed organization.

The general communication patterns among U.S. Senate staff professionals are of three types: personal–promotional, administrative, and legislative. These types emerge out of a combination of formal and informal role relations between the professional staff member and persons with whom he may come in contact.

What are the basic dimensions describing these general communication patterns of Senate personal professional staffs?[2a] A different type of staff member is identified for each of the three communication patterns. No aide's communication pattern is characterized exactly by any one of these general types, but the three types are indicative of staff communication patterns.

Type I, the personal–promotional, comes in contact on a regular basis with his Senator and with journalists. This type of aide is most likely to handle the press and promotional activities of the office. He is in contact with the Senator nearly every hour, possibly to clear with him the press releases that are given to journalists.

The administrative type, Type II, is in contact with constituents, staff in other Senate offices, staff in House offices, the bureaucracy, and staff in the executive offices of the President. Many of these aides handle constitutent problems—casework and projects—and are involved in the "political" activities of the office.

The third type (III), legislative, is in communication with the various committee staffs, including House and Senate committees on which his Senator sits and those on which he does not. Since communication for this type is with Congressional committees, most of the role behavior (activities) is related to legislative research and drafting and, possibly, a certain amount of legislative constituent service.

Senate professional staff communicate with a number of different groups. Most obviously, they talk to those within their office. The significance of this intraoffice communication is noted in an administrative assistant's statement: "The important thing is that we get along. One bad apple can ruin a staff operation." All but one staff member responding to the questionnaire communicated (Table 29) with staff in his office more than once a day. This confirms a key point that Senate staffs are tightly knit groups of persons who communicate actively with each other.

Nearly all staff professionals have contact with their Senator at least once each day. The AA generally talks with him most frequently. "At first I went to him on every problem," comments an AA. "He told me to stop it. He was being overwhelmed. On the issues I knew what he thought, I went ahead and did it." How does this relationship develop between the Senator and the AA? A staff aide comments:

"It is often asked, 'How did the stupid jerk get to be the A.A.?' Answer: He's probably the only person except his wife the Senator can trust.

"The A.A. must do two important things. First, he must be secure enough that he can tell the Senator the truth—when he's wrong, when he's making a big mistake, when to take on an issue and when to forget it.

"Second, he must be trusted completely by the Senator, subordinate his personal ambitions to those of the Senator (no candidates for office, please) and defend the Senator's best interests rather than to lobby for his own causes. He should also stay out of and try to stop any intraoffice internecine warfare.

"He should be paid not for his brains but for his strength of character and personal loyalty."

Communication with staff in other Senate personal offices also is frequent; three fourths of the professional aides talk to other Senate personal offices at least once a day. And 11 percent reported very frequent contact of once an hour or more. Outside the office, communications networks also develop through party groups, committees, state delegation groups, congressional classes, and office location. Taken together, they help form the base for power and influence in the Congress.

Party

Party is a major centralizing force in the work of the Senate and the House. Through party, there is a mechanism for both formal and informal communication.

Party whip notices serve to organize and coordinate the work on the Floor, and personal offices set up specific routines for collecting information which may be needed as a result of the whip notice.

In the House, the more senior Democrats rely on leadership offices for substantive information and guidance, as well as for pro forma information, more than do comparatively junior members. Republicans, regardless of seniority, rely less on leadership offices for substantive information and guidance, apparently due both to the Republican Party's role as the Congressional minority in recent years and to the periodic leadership upheavals within the Republican Party in the House which have often resulted in divided if not stalemated leadership. Lack of adequate minority staffing on committees has meant that even very senior Republicans have been forced to rely on assistance from their own personal staff. The ideological split in the party has resulted in perhaps more reliance on groups within the party (the (liberal) Wednesday Group, the (conservative) Study Group) than on leadership.[3]

A House member's position in the party or leadership also affects staff contacts. Personal staffs of assistant whips know, and rely on, leadership staffs more than do other offices.

Within party, more organized groups such as, for example, the Democratic Study Group, the Republican Study Group, and the Wednesday Group have become important sources of information as well as coordinators of strategy in recent years. The some 250-member plus, somewhat structured DSG embraces a variety of viewpoints, including the majority of Democrats except some Southerners and ideological conservatives. Its staff prides itself on making factual research data, including extensive analyses of bills on the weekly whip notice, available not only to its membership, but also to a few Republicans and Democrats, mainly Southern members who regularly vote with the conservative coalition. However, interview data indicate that some of its members do not rely on or actually seem to distrust its information. One reason may be that the chairmen in recent Congresses have come from the more liberal wing of the group and that DGS staff tend to be known as "liberal activist" and actually are on the payrolls of some of the more activist Congressmen.[4] In addition, assistance has been given to "liberal" nomineees in Congressional battles. These factors apparently make DSG material suspect in some offices.

The House Wednesday Group is smaller than the DSG, with approximately thirty members, and ideologically more cohesive. Congressmen in the interview sample who were members of the Wednesday Group relied on the group's material as accurate and useful input for decision making. There is also a high level of communications activity between staff of the Wednesday Group and personal staff of the Group's members.

House staff groups exist which mirror membership in member's party-attitudinal groups. There have been fairly regular meetings of Wednesday Group AA's and occasional meetings of Wednesday Group LA's. On the other side of the aisle, the DSG holds regular briefing sessions for members' staff, and a great deal of individual staff communication is evident. In the Senate, similar groups serve a similar function, although in general they are not so highly organized. For instance, the Steering Committee, a group of conservative Senators, does not produce nearly as many papers or decision memoranda as does its House counterparts. There are fewer such Senate groups, a factor related to the smaller size of the Senate. But party and policy attitude serve as a framework for communications: a small group of AA's to "liberal" Senators, for instance, will meet on occasion to discuss matters of common interest.

Committees

Virtually all personal staff call on committee staff for status of legislation, likelihood of scheduled hearings, and in some instances, for information on committee attitudes toward bills. This type of communication is essentially informational and relatively pro forma. Committee staff will give the information to any caller, although more quickly to a Congressional staffer than to the general public.

Party usually affects who on the committee is called on: that is, Democrats call the majority staff, Republicans the minority staff. The most frequent communications result from structural channels but contain a large element of personal style, general voting conviction of the member, and a relationship built up over time between staff aides.

In congressional offices where a staff member works on committee matters for his boss, he may develop a close, working relationship with one or more committee staff. He may help coordinate hearing schedules and witness lists. When there is a close relationship, personal aides rely on committee aides for information on matters of legislative content, committee attitude, and anticipated response. In these instances, the personal aide is a surrogate committee staffer. In the House, he is on a personal staff primarily because his boss does not have enough seniority to control any committee staff appointments and yet does have interest in committee work and enough seniority to make his input significant. In the Senate he may be an S. Res. 60 aide or personal office legislative assistant, and on occasion the Senator may not even be a member of the committee. Both committee and personal staff find themselves communicating within a relatively stable and known environment and trust each other to use information discretely. Hence, the information exchange will generally be frank, open, and substantive.

For House members of low seniority, personal staff handle committee work without the in-depth information available to more senior colleagues. Committee staff will give them more information than would be available to a noncommittee member, but information regarding committee members' attitudes or strategies generally is not part of the communications exchange. This situation exists to a lesser degree in the Senate, and there is a wide variation among committees.

House staffers of more senior minority members, those in the upper 50 percent in seniority who do not control staff, occupy a middle ground. Often, they play a major role in the Congressman's committee work, but feel keenly that committee staff is not to be trusted. Thus, factual information is exchanged, hearings and witnesses are coordinated, attitudes may be discussed, but data on strategy and major substantive changes are closely guarded from each other.

Senate personal staff aides also communicate with committee aides frequently (see Table 29). They talk with staff of their Senator's committees several times a week; 13 percent talk with these aides as frequently as every hour, and another 49.5 percent talk with them once a day or more. The pattern is similar to that of the House, where in many instances there is close, continuing contact.

Personal aides talk with committee staff of Senate committees on which their Senator does not serve about once a week, on average; 28 percent of the aides are in contact once a day or more. Senate committee aides perceive even more frequent contact with personal staff aides (on average, several times a day), than those aides report (see Table 30).

Personal staff talk with House committee staff less frequently: on average, about once a month, with 5.4 percent in communication once a day or more, 21.3 percent in contact once a week or more, and nearly half (45.2) percent in contact once a month or more. What may be important about this finding is that, in spite of the traditional separatism between the two Houses, there is in fact quite a bit of communication.

Overall, the pattern which emerges is one of frequent contact among a subset of aides: those on both personal and committee staff who deal with legislation and policy issues.

State Delegation Groups

State delegations serve as initial sources of information for freshmen Representatives and over the years both staff and Congressmen develop specific communication channels within the delegation group. Regular delegation meetings occur but depend to a large extent on leadership of the delegation. In some cases this may be the dean of the delegation: Alabama, for example, regularly held delegation meetings under George Andrews. After his death and the assumption of the leadership by a new dean, who felt that delegation meetings were not so useful, no regular meetings were held. Staff and Congressmen continued to rely, however, on the informal communications nets already in existence. A similar situation occurred in the California delegation several years ago. When the Congressman who called meetings changed, the regular meetings tended to become less frequent and less useful.

The delegation meeting, as a useful information exchange device, is based on a similarity of background and similar knowledge and perception of common problems. Both Feillin and Truman have pointed to the importance of the delegation, or groups within it, as a voting cue-giver.[5] Out of the regularized meeting structure, if there is one, and the relationship which comes as a result of association on procedural and structural matters, emerges the communications network which Feillin describes. This network expands to include staff—so that in the House there are staff-to-Congressmen channels, staff-to-staff channels, and in some cases, staff-to-committee-staff channels via personal staff of an inter-mediary Congressman.[6]

Staff groups mirroring state delegation groups exist in the House, although not for all delegations. AA's and LA's to the Democrats of one Southern state meet regularly for lunch. AA's of Democratic Congressmen from one Western state meet weekly, and LA's to these members also meet, for example.

Regular and frequent staff communication exists among subsets of a state delegation and often includes staff of both House and Senate. The staffs of two midwestern state Democrats, for example, mentioned frequent coordination with each other and with the staffs of the two Senators on a variety of matters: legislation concerning the state as a whole; legislation on which there was attitu-dinal agreement but which did not directly affect the state; and Federal projects which concerned only one Congressman, but on which ranking staff members of the Senators and the other Congressman offered information and support in meetings with the executive branch. Here, it appears that a key element, in addition to joint membership on a state delegation, is attitudinal agreement; information can be trusted and judgment and "bias" respected and shared.

On some issues communications nets extend across party as well as Chamber lines and coordination and joint effort may occur on specific matters.

House–Senate communication is occasionally facilitated by staff movement from one office or committee to another, although it is not usually across party lines. A legislative assistant in the House had come from the staff of that state's Senator; both members were from the same party. The staffer's contacts with the Senate staff were, of course, close, and a special entree was available. Because the Congressman and the Senator shared similar views on many issues, the communications process was clearly enhanced.

In the Senate there exists some cooperation and communication between the offices of each state's Senators. The personalities of the Senator and his aides, party, and ideology affect the degree of cooperation. There may be competitive-ness, which results in a minimum of cooperation; in other instances Senators have introduced legislation and established state offices jointly. Although coop-eration and information exchange does exist, it is more informal and less struc-tured than in the House.

Recently, regional cooperation, which has always existed, has expanded, as a result of specific issues and resulting in the use of developing communications nets in a variety of matters. The New England Congressional Caucus and a Northeast-Midwest Coalition are examples. These reflect another trend also—increasing bipartisan cooperation. The executive director of the New England Caucus notes, "They (the 25 members of the New England delegation) haven't shown any signs of dividing on party lines"[7] and lists several issues, such as oil import quotas and Amtrak routes, with which the Caucus has been concerned and on which the Caucus is united. In instances such as this, both delegation and staff communication has been facilitated by establishing a formal structure and hiring a staff "coordinator."

Congressional "Class"

Class also influences communications nets, not only among Congressmen but among their staffs as well. There is a cohesiveness, of course, which arises from being freshmen together. Although for advice and guidance freshmen go to senior members, they also share their frustrations and queries with their fellow freshmen. As seniority increases, the members feel comfortable in exchange of information. One AA to a senior Representative said, "I go to others for information a lot. Over the years we've made moves from Cannon to Longworth to Rayburn together and the staffs get to know each other." The professional in this office, and professional staffers of the other senior members, exchange information on substantive legislative matters frequently, and often across party lines.

The House freshmen in the 94th Congress (1975–1976) organized early and cohesively and were instrumental in many of the 1975 reforms. Some observers maintain that this class has been dysfunctionally cohesive and never fully assimilated. Although class communication lessens as members develop other ties and commitments, ease of communication exchange among class members continues to be important.

Social clubs, more prevalent among Republicans than Democrats and in the House than the Senate, facilitate communication in much the same way as state delegations.[8] As one freshman Congressman said, when asked with whom he sat on the Floor, "One tends to gravitate to people of their own class, or the one immediately preceding it, so I usually sit with the 93rd freshmen Republicans, or friends from Chowder and Marching."[9]

Where Is Your Office? Office Building Geography

The location of offices also helps to determine staff communication channels and information sources. Just as partisan differences may be muted in committee and subcommittee work, office geography emphasizes bipartisanship and cooperation, rather than partisan conflict. Much of the information exchange involves both substantive and procedural matters, as well as routine information on bill status or White House tours.

Staffs of liberal Republicans and liberal Democrats, in neighboring offices on an upper floor of the Longworth Building, shared information on a wide variety of substantive matters at all stages of the legislative process, including research on emerging issues which were important to the Congressmen but which were not yet in the legislative mill. But this type of information exchange is not confined to junior members. An aide to a senior Republican talked of "going across the hall" for discussion on legislative matters with an assistant to a senior Democrat. The discussion covered not only bill status, but apparently committee reaction by party and leadership (both sides) positions. It should be noted that other variables, such as class, reinforce the "office geography" variable. Many freshmen have offices on the less desirable floors of the Longworth House Office Building. Communications exchange is thus enhanced both by closeness of offices and by congressional class.

In some offices, primarily heirarchical ones where functions are separated and status delineated clearly, the type of information exchange varies with staff position in the office hierarchy. Thus, senior professionals discuss legislative substance and at times strategy, across party lines, using their own judgment as to what ought or ought not to be discussed. Secretaries eat lunch together, call or ask for copies of bills, or put neighbors' constituents into their own White House tour spaces, but they are not expected—nor allowed—to discuss the substance of legislation or cases. One AA, after describing the people he called on for information and advice, including several neighbors of the other party, said, "The girls don't have the same freedom."

Each office building appears to have its own "information exchange" atmosphere. Staff develop loyalty to nearby groups based to some extent on office building geography. Aides agreed that the Rayburn Building is more formal and less conducive to making new contacts than either Longworth or Cannon. A pattern of helpfulness and exchange does exist, but the norm of assistance and many of the channels of communication are forged prior to the move to Rayburn. Some Congressmen with enough seniority to choose a suite in Rayburn have declined to make such a move, preferring the informality and at times apparent chaos of the other office buildings.

Within Longworth, the geography of the building throws Congressmen from diverse backgrounds together, many in offices which are vastly overcrowded. Aides to Congressmen housed in Longworth pointed to the "warmth" of LHOB, in contrast to RHOB, and said, "There's a lot of socializing." One LA to a Southern Democrat specifically mentioned exchange with staff of a West Coast Republican Congressman because "Our workrooms [annexes] are next to each other....There's much jollying back and forth." The same aide talked about "block parties" (that is, corridor parties), and thus indicated there is at times a "corridor feeling" which enhances solidarity and communication too. Another aide talked about Longworth: "It's got annexes where staff can really let their hair down. It's important in keeping the staff happy."

Cannon House Office Building, comfortable, a little less crowded, and vaguely elegant, is closer in style to the Longworth Building than to Rayburn. Some senior Congressmen remain here rather than moving to Rayburn when the opportunity arises; its "worst" offices probably do not have as many drawbacks as those in the LHOB, so that although freshmen do have offices here, there is not quite the same bond of being lowest in prerequisites which is found in certain corridors of Longworth. Moreover, there remains an informality not found in Rayburn.

Of those House offices surveyed in this study, a number of Congressmen of similar voting persuasion were in the Cannon House Office Building together.

Interview data indicate constant and frequent communication among these Congressmen and their staffs. At the opening of the 93rd Congress, several of these members moved to another office building: communication channels, built partially on CHOB days, continued to be used.

Of those in the most junior quartile, 83 percent had offices in Longworth; of those 40 percent were in ground-level offices (1000 level) and 60 percent on either the fifth or sixth floors (1500 and 1600). In contrast, 80 percent of those in the most senior quartile and 73 percent of those in the second most senior quartile were in Rayburn. The rest of the most senior were in Longworth; the remaining second most senior were in Cannon. These concentrations give an indication of the way office geography reinforces other bonds, such as class.

Additional support for the finding that geography of offices is an important factor in House communications comes from observation in 1959–1960 of one corridor of the Cannon Building. Close relationships developed during that session between Congressmen and their staffs in several offices, all situated on the same corridor: William H. Meyer (D-Vt.); Frank Coffin (D-Me.); Clem Miller (D-Calif.); and, to a lesser extent, Ken Hechler (D-W. Va.). In this instance, communications were clearly enhanced by party ties, generally similar voting stance, and similar seniority ranking. The ties between Congressman Meyer and Congressman Coffin were further cemented by their New England constituencies and the same committee assignment. There was also a good deal of communication between this group and Hastings Keith (R-Mass.), whose office was next to Congressman Miller's. There were, of course, other Congressmen, of both parties, on the corridor, and relationships not as close developed. Thus, it appears to be a mix of shared interests and approaches as well as geography which facilitates communication.

Office geography affects communications within the office also. The personal staff functions as a small group. In both Cannon and Rayburn the suites are large enough to house all personal staff. In Longworth, a majority of the staff are housed in a suite with the Congressman's office, but an additional room—the annex—is available for some staff. Many annexes house legislative aides. One Congressman uses it for interns and "think-tank" research. Others house primarily clerks and file cabinets. All, even RHOB occupants, agree that there is little office space, and most aides share offices. One functional consequence which flows from this, however, is that communications are facilitated—not only among staff members but between staff and the Congressmen. One LA, who had served on Senate staffs with their larger and often separate suites, noted, "The architecture is important. Here, the staff is right next door, so you really know the Congressman." At any rate, what *does* seem clear is that architecture does influence both communications nets and staff performance.

Senate office buildings do not appear to be so clearly differentiated, although after an initial rush to move to the new Dirksen building, many senior Senators moved back to the more elegant Russell Building. Senate staffs suffer even more severely from the annex problem. Space is at such a premium that large staffs may be housed in several difficult locations, in some cases, in as many as four different buildings. Coordination of staff activity and communication is difficult. Senate personal offices appear to be more isolated and apparently more self-contained than those of the House; in a smaller membership group office geography seems to be less important to the communication process among offices. But it is of great importance for internal office communication.

Other Internal Links

The norms of political life as well as of Congress, emphasizing courtesy and reciprocity, contribute to a general feeling of camaraderie which finds expression not only in the backslapping socializing of the House Floor so well described by Senator Riegle[10] and in the cordial reception of a visiting constituent, but also in the partying and "socializing" of staffs.[11] To counter the decentralization of the Congressional organization, Congressmen form groups—the DSG, the Wednesday Group, class clubs. Staff form groups too—the Bull Elephants, the Congressional Staff Club, the Republican Communications Association—which mirror, in some degree, the associations of Congressmen. The Republican organizations are more numerous and apparently more formally organized. State delegations are mirrored: both AAs and LAs of California Congressmen meet regularly. And then there are general, bipartisan, get-togethers, where the major purpose is to have a good time and meet people. Contacts made at these affairs may be helpful in two ways: a contact, with specific expertise, becomes a useful information source, and an information source, previously only a name, becomes a face and personality and hence far more useful than previously. In addition, such gatherings offer an opportunity for exchange of information, including shoptalk.

In addition to meetings arranged by staff organizations, during the 92nd Congress there was a social mixer every Friday evening, to which anyone who worked on the Hill was invited. Staff who attended this bipartisan (or "nonpartisan," as one staffer described it) get-together considered it an excellent way to pick up information and make contacts. Other informal get-togethers, such as softball games, serve a similar purpose.

One other type of internal communications link frequently mentioned was contact with "other staffs," based on aides' previous positions. One staffer said, "We've got ties to Senator X, Senator Y, and (several) Congressmen—anywhere [previous] Senator Z's staff went." Staff called on their colleagues from Senator Z's staff for (informational) assistance on the basis of their expertise, but without regard to class, region, delegation, or issue-specific cooperation. For a number of offices, these are very important and useful sources of information. One office noted that aides might call on men and women who had previously worked for the Congressman but presently served on committee staff or worked for another Congressman, for reaction to an office problem—thus using them not in their new role, but in their old role expertise.

Contact with the support agencies of Congress is frequent. These contacts are discussed more fully in Chapter 8 below. As the agencies have increased staffs and staff expertise, they have begun to work more directly with both personal and committee aides.

Issue-specific communications nets are an important factor in Congressional functioning. Although these may involve only one party, the increase in bipartisan issue-specific cooperation is significant. Cooperation may have its genesis in regional concerns or in a shared policy attitude. But communications exchange embraces substantive, procedural, and strategic aspects of the issue and involves both Congressmen and staff. The effect of such communications exchange is cumulative: work on one issue may lead to a continuing relationship and to cooperation on a subsequent issue.

Although there are certain elements of continuity which stem from issue-specific cooperation, the communications nets by their very nature shift with the issue. And as issues change, a cooperating group may develop and maintain an existence, only to dissolve when the issue is no longer of major congressional concern. "The Group" made up of Democratic Representatives opposed to the Vietnam war and "to the left" of the DSG on this issue, is a good illustrative example. Formed in the mid-sixties, as new members were admitted and the war became a less central issue, it was inactive by the middle of the 93rd Congress. One of its members, Congressman Robert Kastenmeier (D-Wis.), attributed its demise to loss of its staff aide, the wind-down of the Vietnam war, and the press of the committee work on its now fairly high-seniority members.[12]

EXTERNAL COMMUNICATION CHANNELS

External communication links are important both to the maintenance of Congress as an organization and to the performance of the constituent service and legislative and policy-making function in the governmental system. For the purposes of this study, groups and individuals external to Congress are those which are not part of the legislative branch but which may be within the Federal government. Thus, interest groups, constituent contacts, academic advisors to Congressmen not actually on the congressional payroll are all considered external to Congress, as are executive departments and the White House.

As would be expected, all Senators and Representatives communicate with and obtain information from similar sources external to Congress. However, frequency and depth of contact with specific groups varies. Major factors shaping office use of information sources appear to be office organization, role emphasis of the Congressman, and party.

In the House, office organization and role emphasis of the Congressman interact and reinforce each other. For example, offices of the most senior Democrats with hierarchical office organization and personal staff concerned primarily with constituent service, contact executive agencies for assistance, read newspapers and magazines, listen to constituents, but do not attempt to generate their own sources of information and analysis to any great extent. In contrast, the offices of Congressmen of both parties with middle-range seniority and developing expertise, and with interest in legislative policy making—whether related to committee work or not—have a wide range of links to external sources.

Office organization is important in two ways. The hierarchical office, simply by the fact that all work finally flows through one person, constrains to some extent the number of contacts possible. This is reinforced by the fact that virtually all hierarchical offices have fewer professionals than other offices. Secondly, in more loosely organized offices, professionals appear to be more "freewheeling" in their various contacts and, hence, are apparently encouraged more to develop information sources.

Links to constituents are many and varied. All the Congressmen in this study responded when contacted by constituents: that is, mail was answered, constituents visiting the office saw the Congressman if he was in, staff aides, very often the LA or the AA, took visiting groups on tours of the Capitol. One LA explained that he and the AA preferred to do this themselves because they were able to give a "substantive-issue" tour, rather than a "pointing-out-the-statues" tour.

Most of the Congressmen sent out newsletters to constituents, prepared weekly columns for district newspapers, and taped radio and TV spots for district use. In addition, a majority of the offices sent questionnaires to constituents to determine positions on a variety of issues. All offices found the processing of returns an extremely time-consuming job. Many feel that questionnaires are perhaps a useful device for letting constituents know the Congressman cares about district attitudes, but most question whether the results are useful for policy guidance. An effort is generally made to write neutral questions, but most aides have neither the training nor the time to devise a questionnaire which is completely neutral and statistically reliable. Keeping up mailing lists for questionnaires and newsletters had cut down on the number of mailings per year.

The Senate provides virtually unlimited communication opportunities. Each Senate office may have three direct telephone links to the state. Newsletters, *Congressional Record* reprints, and other material may be sent to constituents each month through the Senate's service facilities. In addition, party committees provide funds for TV and radio tapes that are sent to local stations. In the smaller states, Senators have the opportunity to communicate with constituents every two or three months and Senators from the largest state may communicate, by utilizing the Senate's facilities, at least once a year with each constituent.

Some offices had tried newsletters and questionnaires and have decided not to continue sending them. Seniority and security of tenure (winning by large margins), as well as the type of constituency, appear to be significant factors in such a decision. One Representative representing a low-income, blue-collar district pointed out that his constituents contact him less about issues than about personal casework and that he needed (and has) several "walk-in" offices in the district where constituents can talk to staff without the necessity of writing. He feels that questionnaires and newsletters don't meet the needs of his constituents. He has cut the number of newsletters from twelve per year to three and no longer sends questionnaires at all, saying "It just generated a lot of (individual case) work," and didn't give much guidance on issues.

An AA to a senior Democrat dismissed newsletters, questionnaires, and similar mailings as a waste of time—"X isn't running for anything else"—and as often foolish—"I know of people defeated because of the way they sent out a newsletter reporting a vote. . . . You can't ever really explain it clearly." However, press work is never completely neglected, and part of this AA's job is writing press releases and "dealing with the press." It may be that some of the coolness on the part of senior members toward generating press work is because the press comes to them. The preparation of both newsletters and questionnaires takes a good deal of staff time, but most offices nevertheless feel that these do serve as important communication links with the district.

In all offices, at least one staff aide has close political ties to the district. In most offices, the aide with the most extensive responsibilities in this area is the AA, although in a small minority of cases the Washington office is primarily legislation oriented, and the field representative is the major political advisor on the staff. Most AA's come from the state or district, as noted above, and often have extensive political contacts and campaign experience. These contacts serve as important sources of information to the member, both for assessing the political impact of his actions and for the substantive content and analysis of issues from known sources. Many AA's are back in the state or district regularly to speak to constituent groups. Many leave the Congressman's payroll and join his campaign staff in the months preceding an election, often as a senior campaign aide.

LA's seldom play such a role and, indeed, less often come from the district. Press secretaries resemble more closely the AA in district contacts. One press assistant told in some detail of "keeping out lines to district press people" and regularly attending meetings of his state's press association. He had brought with him to his job extensive press contacts in the state and extended them. In another office, the "special assistant" had similar duties. He felt he really didn't know how to "handle the press" but was trying to build up contacts and to keep open information channels to the press and to the state legislature where many of his own contacts were. Aides in two offices kept in touch with state government departments for information.

Print media are important sources of information for Congressional staffs. Newspapers, both national and district, serve as links to constituencies and also as sources of substantive-issue information. For some offices, newspapers and magazines are the primary sources of information.

A majority also use, for specific subject information, publications such as *Congressional Quarterly* and *The National Journal*. The Democratic National

Committee and the Republican National Committee also serve as sources of information for staffs, although apparently for only a minority of offices.

All offices rely on interest groups for information and data. The particular interest group used reflects the Congressman's interests (and often his biases), staff contact and judgment, and the importance of a group in a district. Congressmen with large union organizations give access to those groups and often rely on their data in legislative activities. But beyond these fairly general and expected relationships, staff becomes important in defining which groups are listened to and trusted.

One Congressman had become interested in highway issues, primarily through his committee assignment. Although relatively senior on his committee, he controlled no staff and often took positions different from those of the ranking member. Being unable to use committee staff, his own personal staff had become deeply involved in committee work and had developed very close ties with the American Automobile Association (AAA) and the Highway Users Association, relying on these groups for data needed for drafting statements and amendments.

Some staff make an effort to develop communication links with interest groups. An LA told of seeking out groups with information and expertise in particular areas, often those in which the Congressman has an interest, but at times with groups working in areas the LA felt were significant and in which he hoped to interest the Congressman. This LA asks groups for data to use in background research, for statements, and eventually for legislation. In the early stages of the relationship, when he is convinced the group has accurate data and the topic is an important one, he may see that the Congressman is invited to speak to the group, in an effort to focus the Congressman's attention and interest on the issue area.

This same office has been active in stimulating the interest and support of citizens' groups in the district on emerging issues, keeping them informed on the status in Congress of issues which are important to them and calling on them for grassroots support in trying to move the Congressman's legislation through the House.

A number of offices are relying increasingly on briefings by outside experts on specific issues or topics. Many of the briefings are bipartisan and reflect the increase in bipartisan cooperation on specific legislative issues. The Institute for Foreign Policy Studies, for example, has held bipartisan briefing sessions on foreign policy. The DSG runs a series of briefing sessions for its members and their staffs on a variety of current legislative matters; CRS holds similar bipartisan briefings for both Senate and House aides. The Brookings Institution and the American Enterprise Institute, nongovernmental research organizations, also hold seminars and debates to which staff are invited from time to time. We do not have longitudinal quantitative data, but there is, we believe, increasing opportunity for exchange of ideas and concerns between Congress and outside groups: Civil Service Commission In-Service Training Programs for mid-level management personnel, various Congressional Fellow programs, informal lectures, discussions, and meetings bring together Congressional staff and outside groups.

Less institutionalized, and far less frequent, are the informal sessions run by one Congressional office when policy experts are in town. Congressmen and staff in neighboring offices are invited, making possible bipartisan brainstorming sessions.

Other nongovernmental communication channels exist between staffers and "friends around town"—often former Hill aides. Thus, one office has previous staffers in an auto dealers' association in a neighboring state, another has an ex-LA in a legislative liaison job with a national interest group, and a third has an ex-employee who is a research librarian in a well-known economic consulting firm. Since there is a good deal of job hopping among lower-level Hill staff, and since at least a substantial minority of AA's use off-the-Hill contacts to find their next job, it would be expected—and is, in fact, found to be true—that a network of contacts exists between the Hill staff and Washington and district professionals.

One final source of external information for Congress is expert constituents. Many Congressmen with universities in their districts are given assistance in shaping legislation by academic advisory panels. One Midwestern Congressman has used medical school professors extensively for help on health care delivery systems. Another Congressman recruited a group of university students, supervised by a professor, for technical assistance on a variety of legislative matters.

In many cases, individual expert constituents will be known to and called on for advice by a Congressman or his staff. But one office told in some detail of going beyond this obvious exchange situation: whenever a constituent came in to see the Congressman about a matter, he was asked his own area of expertise. In this way, the office built a file of constituents who could be called on for assistance later. Staff is important to this system. A staff aide sits in on every conference between constituents and Congressman, in order to assist in any follow-up work necessary in handling the immediate problem, but also to facilitate later communication.

Communication between Congress and the executive is perhaps the most well-defined as well as the most analyzed of any systemic linkages. The classic studies of subsystem operations have illuminated the crucial informal relationships and contributed to understanding of policy formation.[13] Information flow between Congressional personal staff and the executive branch is important to subsystem relationships.

Legislative liaison offices have institutionalized to some degree these communications networks. Thus, executive departments' legislative liaison offices telephone House offices with news of Federal grants for district projects. Courtesy has generally been extended to the Congressman to allow him to announce the grant to news media, prior to the time the departmental release occurred. The timing of the notification, however, is often subject to party considerations, apparently under every administration.

Bad news from departments is also, in general, handled politically. The office of a Southern Democrat had been notified only a day before the official announcement that certain personnel at a district Air Force base were being removed from Civil Service contract, and that the work would be done by a private firm. The press secretary complained, "It was just a political decision. . . .In the next district, which is represented by a Republican, they're hiring because a whole (federal agency) section is moving in."

Individual casework, federal project grants, and legislative mail about matters on which departments have information mean constant communication with legislative liaison staff. The contacts, which may at first be fairly formal and routine, over time often develop into close and frequent relationships. The relationships may be affected to some extent by party (is the Congressman of the same party as the President), by continuity in personnel (both executive and congressional), and also by the type of leadership given the executive department's liaison staff.

In some cases, liaison staff, particularly if based on the Hill, appear to perceive themselves more as Hill employees than as executive branch employees; they will handle casework requests on a basis which is similar to some of the technical committee work, i.e., on a nonpartisan, subject-matter basis. Other liaison staff, although based in the department, appear to make extraordinary efforts to assist congressional offices, perceiving their job as one of facilitating communication between Congressman and constituent, very often regardless of party; this attitude is heavily influenced apparently by executive department liaison leadership. One LA, who had served on a departmental liaison staff in a previous administration, pointed to some of the considerations in this communications linkage when he said (in 1971),

> "There's really been a big change in liaison (since 1969 when the Republicans came in). . . .It's pretty poor right now. There's no stopping by to keep in touch, there's a lag in answering mail, and in sending up legislation. Why, when I was in —————— Department, we'd be up on the Hill all the time. We'd make a real effort to meet new members and to offer our services. We'd keep in touch with the Representative and his staff. We'd try to get the mail out fast. And legislation went up much sooner after the message."

He went on to say that he'd worked under two "extraordinary" men at the Department, one with a great deal of subject-matter expertise, the other with long background in, and sympathy for, Congressional operations.

A number of offices are in contact with departments also for departmental reports and data on pending legislative issues. This is true both of Republicans and Democrats, activist and nonactivist offices. For example, the staff of one freshman Democrat with a lot of policy interests, mentioned "agencies and departments" as very useful sources of information. This particular office often identifies an emerging problem and then approaches experts in the executive branch for information and advice, going beyond the legislative liaison offices and looking for experts in the bureaucracy familiar with a particular problem. The staff, although relatively young, has cumulative work experience in Washington which is both varied and extensive and also has no hesitation about calling on the staffs of the state's Senators for contacts and support—this may be the reason they feel comfortable using "downtown" experts.

Contacts with experts in the executive branch are carefully cultivated and considered important. Just as committee staff develop long-term relationships with their professional counterparts in the bureaucracy,[14] so apparently do some personal staff. The LA to a Democrat of middle-level seniority told of regular meetings of AA's and LA's prior to 1969 for briefing and contact with their counterparts in the bureaucracy. He said, "Most staffers consciously build up those channels." Another office said, "We've got a lot of our alumni in the bureaucracy now."

Of the House personal offices in the sample, only one mentioned specificially having staffers leave for a variety of executive branch jobs. And of the professional staff in those offices, only 25 percent had previously held jobs in the executive branch. As noted above it appears that personal staff jobs are filled primarily by men and women with a legislative and local orientation. No large number of personal office staff move to the executive branch, and therefore if staffers want to find trusted experts in government they are better off building up contacts and communications linkages with the present employees of the executive branch, rather than relying on the movement of staff from the Hill to downtown. On committees, there is more movement between executive and legislative branches, as our data indicate. But here, too, seeking executive branch contacts is important.

Committee assignment is also a significant factor in staff–downtown relations. In offices where the Congressman serves on an important committee, and particularly where he may have some seniority, departments contact the personal staff and make themselves available for all the help they can give. This extends to all professional staff, especially if staff are involved in substantive legislative work, and particularly in committee work.

One Congressional office noted a change in departmental initiative immediately upon the Congressman's change of committee: within hours high-ranking department personnel (an Assistant Secretary, among others) were making calls in person to facilitate information linkage. Trusting the information is another matter; but with a personal relationship built up over time and enhanced through travel together on inspection trips, the staff felt they had access to data which they might not otherwise have and personal knowledge to draw on in judging when to ask for more data or to probe for underlying motivation.

Staff also tended to have closer relationships with persons in the departments affected by the Congressman's committee assignment. Thus, they seem to know whom to contact for information beyond the legislative liaison people. Of Senate personal staff aides, 22 percent report contact with the bureaucracy at least every hour; 68.1 percent are in touch once a day or more; and a full 90 percent communicate with the bureaucracy at least once a week or oftener. Rather surprisingly, these figures are almost exactly those of Senate committee aides (see Table 30 below).

Most offices do not deal frequently with White House staff people,[15] but, rather, will work with departments when legislation is being shaped. This appears, however, to vary with the issues, the existing contacts, and with the willingness of the Congressman to pull out all the stops in dealing with an issue.

Few aides contact the staff in the executive office of the President as frequently as they contact the bureaucracy: Only 1.1 percent report communication as frequently as every hour. However, 17.6 percent are in touch daily, and 41.5 percent communicate at least once a month. The White House contact tends to show up when there is an "important" vote pending and during committee consideration of major legislative issues. We think the personal aides have more involvement in both (1) matters with a political angle, and (2) legislative matters in their final stages (e.g., Floor votes). This may reflect the fact that on matters of political judgment committee staff tend to be responsive primarily to the chairman or the ranking minority member; if the assignment of committee staffing changes, patterns of communications can also be expected to change.

Communications patterns between Senate personal offices and groups outside the congressional system are similar to those of the House. Senate staffs are able to draw on a more diverse constituent group for information than are most House members. Also, because Senators often are national figures, they may have more ready access to the expertise of men and women outside their constituency. A study comparing expert information sources for Senate and House personal offices would be helpful in analyzing the policy-making process. Overall, however, the state is a prime focus of communication. Senators' offices handle a heavy load of mail, casework, and constituent requests. A California Senator reports receiving 12,000 letters a week. For many Senate offices, keeping up with the volume of mail requires the time of most of their staff. Senator Cranston, of California, has noted how difficult it is to staff legislative activity adequately because of the volume of mail and casework.[16]

Mail, however, does not vary systematically by state population. Some Senators from smaller states have a fairly heavy volume of mail. Other Senators, from states with quite large populations, have relatively small mail loads. And, two Senators from the same state will have quite different mail loads.

Senators, like their House counterparts, send out questionnaires, newsletters, newspaper columns, and radio and TV tapes. They see groups of constituents regularly. In fact, a study of Senators' time-use by the Commission on the Operation of the Senate indicates that *on average* Senators spend one hour and forty minutes each day meeting with constituents and interest groups in their Senate offices; additional time is spent meeting with interest groups not from their home state.[17]

Senators' personal staffs communicate frequently with constituents: 35 percent of staff report contact once an hour or more; another 43 percent report communication with constituents once a day or more (See table 29).

Occasionally, in both the Senate and House, a staff member will do original, basic research on an issue. For example, in the office of a Southern Representative, the LA went to a Western Indian reservation to interview and to read archives pertaining to Indian problems. This activity was the result of a problem in the district and the Representative hoped the findings would provide a solution to that problem. This type of research—an external communications link—is, however, rare. Committee staff do conduct on-site investigations and research. But for both groups of aides, most frequently, "research" means reviewing and synthesizing previous studies. Staff act as conduits to members from experts. With about 1,000 professional committee staff and a larger but still relatively small number of professional personal aides, the Congress will continue to utilize a great deal of outside information in their legislative work.

COMMITTEES

As with personal staffs, the communication channels and nets of committee professionals are based on formal and informal contacts.

On the average, committee staffs work with executive branch personnel at least once a day and often, more frequently. This is about as frequently as with the Congressional Research Service. Committee staffs on the average contact Presidential staff less frequently, about once a month. Nearly 29 percent of House professionals talk with the Presidential staff once a week or more; only 8 percent are in contact once a day or more, and the average frequency of contact is once a month. The pattern for the Senate is quite similar: 24.5 percent report contact once a week or more, 8.8 percent once a day or more, and the average frequency again is about once a month. The similarity of the contact patterns for all the groups of professional aides is striking. The variations raise interesting questions about the role of committee and personal staff aides. Although, as might be expected, Senate committee aides contact the bureaucracy slightly more frequently than aides on Senators' personal staffs, they are in contact with Presidential staff quite a bit less frequently than personal staff aides.

As would be expected, Senate committee staff aides are in frequent contact with Senators, Senators' personal staffs, and often Senate committees. Intra-House communication patterns are fairly similar to intra-Senate ones. However, House aides are in more frequent contact with Representatives than their Senate counterparts with Senators. Our data parallel those of Patterson in this regard. However, we find there is more staff contact among committees within a Chamber than between Chambers.[18] This may reflect the increasing incidence of multiple-referrals and intercommittee cooperation. It may be a reflection of House specialization, or one measure of somewhat more "independence" and autonomy of Senate aides. Where differences in communication patterns appear they tend to be intra-Chamber. In contacting external groups, whether in government (bureaucracy or Presidential office staff) or outside it (press or constituents), committee staff patterns of communication are remarkably similar. (See Table 30.)

Another way of looking at communication patterns is to examine where aides obtain information. Who are the information sources? To whom do aides turn for information on the substantive aspects of their work? The question aides responded to was, "How often do you rely on the following sources of information?" It is clear that legislative branch personnel and executive department personnel are the major information sources for Congressional committees (see Table 31). These data confirm conclusions of various case studies regarding the close working relationships of departmental and committee personnel. They also give added reason for the recent Congressional efforts to establish analytic support staffs, such as the Office of Technology Assessment and the Congressional Budget Office, within the legislative branch.

Other sources of information mentioned by committee aides are the press, other committee staffs, and other (undetermined) groups. A committee aide described his information system to us, illuminating important aspects of the legislative process:

"I keep an open door and anyone can see me. I make it my business to be accessible. This is my 'intelligence system.' I try to be on a friendly personal basis with all of the special interest groups so I can understand them and their motives, and use them to the committee's interest. I make a special effort to accommodate other Congressional offices. I try to maintain a personal relationship with executive officials, White House, etc. One must be personally involved if he expects to understand the many conflicting political viewpoints."

The data confirm much of the previous evidence on information sources: heavy reliance on departmental personnel, a good deal of help from the congressional support agencies, and fairly close relationships with various interest groups. One aide told us, "Most information given staffers by businessmen, labor leaders, etc. is obviously both *interested* and *parochial,* but may nevertheless be very useful." There is far less reliance on Presidential staff, hired consultants, or volunteer experts—although interviews indicate that the use of committee consultants may be increasing. The data illuminate some Senate–House differences, although, as with communication patterns, the similarities are more striking than the differences. In short, the data confirm that much of the staff work of standing committees is conducted through experts.

DEVELOPMENT OF COMMUNICATIONS NETS

It is apparent from the preceding discussion that staff communications nets develop in a number of ways. The structure of the Congress is one causal factor, and both formal and informal nets develop from it. Issues also play an important role and lead both to partisan and bipartisan communication, some of which is the basis for continuing interaction.

Staff members bring their own contacts and communication links to the committee or congressional office hiring them. Freshmen Congressmen often try to balance Washington and district expertise when hiring, and, for purposes of legislative impact, both Washington and district nets are important.

Some feedback from constituents on issues, concerns, implementation of government programs, and so forth comes more or less automatically to the Representative and Senator and his staff. Offices make varied use of these communications, but in a large majority of offices the result is often a continuing communication link and a legislative impact (as well as problem solution specific to the issue and the individual).

Some specific examples will serve to illuminate these observations. What we have called "structural" communication links were important in nets mentioned by every office. In addition to nets which might be predicted, such as those between leadership and office staff, there are others, less obvious, which also appear to be important. Thus, in most offices there is frequent contact between staffs of a state's Senators and its Representatives. Very often the contact is between two staff members who have personal knowledge of each other's expertise in a specific area. Some House offices coordinate with offices of Congressmen from neighboring districts, and on specific issue areas one staff aide will coordinate information for all. This happened with, for example, a California Congressman and those of neighboring states on the problem of forest fires.

The interaction of the Presidency and Congress is apparent. Several staff aides to Democrats mentioned regular briefing sessions and meetings with administration officials during Lyndon Johnson's presidency. One then noted, "during a Republican administration we don't have any Cabinet members to listen to, and we haven't had any such meetings."

In the House, issue-specific network development abounds, although in offices of most-senior majority party Congressmen it is less common than in others. A group has met regularly on nuclear safety. Another group of aides had held regular dinner meetings to hear speakers—often ambassadors—and to discuss African affairs. Ten Congressmen in the 92nd Congress pooled resources to hire a staff man on military issues. In addition to serving as an in-house expert, he arranged information and discussion conferences for staff and members.

Because individual staff contacts are so important to the functioning of Congress, it may be useful to look briefly at specific communications nets of several offices.

One freshman Representative from the Midwest hired a staff balanced fairly evenly between district and Hill professionals. Those aides who joined the staff from other jobs in Washington had contacts in and detailed knowledge of a number of other offices, having worked previously for two other Senators (one from the new Congressman's home state), a very senior Midwestern liberal Representative, a conservative Eastern Representative, and a moderate Western Representative.

On the basis of similar interest in and attitude toward issues, the Representative and his staff worked frequently with another Democrat of the state delegation and with both of the state's Senators. The new Representative's staff relied heavily on the staff of the delegation colleague, through them developing ties to the staff of a Western Representative of similar policy attitude for advice on tax issues, and the staff of another Midwestern Representative for assistance on social security issues. They also established links to staffs of Midwest Democrats with similar rural districts, and on some matters, primarily agricultural, cooperated with staff of rural Republicans facing similar district problems.

Another way of looking at nets is to trace the present positions of previous colleagues. Using only those in the House study sample as examples, staff dispersed through several offices of Midwestern Democrats had previously served together on the staff of a Midwestern Senator. The Senator's ex-aides also were employed in other senatorial offices, in other House offices, and a few in executive departments.

Senators and Representatives and their staff aides also become known for expertise in a given area, and numerous colleagues will call on them for assistance. This occurs primarily within party and among offices holding similar policy attitudes, although there are exceptions. One staff aide to a somewhat conservative senior Democratic Representative named two very liberal, very activist, offices as his information sources on two important legislative matters. These two offices were also named as information sources by several very liberal, very activist Democrats.

Much of the information exchange which occurs is haphazard, and within certain general structural constraints based on personal contact and predilection. Staff, however, do work within guidelines set by the Congressman for whom they work and may feel some constraint in pursuing communication links too actively. Severe constraints were evident in only a very small percentage of the House offices surveyed (8 percent, or two offices). That staff may feel hampered is evident from a comment of one staff aide, "The boss is pretty individualistic, and also has a party position and some seniority. He's got his own sources of information, but is something of a lone operator, so that the staff has some difficulty forging internal links. We need them, but you can't do what your boss doesn't care about."

There is increasing coordination of information and strategy but also a great deal of duplicated work. At present, one of the primary causal factors in Hill information exchange appears to be staff aggressively attempting to widen communications nets.

STAFF COMMUNICATIONS CONTROL

Implicit in the establishment and maintenance of communications nets is the staff capacity to control information flow into and out of the congressional office. Clearly, the capacity to affect information flow, as well as staff impact on communications, varies with the office. It is also clear, however, that staff have potential for affecting office communications and in fact do have impact. As staffs become more involved in the policy process, this can be expected to accelerate.

At any number of points in the communications flow process staff impact is possible. It is based on a combination of access to the information flow and judgment—the latter a blend of expertise and perception of the issues and/or the actors. "Dear Colleague" letters, for example, are one area for staff control. In some instances, co-sponsorship may be primarily dependent on staff-to-staff communication. Others are control over who sees a Representative or Senator and the choice of information to bring to the Congressman's attention. Lobbyists and district groups may see staff aides and staff perceptions of those meetings shape the information flow to the Congressman.

Or staff aides may represent their boss before district or interest groups. In House offices where Congressmen do not sign their own mail (a minority), staff exercise very nearly complete control over this type of communication. In the Senate, mail flow is more routine, and Senators handle only a small sample. Staff have an impact on newsletters by advising on issues to emphasize or neglect, and by the way certain points are stressed or de-emphasized in articles.

As Federal project casework increases, relationships with Federal agencies and personnel become more complex. Most of these contacts are handled by the staff, and the final outcome is judged, on behalf of the Senator or Congressman, by the constituency.

CONCLUSION

The following propositions summarize our findings about staff communications:

- Communication channels follow the expected structural lines, but also important are channels unrelated to the structure of Congress. Among the former are party, leadership, committee, personal office, and executive agency channels. Among the latter are office location, previous job, ideology, and "class."
- Seniority affects communication, particularly in the House. Representatives of middle-range seniority generate their own sources of information more frequently than those of highest seniority, who rely most exclusively on committee staffs. Junior Representatives may initiate information exchange, but the impact on the policy process is less because of their own junior status in legislative decision making; the information generated becomes a base for action in subsequent terms.

- Party affects communication. In the House, Republicans at all seniority levels rely less on leadership offices for substantive information on legislation than do Democrats. Senators of the majority party have access to more staff and generally dictate legislative strategy based on the communications networks established by their personal and committee staff. Some minority Senators have been able to build up extensive staffs and thus rely more heavily on communication from outside groups and from the executive when it is in the control of their party.
- Organized subgroups are formed to facilitate information exchange in both House and Senate. These may be intra-party (DGS, Wednesday Group), regional (New England Caucus), or issue specific for example.
- Staff groups exist which mirror those of the principal actors (State delegation AA's and LA's; DSG LA's). In the Senate, information exchange occurs, but the groups are not usually as formally organized.
- The way personal offices are organized affects communication. In hierarchical offices in the Senate and House, there are fewer professionals and the professionals are less "freewheeling" than in more loosely coordinated offices.
- Committee assignment affects communication, particularly with the executive branch. Congressmen on authorizing committees, or appropriations subcommittees for a particular agency, can expect frequent staff contact and immediate and fuller response to queries.
- The political content of information exchange affects the communications pattern. For instance, personal aides are in more frequent contact with the executive office of the President than are committee staff, because they are generally geographically closer and more attuned to the local political issues than committee staff.
- Overall, on average, patterns of communication are similar for both committee and personal professionals. What this means is that although there may be individual variations in content, or in constituent service versus policy, by and large all staff groups are performing similar communication activities in the legislative process.[19]

We have shown quantitatively some differences between communication patterns in the Senate and in the House. A former House administrative assistant, now a Senate AA, assessed the impact of the difference, and the role of committee versus personal staff.

"If you wanted to find out about some piece of legislation on the House side there was always a Congressman who knew all about it. You could get him aside and he would go down the list of political as well as practical matters. Here in the Senate the Senators are not experts. You have to go to the staff. First, I call the office and find out as much as possible. Then they usually refer me to a committee staff person. Committee staff many times know the practical but not the political issues. You have to know both to make a decision on a bill."

Another aide commented on House–Senate differences.

> "Staff on the Senate side are more pompous than those on the House side. You have a system of layers here—the Senators only talk to Senators, the administrative assistants to administrative assistants, the legislative assistants to legislative assistants, etc. On the House side, you could find out what was going on in forty-five minutes by going from group to group in the cafeteria. Over here, I go down to the cafeteria and eat alone."

We do not know how widely held this view is. Some differences may derive from the larger and more specialized Senate personal staffs. We suspect that staff age and ambition may also make a difference.

The quality of staff advice is based on the quality of information obtained, filtered through staff expertise and perceptions of both issues and actors. Hence, communications nets developed and maintained by staff become extremely important.

In any organization staff work is vital, with Congress being no exception. Although much of the literature has ignored the staff role, it seems clear that as the Congressional workload has increased in amount and complexity, staff have become more important to congressional communications. Although Congressmen have their own lines of communication, both internally and externally, the number who do not rely on personal staff for policy input is decreasing. Hence, for both personal and committee staff, position astride the office communications network is today a significant factor in constituent service and legislative policy making.

NOTES

1. A considerable literature focuses on organizational communications. See, for example, Herbert Simon, *Administrative Behavior,* 2d ed. (New York: The Free Press, 1957), and Harold L. Wilonsky, *Intellectuals in Labor Unions* (Glencoe, Ill.: The Free Press, 1956). Studies of Congressional communications include: the work of Lewis Anthony Dexter; de Grazia, ed., *Congress;* Melvin Laird, ed., *Republican Papers* (Garden City, N.Y.: Doubleday Anchor, 1968); John W. Kingdon, *Congressmen's Voting Decisions* (New York: Harper & Row, 1973); David M. Kovenoc, "Communications and Influence in Congressional Decision Making," paper presented at Annual Meeting, American Political Science Association, Chicago, 1964, and "Influence in the U.S. House of Representatives: Some Preliminary Statistical 'Snapshots,'" paper presented at the Annual Meeting, American Political Science Association, 1967; Leroy M. Rieselbach, *Congressional Politics* (New York: McGraw-Hill, 1973); and Saloma, *Congress.*

2. In early 1977, formally named the Caucus for an Effective Senate. The Caucus includes Senators beyond the first term.

2a. Responses, made by 172 staff members, to 11 questions about their frequency of contact with other persons were intercorrelated, and a factor analysis using the principal axes method was performed. Three factors thus obtained were blindly rotated utilizing the Varimax method.

3. See Table 3 for minority staff figures. Democrats suffer from this, too, of course. The DSG started earlier and may have filled a gap. Also see Kingdon, *Voting Decisions,* especially chapter 4. Our findings agree with his on the relationship between leadership and rank-and-file.

4. Liberal activism is measured by ADA ratings, low support of the conservative coalition, and by sponsorship and co-sponsorship of bills and resolutions.

5. *Op. cit.*

6. Barbara Deckard has cited the importance of the highly cohesive and the cohesive state delegation both for socialization of new members and in information sharing for all. She notes that in less cohesive delegations staff input becomes far more important. Our interview data do not always bear this out. "State Party Delegations in the U.S. House of Representatives—A Comparative Study of Group Cohesion," Barbara Deckard, *Journal of Politics,* 34, No. 1 (Feb. 1972), pp. 199–222.

7. *Roll Call,* newspaper of Capitol Hill, March 15, 1973, p. 6.

8. For an analysis of Republican social groups in the House see John Elliott, "Communications and Small Groups in Congress: The Case of Republicans in the House of Representatives," unpublished Ph.D. dissertation, The Johns Hopkins University, 1974.

9. Quoted in Riley Atkins, "The Socialization of The Freshman Congressman: A Study of Eight Representatives Elected to the 93rd Congress." Unpublished Washington Semester paper, The American University, 1973, p. 37.

10. Riegle, *O Congress!*

11. We know of no research on staff socializing, but our impression is that informal partying assists work much more in the Congress than in the executive branch. Executive branch personnel lunch together or attend occasional private dinner parties or once-a-year office gatherings; but there is no regular partying such as is found in the House and Senate. A committee staff in the Senate gathered once a week to "celebrate" a birthday or special event; these gatherings included persons working closely with the committee and often involved an exchange of ideas and information.

12. *Roll Call,* newspaper of Capitol Hill, March 29, 1973, "Within Congress," p. 2.

13. For example, Richard F. Fenno, *The Power of the Purse* (Boston: Little Brown, 1966), and J. Lieper Freeman, *The Political Process: Executive Bureau–Legislative Committee Relations,* rev'd ed. (N.Y.: Random House, 1965).

14. Fenno, *Appropriations,* and John F. Manley, *The Politics of Finance* (Boston: Little, Brown, 1970).

15. White House congressional liaison personnel generally are concerned with passage of legislation which has been shaped. Here, we are dealing primarily with issues in the process of reaching legislative form.

16. *Congressional Record,* June 9, 1975, S.10137.

17. See *Toward A Modern Senate, Final Report,* The Commission on the Operation of the Senate, December, 1976, Senate Document 94–278, 94th congress, 2nd Session.

18. Samuel C. Patterson, "Congressional Committee Professional Staffing," pp. 404

and 410 in Allan Kornberg and Lloyd D. Musoff, eds., *Legislatures in Developmental Perspective* (Durham, N.C.: Duke University Press, 1970). Our frequency data group all communications with committees of the other Chamber and do not separate contacts with the parallel committees.

19. A 1970 study by the Center for Political Studies at the University of Michigan, reporting on the perceived information needs of staff in the House, bears on this point. "Report to the Special Subcommittee on Electrical and Mechanical Office Equipment of the Committee on House Administration, Congress of the United States, House of Representatives, on Perceived Information Requirements of Staff Members," Institute for Fiscal Research, August, 1970.

8. Congressional Support Staffs

Congressional personal and committee staff are augmented by various other supporting staffs—the support agencies, the "legislative secretariat" in each House, and staff of informal groups. Interns, Fellows, and volunteers also assist Congress, most usually by working on a personal or committee staff. These staffs provide a wide range of services that assist the member in his Congressional activities.

SUPPORT AGENCIES

The major support agencies of Congress, the Congressional Research Service of the Library of Congress (CRS), the General Accounting Office (GAO), the Office of Technology Assessment (OTA), and the Congressional Budget Office (CBO), supplement the work of the committee and personal staffs. These nonpartisan agencies enable Congress to draw on the expertise of a pool of specialized professionals, who are able to perform special studies and long-term projects. Although the fields of expertise vary among agencies, each support group provides information and analysis that often influences the legislative decisions of Senators, Representatives and their staff.

In general, the agencies handle both quick-reference requests and longer-term in-depth studies. Some agencies such as CBO and OTA undertake major studies only at the request of a committee; the other agencies generally give priority to committee requests over those of individual Congressmen and staff. Two agencies, the General Accounting Office and the Congressional Research Service, may detail staff to congressional committees for assistance.

Each house also has central support staffs, sometimes referred to as a "legislative secretariat," who work on housekeeping, legislative, and policy matters. These include the Office of Legislative Counsel in both the Senate and the House, staffs of various party groups (policy and research committees), House and

130

Senate officers, Parliamentarians, journal clerks, document room personnel, and others. We will report briefly on the activities of these groups.

The recent establishment of two new congressional support agencies, the Office of Technology Assessment (P.L. 92-484; 1972) and the Congressional Budget Office (P.L. 93-344; 1974) was in response to several factors. One is the challenge to Congress as an institution during the years of the Vietnam war, Presidential impoundments, and Watergate. Conservative and very liberal Congressmen, traditionally on opposite sides of most issues, found themselves voting together on matters which are viewed as crucial to the preservation of Congressional power vis-à-vis the executive branch. In addition, the increasing impact of technology and science, the saliance of issues with a scientific component such as environment and energy, and the interdependence of issues, all made Congress more aware of the need for experts and expertise. These factors led not only to the establishment of new support agencies, but also to a Congressional mandate increasing the professional staffs of the existing support agencies. The support agencies show a staffing pattern similar to that for committee and personal staff—more staff, more professional staff, and increased and more diverse responsibilities.

The most often used of the support agencies is the Congressional Research Service, which is part of the Library of Congress. It was established in 1914, at the direction of Congress, as the Legislative Reference Service by the Librarian of Congress. It occupied space in the Library of Congress building. The focus at that time was on assisting Congress by preparing law indices and digests. This continues to be a major service of the CRS. The following year Congress extended the mandate to include providing research services and preparing analyses, gathering data, and preparing legislative materials. The Legislative Reorganization Act of 1946, Section 203, expanded the work of the Service so that direct assistance could be provided to both committees and individual members on various legislative proposals. In 1970 the purposes of the Service were further expanded. The Legislative Reorganization Act of 1970 changed the name of the Service to the Congressional Research Service and emphasized that policy research and analysis for Congress should be an important function. A number of specific points were listed as to ways the CRS was to carry out this mandate.

In 1970 the Congress expected that the staff of the CRS would triple in the following five years; in fact it increased from 323 in 1970 to 778 (565 of them professionals) in 1975. In addition, the Service has equipped itself more fully to provide assistance on a broad range of policy matters. (The staff was 180 in 1960 and 323 in 1970.)

The CRS performs various support activities for Congress. It shows traces of its library origins in its quick response to a great many requests for factual information, especially through the Quick Reference Division. Requests for specific items of information concerning population statistics, the provisions of a new law, or Federal employment, for example, go to this division. In recent years, and particularly since the 1970 Legislative Reorganization Act, it has emphasized more fully the research and analysis mandate. The workload has increased greatly in recent years: an increase of 21 percent in FY 1975 over FY 1974 and in the first part of FY 1976, an increase of 38 percent above its FY 1975 workload.[1]

Regular reports are issued for use by Congress, such as Issue Briefs on various matters, a Digest of Public General Bills and Resolutions (which includes sponsors and co-sponsors), multilith reports on a variety of topics, and, during the sessions of Congress, a summary of major legislation of the Congress. It also operates various computer information systems, including a legislative bill status system. In addition, the CRS will, on request, prepare speech drafts, analyses of pending issues, briefing reports on issues, and will respond to other requests insofar as possible. CRS holds seminars for Congressmen and senior staff on various policy issues. Its senior analysts and specialists conduct in-depth research on issues within their areas of expertise, and they work closely with committees and can be assigned to work on a committee staff during the term of a particular project. For instance, CRS personnel worked on the Bolling Committee and the Senate Temporary Select Committee to Study the Committee System in 1973–1974 and 1976–1977, respectively. They served as staff for the Rules Committee subcommittee which handled the Legislative Reorganization Act of 1970 and, briefly, on the House Budget Committee staff. Other CRS personnel have worked closely with the Commission on the Operation of the Senate while remaining at the Library and have worked closely with a number of Senate and House Committees.

Since 1970, the CRS has expanded its assistance to Congressional committees, preparing lists of programs under the authority of each committee which will require reauthorization during the coming Congress; it has also identified areas which committees might wish to study.

The increasing demand for CRS assistance has occurred for several reasons, among them more congressional staff and increasingly complex decision-making requirements. Because it handles such a wide range of requests and its role has, pursuant to congressional mandate, shifted from the quick informational response to greater emphasis on policy research and analysis, its future role is not entirely clear. Some staff of Congressmen and committees feel strongly that CRS responses are superficial; other aides report excellent assistance, particularly if there is direct communication with the CRS staff aide involved. At any rate, CRS is aware of the criticisms, and is endeavoring to respond to them.[2]

The General Accounting Office, with over 5,000 employees, has been a legislative agency since its establishment in 1921 by the Budget and Accounting Act of that year. Recent legislation has mandated expanded assistance to Congress. The Legislative Reorganization Act of 1970 expanded the oversight assistance function (Sec. 204; ". . .shall review and analyze the results of Government programs and activities carried on under existing law, including the making of cost benefit studies. . .''). Also Congress directed that GAO reports be widely available to members. The Congressional Budget and Impoundment Control Act of 1974 furthers the expanded GAO support role for Congress, particularly in program evaluation, program data, and oversight work. Other Federal laws have directed GAO to study and evaluate various programs and issues.

The staff of the GAO has increased from 4471 in 1970 to 4,954 in 1974, and to 5,126 in 1976. During that period, the proportion of professionals increased at a faster rate, with 2,769 professionals in 1970 and 3,600 in 1970, a result, it would seem, of the emphasis on diversification of staff background. As with CRS, the workload of GAO for Congress has increased in recent years. Presently, approximately 34 percent of GAO's work is in response to Congressional requests, up from 8 percent in 1966. As is evident from these figures, however, a large portion of GAO's work is not for Congress. Traditionally, GAO has been an audit agency, auditing agencies and programs for the entire executive branch. In recent years, in response to increased responsibilities for Congress, the professional staff has been diversified, and analysts trained as economists, political scientists, and psychologists are being hired.

We think that one of the most significant trends in GAO–Congressional staffing is the cooperative program evaluation work of GAO and committee staff. Partly in response to the new budget cycle, congressional committees are increasingly aware of the need to justify program budget requests. Paralleling this is an increased interest in oversight and a growing willingness on the part of staff and Congressmen to use more sophisticated program evaluation techniques. This may partially be a response to the increasing interdependence of policy issues and the movement into an era of resource scarcity. The outgrowth, for Congress and GAO, has been that information systems providing extensive data for problem identification and oversight analysis are being developed. This is occurring on a committee-to-GAO basis and, although hardly widespread, offers a glimpse of the future.

The Office of Technology Assessment was established by the 92nd Congress (P.L. 92-484) and began operations in 1973–1974. It currently has a staff of ninety-three and a budget, for FY 1977, of about $8 million. OTA was established to assist Congress in evaluating the technological implications of proposed legislation and to study and assess the impact of scientific and technological developments. The Office has been particularly active in assessing proposals for oil exploration and leasing on the Outer Continental Shelf (the Oceans Assessment Study), in the area of transportation, health, food, and materials assessment. Initially, a major portion of the work was handled by contracts; recently, however, OTA has increased its in-house capability for performing studies.

OTA policies are set by a bipartisan board, the Technology Assessment Board, of six Senators and six Representatives. An advisory council is made up of ten public members and the Comptroller General and CRS Director. There appear to have been some problems of focus within OTA. Should OTA perform quick analyses of pending legislation or should it devote a major portion of staff time to long-term assessment studies? A number of congressional aides and members are really not aware of OTA's work or the support services that are available. It may be that the matters are so technical the studies do not lend themselves to wide distribution and request. On the other hand. OTA appears to have a capability which has potential for significant congressional assistance. It is simply too early to tell how it will fit into the Congressional information structure.

The Congressional Budget Office (CBO) was established by the Congressional Budget and Impoundment Control Act of 1974. The CBO staff of fiscal and economic experts with extensive training, contacts, and experience provide independent economic and fiscal analysis to the Congress. The Director was appointed in 1975, and the office became operational later that year. As the newest of the support agencies, it is still finding its niche, although it has already been deeply involved in the budget process. CBO is the legislative branch's counterpart to the executive's Office of Management and Budget.

Many of the professionals within CBO have previous executive branch experience, which plugs Congress directly into an information network of fiscal and economic policy experts and offers a sophisticated, independent source of information and analysis.

During 1975, CBO assisted in the "dry run," generally perceived as successful, of the new budget cycle. Relationships were worked out with the new Budget Committees in each house, and with other standing committees, as well as with the other support agencies. By 1976, with the new budget process machinery in place, the FY 1977 budget process seems to have worked in a timely and fairly comprehensive manner. CBO reports are being relied on by members and their staff. CBO is working with authorizing committees in costing-out programs.

The road has not been entirely smooth. Congress's uneasiness with staff increases is perhaps most evident in recent hearings reviewing the budget of CBO. Although the CBO professional staff is highly trained, few have had previous Hill experience. In addition, the concern about duplication of effort, evident in a number of areas, has focused on some of the CBO activities.

CBO publishes various reports on the budget, including scorekeeping reports, at regular intervals. It makes estimates of tax receipts and expenditures, economic forecasts and projections, estimates the cost of proposed legislative programs, and conducts background studies and analyses in major policy areas, presenting analyses of various policy alternatives. It has had to resist quick-answer requests from staffs and members and has been directed by the Legislative Appropriations Subcommittee in the Senate to give priority to its primary mission: "Providing accurate fiscal and budgetary information."[3]

There has been some hostility to CBO, stemming particularly from the staff's lack of Hill experience and the perceived duplication of effort. CBO's relationship with committees and in turn the Office's work focus are still evolving. In our view, it brings a needed expert source of independent analysis to the Hill.

There has been a good deal of talk and concern recently that the support agencies are simply duplicating each others' work. In various ways, Congress has made this concern clear through questioning at hearings and in committee reports. The four agencies have established, in response to this concern, a group of top-level personnel, which meets regularly to coordinate requests and to avoid duplication and overlap. A list of new projects undertaken by each agency and a research notification system of projects in process and recently completed are published regularly. The agencies also exchange information, and publications on various specific matters, and cooperate on projects such as the GAO–CRS Staff Training Seminars and a GAO–CBO joint budgetary task force.

Most recently, the Legislative Appropriations Subcommittee in the Senate noted that,

> During the hearings the coordinating arrangements were discussed with each of the agencies, and the Committee was assured that procedures have been put in effect. Nevertheless, the Committee continues to have some concern about duplication between the agencies, and in particular the lack of OTA input into recent studies evaluating the technology of Federal agencies. . . .The Congress has established a strong staff to evaluate technology in the OTA and the Committee believes that the other three units should look first to that staff for such evaluations before adding duplicative staff or contracting for the capability OTA already has available. . . .The Committee. . .will be following closely the coordinating efforts in preparation for next years' hearings.[4]

Clearly, the agencies are on notice, both about the uneasiness with growing staffs and the management of those staffs. In a study of the four support agencies, one observer concludes that "the problem of duplication (is) all but solved." He points out that the potential for cooperation is great and that attention should be focused on this.[5]

INFORMAL GROUPS

Informal groups, both members and staff, within the Congress are little known to the average citizen but can have policy, oversight, and constituent-service impact. Among the member groups are: the Democratic Study Group (House); the Republican Study Group (House); The Wednesday Group (House); The Black Caucus; Freshman Senators Group (Senate); Prayer Breakfast Group (Senate); and The Chowder and Marching Society.[6]

Staff groups include RAMS, The Bull Elephants (House), The Burro Club (House), Senate Staff Club, Congressional Staff Club, Republican Communications Association, Republican Women on Capitol Hill, Senate Association of Administrative Assistants and Secretaries, and Senate Press Secretaries Association.

Informal groups are formed, as noted earlier, on the basis of region (New England Caucus), attitude (Democratic Research Organization), or class (New

Members Caucus) for example. They serve as information sources and communications exchange mechanisms. Some groups hire staff aides and set up a formal office. Others function more as informal get-togethers on a regular basis. And for others, the organizational aspects are handled by aides in members' offices. All are, in some way, an effort to organize and structure the work of individuals within the House and Senate. These groups are not formal support staff; their establishment and life tend to be somewhat fluid, although in recent years more have been established than previously. Also in recent years, some groups previously established have become more institutionalized, and appear to be permanent subunits of the Congress. These groups may provide briefing papers, whip action, and forums for discussion of issues. Some are basically social in their purpose but, in fact, often are forums for "pressure" issues. But all, whatever the degree of organizational complexity or permanence, offer important support, whether informational or social or psychological, to Congressmen.

OUTSIDE SUPPORT GROUPS AND PERSONS

Outside support groups and persons also provide assistance to the Congress. They bring information, analysis, secretarial support, evaluation, and policy hints. Occasionally, outside groups and Congressional staff work closely together on an issue. As an example, the Senate Agriculture and Forestry Committee recently developed comprehensive forestry legislation in a collegial setting involving representatives of the forestry industry, wildlife and conservation groups, the U.S. Department of Agriculture, and committee staff.

Included in the outside support groups and persons are the national, state, and local party committees; lobbyists, including business, labor, public interest, religious and ethnic groups; consultants; constituents; volunteers; research organizations; and fellows, researchers, and interns. Political parties at all levels usually provide campaign rather than policy or constituent-service assistance. During the 1976 election period, national parties cooperated with House and Senate candidates in setting up such campaign tools as phone banks and by polling their constituencies.

Lobbyists can provide important information and assistance to Congressmen and staff, bringing citizen input and some assessment of citizen response to policy matters. Lobbyists, be they representing business, labor, or a public interest, are often consulted when "their" issue comes up. Congress would be unlikely to change highway construction standards without seeking the views of the highway engineers; to write new labor laws without contacting various unions; or to create a national park without hearing from the conservation and wildlife groups. With over 1,400 special-interest group offices in Washington, there is a great deal of communication with the Congress. As noted in Table 31, these contacts take place on a regular basis but not as often as communication with the CRS or executive department personnel. And, information is used with awareness of the source.

Consultants are utilized mainly by committees. They usually assist on a single project that committee staff has neither the time nor expertise to undertake. For instance, the Temporary Select Committee to Study the Senate Committee System hired consultants to construct a computer-based model of the senatorial committee assignment system. This system helped the Select Committee to test out various alternative committee systems and is now being used to assist each party in making their committee and subcommittee assignments.

Constituents are often the most powerful information source. Letters, telegrams, phone calls, and visits from constituents will almost always have an impact on the member and his staff. Opinions and information are fed into the decision-making machinery, and if a dozen or more constituents communicate a similar message then this message will often be discussed by the member and his staff.

Volunteers assist the member in both his Washington and local offices. They most usually perform secretarial tasks. At campaign time they take on a special significance and are recruited in great numbers to perform various campaign-related activities.

Various private research organizations e.g., The Brookings Institution, The American Enterprise Institute, and The Urban Institute, supplement the policy information and analysis available to the Hill. Through publications, seminars, and individual conferences, they supplement the work of congressional staffs. Most recently, a group of former Senators, Representatives, and congressional staff have supported the establishment of an Institute for Congress, designed to provide policy analysis for Congress in major issue areas. Foundation funded, the Institute began operation in 1977, and is working with Senate and House leaders to design and conduct studies on matters of concern. The Institute for Congress is presently working out relationships with Congressional committees and individual members and their staffs. It is clearly a response to the difficulty of Congress-conducted long-range analyses. The assumption is that this kind of policy analysis is needed, and that a suitable vehicle can be developed outside the Congress rather than in-house. Our guess is that it will make an impact within a few substantive areas, becoming known for its expertise in health, education, or other major topic(s). These research groups, removed from the frantic daily pace on Capitol Hill, are an effort to bring to Congressional decision making some long-range planning and thinking, which there is not often time for during the press of daily business.

Interns, fellows, and researchers contribute both to the analytical and clerical support of Congress. For instance, especially capable interns have developed resolutions that would change conference committee procedures, or respond to the needs of the aged. But many interns open mail, copy materials, run errands, or visit Washington's sights. Fellows sponsored by the American Political Science Association, the American Association for the Advancement of Science, and The National Industrial Conference Board over the years have worked on legislative issues. For example, an economist sponsored by the APSA assisted in the development of the Congressional Budget and Impoundment Control Act of 1974 and had a major role in the drafting of Title VII, Program Review and Evaluation, of that Act. Hundreds of researchers, interns, and fellows find positions on Capitol Hill each year. Their presence brings fresh ideas, new approaches, and enthusiasm to the Congress.

There are a number of intern programs on the Hill, and the House now appropriates funds for minimal salaries for interns. Any program which brings in short-term personnel has certain dysfunctional aspects, such as time required of the permanent staff for supervision, which must be considered. In fact, a majority of intern programs can perhaps better be considered constituent services, with the consequences evaluated as a learning experience for the intern (and in terms of long-range citizen knowledge of government). Other programs do have important functional workload and legislative consequences.

Both staff and Congressmen interviewed for the House study discussed the use of interns (most often college students). One administrative assistant noted that the office tried to be sure that interns would have substantive work to perform, and that there would be visible achievement: "We use interns on a professional basis—maybe (as many as) thirty during a year. We assure them of at least one publishable thing." (Presumably he meant testimony or a Floor statement, for example.) A Congressman told of having interns go to the gallery to hear him deliver a statement the interns had written.

Another office gives interns a chance to work on research in addition to doing routine jobs such as filing letters and answering the telephone. The staff aide supervising interns sets up staff meetings (often with staff of other Congressmen) for presentation of the research. One legislative assistant was disdainful of many offices using interns, "There are perhaps 100 offices using interns. Only twenty use them well." But most staff and Congressmen agree that interns can be a useful substantive resource for congressional offices.

Outside advisors assist in a number of ways. In two offices, volunteers handled committee work. They acted as legislative assistants in one very specific area, coordinating with the AA but working directly with the Representative on the substantive aspects of the work. They do background research, brief for hearings, coordinate the work of interns assigned to assist them, and are, in effect, adjunct staff.

Other offices have set up informal advisory committees on specific issues, often asking professors from universities in their districts to help staff design and draft legislation. An added payoff here is that "It's useful for constituents to know he (the Congressman) cares what they think," as one legislative assistant noted.

Over a period of several years, a university group worked on various issues of concern to a Congressman and one of the state's Senators. The students in the group were paid on the basis of ten hours' work per week and often later served as summer staff aides. Another office has used various experts, not necessarily from the district, for assistance on specific legislative issues and for briefing and brain-storming sessions with both Congressman and staff.

Interview data indicate that Congress is increasingly using all types of supplemental assistance. Professional experts draft background information papers; outside resource people meet with groups of Congressmen or staff personnel for discussion or specific legislative drafting assistance. Although some Congressmen or committees add a "consultant" to their staff for a temporary period, much of the outside assistance is available to the Congressman without fee.

What particularly distinguishes the assistance given by outside advisors and consultants described above as a "staff supplement" is the formalized, ongoing relationship which develops, where the advisor is at times quasi-staff.

LEGISLATIVE SECRETARIAT

The legislative secretariats include over three dozen separate organizational entities. Within the Senate these include the Majority and Minority Leaders' offices, Majority and Minority Whips' offices, the Vice President's office, Secretaries to the majority and minority and the related cloakroom staff, the Democratic and Republican policy committees, the Senate Chaplain, Disbursing Office, Secretary of the Senate, Sergeant-at-Arms, Service Department, Superintendent's Office, folding room, various physicians and nurses, Office of Legislative Counsel, Parliamentarian, journal clerk, printing clerk, executive clerk, legislative clerk, bill clerk, enrolling clerk, reporters of debate, document room, Senate library, Daily Digest, and Senate capitol police.[7]

House of Representatives

Within the House, similar support staff make up a "legislative secretariat." The leaders of the House—the Speaker, the Majority and Minority Leaders and Whips—have staff usually in Capitol offices near the Floor to assist them in their leadership duties. The party caucuses and committees employ staff for research and assistance to party members. And the Parliamentarian, the Legislative Counsel, and the Law Revision Office employ nonpartisan, expert staff to assist the House, its committees, and individual Members, on specific highly technical legislative and parliamentary matters. During the 94th Congress (1975–1976) a total of 130 aides served on these various staffs.

For both Democratic and Republican leaders and committees, staff may be carried on a personal office payroll but actually assist the Representative in his official leadership or party duties. The House authorizes appropriations of funds for the Democratic Caucus and Steering Committee and Republican Conference (Caucus) staff.[8]

The staff of the House and party leaders engage in many of the same legislative-related activities as other committee and personal staff professionals, but they are more often concerned with the flow and processing of legislation and with monitoring Floor activity. Aides staff the regular whip meetings and work with committees on legislative timetables and to manage intercommittee conflict. When the House is in session, they are on the Floor assisting their bosses in monitoring Floor proceedings. (Personal and committee aides in the House accompany members to the Floor less frequently than in the Senate; aides to House leaders are the exception.) Aides also draft Floor statements, work on amendments, and assist on speeches, as do their committee and personal staff counterparts. Most usually, their activities are focused on matters relating to party role and interests in the House, rather than on specific legislation or policy interests of a committee or an individual member.

Staff of party committees also work on matters of interest and concern to the party as a whole or to a group of Representatives. They, too, often deal with matters of procedure and strategy. Party caucus and committee staff keep voting records for each party member, staff the caucus and committee meetings by assisting on record keeping, notifying members of matters in which they have expressed an interest, and monitoring legislation which may be called up. Particularly for Republicans, who do not control most committee positions, research and briefing for members is an important aspect of the work of central party staff.

The staffs of the Parliamentarian and the Office of Legislative Counsel are quite different: highly trained, with an apprenticeship period, they are nonpartisan and serve the House as an institution, as well as, on request, committees and individual members. In the more senior positions in these offices, there is little turnover.

The Parliamentarian's office assists the Chair in ruling on procedures and precedents of the House. The Office of Legislative Counsel assists in writing legislation, including amendments, and often works closely with a committee for a period of time as legislation is being drafted and "marked up."

The Office of Legislative Counsel was established in 1919 as the Legislative Drafting Service (Revenue Act of 1918). Since that time, each House has had its own Office of Legislative Counsel. The Senate Office continues to operate under the basic authority of the 1918 law; Title V of the Legislative Reorganization Act of 1970 expanded the mandate of the House Legislative Counsel Office, explicitly directing that the office assist both committees and individual members, for example, stating the role of the office more generally, "[to assist in] achievement of a clear, faithful, and coherent expression of legislative policy," and providing that "at the direction of the speaker. . . .(the office is to) perform on behalf of the House. . .any legal services which are within the capabilities of the office."[9]

The primary role of the office has not changed over the years, however, but the workload has increased substantially. Some workload figures make this explicit. Between the 82nd Congress (1951–1952) and the 93rd Congress (1973–1974) the total number of jobs increased from 2,873 to 7,003. Jobs for members increased from 2,560 to 5,877; jobs for committees from 313 to 1,126.[10]

The office began operations in 1919 with three lawyers and one clerk; by 1947 four lawyers were added, and since 1970 the number of professionals has increased from twelve to twenty-six.

Interview data indicate that staff professionals on the personal staffs of Congressmen call on the Office of Legislative Counsel for assistance in drafting legislation, whether or not that staffer has had legal training and/or experience. The expertise and experience in the intricacies of legislative drafting which the Office has are considered necessary inputs for effective staff work. That a major increase has occurred in jobs for individual members appears to be due not only to the increasing complexity of legislation and number of Federal programs, but also to the extensive involvement of personal staff in assisting Congressmen on legislative matters.

The office works closely with committee staffs, often through the conference stage of legislation. In some instances, lawyers are assigned to committees or subcommittees for long periods, in actuality serving as committee staff. This was the case in the 90th Congress, when Ways and Means was working on the tax reform bill, for example.

CONCLUSION

Congressional support staffs are derived from a number of sources. Some are internal to Congress (House and Senate); others are funded within the legislative branch. Still others are external in their origin.

The impact of these staffs varies according to the issue. In some cases a single group or person may be a prime causal factor for congressional action. Most often an aggregate of actors is involved in generating activity in the Congress. Input from the various support agencies—CBO, CRS, GAO, and OTA—have major influence. A variety of support staffs are involved in the policy, legislative development, oversight, and constituent-service activities performed within the Congress.

NOTES

1. See Legislative Branch Appropriations Hearings, FY1960-FY1977, U.S. Senate and U.S. House of Representatives for data on work load and staff size of all the agencies.
2. Studies of the activities of each of the support agencies as well as a comparative study

of the four agencies were made in 1976 for the Commission on the Operation of the Senate. See *Congressional Support Agencies, A Compilation of Papers,* Committee Print (80–189), 94th Congress, 2d Session, 1976.

3. 94th Congress, 2nd Session, S. Rept. 94-1201, to accompany H.R. 14238, Legislative Branch Appropriations, 1977, p. 27.

4. *Report,* (S. Rept. 94-2401), pp. 25 and 26.

5. Ernest S. Griffith, "Four Agency Comparative Study," in *Congressional Support Agencies,* 1977, p. 110.

6. See Elliott, "Communications and Small Groups," and Arthur G. Stevens et al. "Mobilization of Liberal Strength in the House, 1955–1970: The Democratic Study Group," *American Political Science Review,* Vol. 68, #2, 1974, pp. 667–681.

7. For a description of a portion of the above, see "APPENDIX I, Functional Descriptions Legislative Secretariat," *Automated Legislative Record Keeping System for the United States Senate,* Committee on Rules and Administration, U.S. Senate, February 29, 1972, pp. 117–235.

8. *Hearings* on Legislative Branch Appropriations, U.S. House of Representatives, FY 1977, pp. 641–643.

9. Sec. 502 and 503, PL 91–510.

10. *Hearings,* FY1964, p. 298; FY1970, p. 444; FY1977, p. 655ff.

9. Staff Impact

What difference do staff make? The constellation of factors that have been presented so far have demonstrated the importance of staff. Our contention is that staffs perform much of the congressional work: they perform almost exclusively the constituent-service function; do most of the preliminary legislative research; help generate policy ideas; set up hearings, meetings, and conferences; carry out oversight activities—program evaluations, investigations, etc.; draft bills; and meet and talk with executive, interest, and constituent groups on substantive matters. The member spends most of his or her time chairing hearings; debating, conferring with colleagues, and voting on the House or Senate Floor; talking to constituents; marking up bills; and directing and working with his personal and committee staff.

As demands on Congressmen have grown, congressional staff members have also had to assume a greater role in policy making. For instance, often they are called on to develop substantive legislation. The Congressional Budget and Impoundment Control Act of 1974, surely one of the most important bills enacted by Congress in the last twenty-five years, was largely formulated by staff in a long series of "mark-up" sessions. Staff aides from the Senate Government Operations Committee began consideration of this bill. It was redrafted by a conference of a few select staff members from the major committees and joint committees that were concerned with the bill and subsequently approved by the Senators and Representatives on the Conference Committee. Senators, indeed, are functioning more and more like the president or chief operating officer of a corporation, giving direction to policy and giving staff the responsibility for details.

When members could count government programs in the hundreds and not the thousands;[1] received 30 or even 100 letters a week and not hundreds or thousands; took the few constituents who came to Washington on personal tours instead of having a receptionist hand out hundreds of Washington maps imprinted with the member's name and picture—those were the days, not so long ago, when the staff employed in Congress consisted mainly of a few clerks and secretaries. Those days are gone. Today the member must depend on his staff to do most of "his" work. The personal nature of this work elicits norms that differ from the usual bureaucratic setting.

The effectiveness of each member's personal team depends on a constellation of factors. The most important of these have been discussed earlier— organization, attributes, tenure, communication, activity, and role.

Various aspects of our earlier discussion merit review to summarize the staff-member relationship, staff role in constituent-service activities, and staff work on legislative issues as they bear on the Congressional process.

We have been concerned throughout this study with the role of professional staff in the policy output of Congress. Office organization, structures for decision making, and recruitment and educational background of aides, as well as activity and communication patterns have been analyzed to provide a basis for assessing the extent of staff input in the legislative and policy process and to identify particular points at which it occurs. The study has also sought to analyze the importance of several key variables such as party and seniority on the organization and function of professional staff in congressional offices, and to compare and contrast the operations of professionals on committee and personal staffs. The similarities between the duties, responsibilities, and influence of committee and personal staff aides are more striking than the differences—although, as detailed earlier, there are differences which should not be overlooked.

Staffers exert a strong influence on the material with which they deal because of their position astride the office communications process, their control of factual data, and the expertise and professional judgment which they bring to their jobs. And most significant to the actual policy activity is a member's expectation that staff are hired for ideas, judgment, and counsel. This is evident from statements of both staff and Congressmen, and from the activities which staff do indeed perform.

Today staff are more expert and are becoming increasingly specialized. As we have noted most staff have assumed positions that require them to specialize in one, two, and sometimes three roles. Senate and commitee staff have to be more specialized than House personal staff. In the House of Representatives, with its range of responsibilities and relatively limited staffing (as compared, for example, with both the Senate and the executive branch), personal staff professionals are generalists to a greater degree than their Senate counterparts. Committee staff in both Houses perform similar functions; there is somewhat more opportunity for specialization, and for many, more time to devote to legislative and oversight work than is possible for personal aides.

Congressional staff perform a variety of legislative and policy-related activities. On occasion they argue vigorously for or against a certain policy position. Personal aides have substantial responsibilities for the Congressman's committee work. The intensity of involvement varies with the committee assignment, with the issue, and with the Congressman's seniority and control of committee staff.

Personal staff responsibility for coordinating legislative strategy is increasing. It may involve coordinating committee-related matters with committee aides as well as with personal staff of other committee members, or it may entail work on general legislative matters unrelated to the Congressman's committee assignment. In both these areas, staff work on a bipartisan basis also appears to be increasing. Both the SST and Congressional reform issues in the House involved staff and Congressmen from both parties; budget reform, strip mining, and health insurance are continuing issues which involve bipartisan, and in some cases, across-Chamber aides. Such coordination may be initiated by staff of a committee, a particular group (for example, the Democratic Study Group) or by personal staff aides.

Finally, in what appears to be a growing number of offices, professional staff participate in the identification and development of issues to be introduced into the legislative process, as committee staff regularly do. This activity is in addition to assisting in the formulation of specific legislative provisions after an issue has been identified. As staffs increase and specialization occurs, it may be that this type of staff input will become more prevalent.

Personal staff also participate in the Congressional function of legislative oversight, although most prior studies deal only with committee activity in this area. Where personal staff are concerned, oversight is linked primarily to office casework or state or district problems. A number of staff aides, after describing a piece of legislation or an administrative procedure change, noted that the initial impetus for an inquiry stemmed from the constituency. Infrequently, but nevertheless occasionally, a Congressman or aide will become concerned about a matter—perhaps related to the Congressman's committee work—and initiate inquiries. The number of offices actively concerned with oversight is relatively small, but also appears to be increasing.

Congressional staff professionals also affect policy decisions because of their involvement in communication lines within and among offices. Their role in obtaining and analyzing data has been noted. When staff meet with lobbyists, or with constituents to discuss their concerns, their report of the interview is filtered through their own perceptions. The accuracy and extensiveness of the report to the Congressman, as well as the priorities they may assign to various requests, become significant in terms of input into the policy-making process.

Similarly, staff work on communications which emanate from the office shape outside perceptions of the Congressman. Although in general this is an area over which Congressmen hold final control, the Congressman cannot do everything and may not have time, for example, to rewrite a newsletter drafted by his staff. Most Senators rely heavily on staff and do not have time to oversee closely the letters, phone calls, and telegrams that are prepared in their offices. In both the Senate and House, staff determine content and issues to be considered in newsletters, in questionnaires, and in many "low priority" statements.

In the aggregate, various attributes of the staff member can impact through the Congress, on policy and on citizens and organizations.

Age and Tenure

Staff are younger than might generally be expected. The average age of Senate personal staff professionals is 38.6, with nearly 50 percent 35 or less. In the House during the 92nd Congress, 69 percent of the legislative assistants in personal offices, and 90 percent of professional assistants in jobs other than that of AA or LA were thirty or less. Committee staff are only somewhat older. In 1973–1974, 16 percent of committee professionals were under thirty (18 percent in the Senate and 12 percent in the House); 40 percent of the committee staff aides were less than forty. Senate committee aides, like personal staff aides, are younger than their House counterparts.[2]

Tenure of many aides is, on the average, quite brief. Nearly 50 percent of Congressional committee aides have been in their jobs less than four years; another 36 percent have served four to ten years on that committee. LA's on personal staffs in the House had an average tenure of 2.3 years, with 6 years the longest any LA had been in his or her job. The junior professional may help set up hearings, attend executive briefings, and deal with high level executives and senior corporate officials. Junior staff members can move up to senior professional positions quickly, on occasion in three to five years. The lack of experience on the part of aides actively involved in legislative decision making may contribute to some of the mistakes and omissions found in public laws, particularly in measures concerning technical aspects of business, social, and scientific areas. Brief tenure, whatever the aide's age, means frequent training of new aides. In addition, there is lack of what we would call a committee or office history. Most legislation is approved only after consideration by several Congresses. New aides have not participated in, and often do not know, this background. Research, previously done, may be duplicated. On the most mundane level, it may take longer to find a needed file.

Education

The most prevalent educational background among staff members is the liberal arts and law. A limited number of staff have training in other fields of expertise—business, science, medicine, or engineering, for example. Although drafting legislation requires technical skill, knowledge of a substantive field is also important. Because time is at a premium, particularly during a session, it may be difficult to become knowledgeable rapidly. Some observers, noting the preponderance of lawyers, have argued that Congress would be better served by staff with more diverse training and experience, even with an emphasis on fields which differ from those of Congressmen.[3] But many Congressmen prefer aides with similar backgrounds, and ease of communication with aides is an important consideration. The consequence of similar experiential and educational backgrounds, may be that the process of bargaining and negotiation is overemphasized.

The trend is for younger staff to have higher levels of education than older staff. For example, over 50 percent of House LA's have M.A.'s or law degrees. In contrast, the highest degree held by 46 percent of House AA's is a B.A., with an additional 9 percent holding no degree. Opportunities for persons with advanced training appear to be increasing, and there is some movement toward more diversity of training (within OTA and CRS, for example).

In a more complicated and specialized legislative work world, this drawing on expertise is in line with other areas of government and with nongovernmental activity. But a tension exists between expertise and the more generalist norms of the Hill, a situation which we discuss below.

Prior Experience

The professional experience of personal office staff tends to be similar to that of their bosses: legislative and local. In nearly a third of House offices, no professional staff member had worked in any other branch of the Federal government. Even on committee staff, 57.2 percent had not worked in a Federal department. But over 50 percent of House LA's do bring a knowledge of legislative work, attained through law, political science, or practical political experience, to their job. This background may reinforce existing Congressional norms and the views, not altogether positive, of executive decision making. In the Senate, where fully six of ten professional staff members knew their boss in some capacity before they were hired, the consequence of staff experience and previous staff–member contact are baseline characteristics that help to establish the personal team relationship within offices and committees.

Residence

Within personal offices a state-centered attitude is often found, reinforced by hiring. For example, as previously noted, nearly two-thirds of Senate personal office staff maintain legal residence in their Senator's home state. It is not uncommon to hear a staffer explain, "We throw away any mail from out-of-state," or "My Senator is a budget-cutter until our state is affected." By hiring staff from the home state or district, the member keeps up home ties and buys talent that knows the policy needs and expectations of his constituents. When a bill is proposed that changes a formula for domestic assistance, it is now common practice to show on a state-by-state basis, and often by congressional district, that the modified program will not cause loss in revenue to any jurisdiction. LA's and committee staff often analyze proposed measures to anticipate the question from the member, ''Does it make any difference to our people?''

In contrast, a large proportion of committee staff maintain legal residence in the District of Columbia, Maryland, or Virginia. Do the patterns of residence indicate a difference in role orientation? As noted earlier, we think so. How do these different patterns affect policy? From our study data and observation, it appears that ''local'' aides with backgrounds similar to that of their Senator or Representative may be attuned to the state or district aspect of legislation. However, measurement of different influence is difficult, and further research is needed. The location of the aide may be less important than the situation of serving on a personal rather than a committee staff. Do these differences mean that increasing one type of staff resource rather than another will affect policy outcomes? There is no definitive answer. Congressmen prefer to have state aides in some jobs and do not have any strong preference for other jobs. Certainly, however, localism is an important factor in the Capitol Hill policy-making process.

Political Values

Professional staff, whether in a personal office or on a committee, have a tendency to hold political values similar to those of their Senator or Representative. Of course, there are staff aides with differing values from their sponsors, but on the whole staff are able to reflect their member's basic philosphy even though it might not be their own. The overall policy impact appears to occur in several ways. Many staffs actually hold slightly stronger, more ''liberal'' or more ''conservative'' views than the member; hence, aides may reinforce a member's views and values. The tendency of Congressmen to listen selectively[4] and the natural predilection of aides to bring information which the member wants to hear may filter out some political values, but it would appear that, generally, shared political values serve as a base for the impact of professional judgment and expertise.

Personality

In addition to political values, other personal factors give insight into how staff behavior influences policy. The general personality type found among Senate personal professional staff was of a conservative task leader who evidences persistence, activeness, and social participation. Professional aides, as would be expected, join clubs, participate in the various phases of legislative activity, legislative bargaining, and may initiate activity. Committee staff may self-initiate oversight of a program and report the results to a member. Personal aides initiate interest by members in proposed areas or pending legislation.

Communications

Communication patterns among members and their staff are very intense. Aides talk on at least a daily basis and nearly half of the Senate personal staff see the member every hour or more; the average Senate committee professional communicates with a Senator frequently. House committee staff see their member slightly more than their Senate counterpart. This close contact helps maintain the personal relationship that each member generally has with his professional staff. It also is a product of, and now tends to reinforce, the informality and lack of hierarchy in the organizational structure of Congress and its subunits.

Member–staff Relationships

Staff may have positive, neutral, negative, symmetrical or asymmetrical relationships with their boss. From the data on Senate personal staff, it is clear that many relationships of mutual respect and cooperation are found among members and their staff. This is especially true of the senior professionals on personal and committee staffs. The very personal nature of these relationships is the basis for the common observation that "talking to a member's AA or staff director is as good and sometimes better than talking to the member."

Members build up personal staff teams with backgrounds and ideologies similar to their own and have at least everyday contact with each other. This relationship between a member and his staff provides the foundation for staff impact both within and outside the Congress.

STAFFING AND OUTPUT

Measurement of staff impact is difficult, and yet measurement data, relating staff and output, are a useful supplement to systematic interviews and survey data.

Measures of output are not entirely satisfactory. Co-sponsorship of bills measures one type of activity but does not measure quality of work, nor can co-sponsorship levels easily be linked to staff activity. Similarly, the number of bills and resolutions reported by a committee measures one kind of activity, but one committee may report ten very complex bills and another may report twenty-five which are less complicated; the measure does not get at the differences and, in fact, the workload may be similar. Hearings, number of meetings, number of pages of bills, etc., are all measures of *something,* but we are skeptical of relying too heavily on these kinds of data to measure staff impact on output. How can we measure impact in the following situations:

- Staff review of budget justifications and preparation of questions for a hearing?
- Staff discussion with executive agency personnel of requests and/or policy changes which the agency is considering?
- Staff work on an amendment which is defeated in committee?

Time surveys and frequency of activity data are attempts to measure this kind of work.[5] They are helpful in describing activity, and some inferences can be made. Case studies give a good indication of quality, but it is difficult to generalize from a case study. With these caveats, in Table 32 we present several indices relating staff size and committee output.

There is a rough correlation between staff size and number of hearings, that is, the larger the staff, the more hearings tend to be held by a committee. The relationship is not perfect, however; that is, the committee with the largest staff does not hold the most hearings, and so on down the ranking list. A similar pattern is evident when all committee meetings are considered. Using these figures as a measure of output and of staff impact is not entirely satisfactory; we realize the figures are indications of quantity, not quality. In addition, the quantity measured is only one type of activity. We can infer, however, that with more hearings, more information is being transmitted; and it is likely that a committee holding a large number of hearings or meetings is either processing more legislation or more complicated legislation.

A recent study demonstrates that as committee staff has increased, oversight activity (measured by hearings) has also increased.[6] Again, a consequence of larger staffs is more activity, with presumably more matters covered.

Ranking the committees by a legislative index (ratio of measures reported to measures referred) can give another measure of output; this method does not distinguish differences in complexity of legislation (a bill of two pages is the equivalent of a bill of fifty pages) and workload variations (e.g., if 10 percent of the bills referred were reported, this could result from an output of 2 of 20 or 50 of 500). Using this measure, as Table 31 indicates, there is a very slight relationship between staff size and bill output.[7]

Communication patterns of Senate committees do not appear to differ with size of staff. (See Table 32.) There is some evidence to suggest that larger staffs may be slightly more entrepreneurial and less local: They contact Senators and constituents less frequently but work with the bureaucracy, Presidential aides, and staffs of Senators more frequently than aides on smaller committee staffs. It should be noted that committee jurisdiction may affect these patterns, as the smaller staffs tend to be those of committeees with limited jurisdiction.

The difference in output figures is striking. Committees with large staffs report more legislation and hold many more hearings and meetings than committees with small staffs. They also appear to be more efficient, holding more meetings and hearings per professional. It also appears that somewhat larger staffs facilitate wider information gathering and greater analytic input.

Analysis of communication and activity patterns by committee indicates that some differences exist. The variation does not seem, however, to be regular. What is evident is that, when communications are more frequent, this extends to all contacts. For example, when aides on a committee contact the bureaucracy frequently, they also often contact Presidential staff, and other committee and personal staff. Increased communication in turn appears to be related to larger committee staffs.

Measurement of output of personal offices can also indicate the effect of staff. As for committees, measures of quantity and output which have been used are not entirely satisfactory. Nevertheless, some analysis of output is helpful to show the general directions of activity.

Using the House sample, Table 34 shows the relationship of output, as measured by cosponsorship of measures (bills and resolutions) during 1971, to several variables.

There is a relationship between the number of professional staff and output; the more professionals, the greater the output. There is a similar relationship between the total number of staff and output. Larger staffs apparently release professionals for legislative and policy work; the larger staffs also seem to be those with more professionals.

Other variables—type of office organization, seniority, and particuarly policy attitude—also appear to affect output.

Output increases from hierarchical to coordinative, and again to individualistic, offices. This supports our earlier observation that hierarchical offices are somewhat more constraining in terms of staff entrepreneurial activity and communication levels.

Output also increases as seniority decreases. This may reflect a focus on committee assignments at the most senior level; it may also be linked to staff numbers—as the more senior members tend to have fewer staff—and to other factors.

The number of staff does not seem to be as important as policy attitude in determining office output. Of those Congressmen with one professional aide, the output varies according to "liberalness" or "conservativeness." Within each policy attitude group, output generally increases with more staff, but the pattern is not always as expected. For example, among moderate Congressmen (20–79 on the Conservative Coalition scale), the output of offices with one or with three or more professional aides was similar (27 and 28); but the offices with two professional aides cosponsored many more measures (52).

In summary, for both personal and committee offices, the measures we have used indicate that staff has impact on output in quantitative terms. But the measures indicate little about the relationship between staff and quality of output.

SENATORS' AND REPRESENTATIVES' PERSPECTIVE

Staff role is illuminated by several interview comments. One senior Republican said, "My staff is savvy. . .and I consider them experts. I rely on their expertise." He went on to illuminate the interplay between staff input on policy and legislation and the Congressman's trust in his staff, "It's very important to have a good staff. . .and I feel I've got a good one. My AA knows (home state); my LA knows cases and is diligently learning. I'm trying to give him more responsibility." A Democratic colleague said, "[A lot] of staff time is spent on the legislative function. I divide the responsibility, pool the effort, share the responsibility and the satisfaction." And a freshman Congressman explained, "The staff feeds me ideas and facts. Often we bat stuff around together. I make the final decision—but I want input not only on facts."

In the House, staff input appears to change during the course of a Representative's career in Congress.[8] Increasing seniority may bring different concerns and different priorities. One near senior Democrat on an exclusive committee felt there were difficulties from "added security" of increasing tenure. He had organized his staff to assure a flow of fresh ideas, as well as continued expertise. He also felt that over time his staff had become less political, and he hired more for expertise and issue interest.

It appears that often around the fourth to sixth terms, Congressmen reassess their priorities and in doing so reorganize their staffs. One Representative, newly re-elected to a sixth term, hired a legislative assistant and began to devote more time to legislative work. Another one of slightly less seniority added a research assistant to his staff to identify and develop legislative issues. Other Congressmen point to heavier reliance on expertise than in early terms and to "reacting more responsively to the legislative function." There is also just "more work," partly due to more subcommittee assignments. One Congressman seemed to be saying that with increased seniority, he didn't rely on his staff as much for factual data—but that he expected them to be useful in creative ways by keeping up with a certain amount of information and building on that.

A change in committee assignment also affects staff function. For example, an appointment to the House Appropriations Committee has meant heavy personal staff involvement in committee work. A new committee assignment, to a committee of first choice, enabled one Representative to blend his expertise with that of his research assistant and to begin development of legislation which he felt might have some chance of passage. And in another office a new committee assignment meant that "more legislative work was needed from staff," and "Our focus is changed. . .it's more national in scope."

We are struck by the similarities in role, activities, and function between personal and committee aides. The organizational context may be somewhat different: committee staffs, for example, are somewhat more hierarchically organized. The job of committee aides may be somewhat (or in some instances, very much) more specialized. Time may be allotted a bit differently, but the differences are really of degree, not of activities or roles.

For both personal and committee professionals, office organization and interest of the principals are major determinants of staff input, particularly at the issue development and priority setting stages. In some offices the staff operate within clearly defined and quite narrow limits, primarily giving technical assistance. In others, the staff are encouraged to act as policy "entrepreneurs," working on issue identification and legislative development as part of wide-ranging responsibilities.

Staff, whether committee or personal, are hired for judgment, as well as loyalty and expertise. Many Congressmen ask for and expect expressions of opinion. One aide, describing his activities, reported of his boss, "He wants our opinion and judgment." And a Congressman, agreeing, said, "The staff must bring pros and cons, but they also must be able to say 'wait.'"

NOTES

1. Harrison W. Fox, Jr. and Beverly Lovelady, Third Staff Report, Temporary Select Committee to Study the Committee System, U.S. Senate, 1976, mimeo.
2. A freshman Senator, who had served ten years in his state's Senate, noted his concern with young, inexperienced aides: "I find too often that many of our staff members are bright, young political scientists with very little experience, who have a bright future some day. But too often they are just using us as a training ground while the system allows them to write major legislation. I am afraid that we are not getting the quality of work that we ought to have. I don't say this to reflect on these young people, but the U.S. Senate ought not to be a training ground...." *Hearings,* Temporary Select Committee to Study the Senate Committee System, 94th Congress, 2nd Session, July 1976, p. 105.
3. See James Robinson in de Grazia, *Congress.*
4. Lewis A. Dexter, "Congressmen and Their Constituents," in *New Perspectives.*
5. See, for example, the time-use survey reported in Commission on the Operation of the Senate, *Toward a Modern Senate* (December, 1976). Additional data on activity are reported in Fox, *Senate Staffs;* see also Saloma, *Politics.*
6. Joel D. Aberbach, "The Development of Oversight in the U.S. Congress: Concepts and Analysis," in *Techniques and Procedures for Analysis and Evaluation,* Commission on the Operation of the Senate, Committee Print (82-042), 1977. Aberbach's data cover the 85th through the 94th Congresses, using the first six months of each session; he points out that this does not necessarily mean that the quality of oversight has improved.
7. The exception is the Finance Committee—with a very low ratio of bills reported to bills referred. The bills reported are extremely complex. However, the number of bills referred is very high in comparison to other committees, perhaps a result of the committee's subject matter.
8. There is perhaps less change in Senate staff activity because the freshman Senator has expectations of affecting policy from his arrival on Capitol Hill. A six-year term encourages this, of course.

10. A Broader View of Congressional Staffs

To this point the major focus has been on legislative staffs. A number of factors linked to the staff have been described as ingredients in Congressional operations. This sets the stage for a broader view of Congressional staffing, with a focus on several themes.

Congressional staff is involved heavily in the three phases of Congressional policymaking—idea generation (foresight), legislative development, and oversight. Much Congressional activity in the first and third categories is performed by staff. During the legislative development stage Congressmen's activity is perhaps most visible, as they chair hearings, mark up bills, debate on the floor of the respective houses the merits, and work out legislative differences in conferences. Staff support these activities very heavily as has been noted earlier.

Foresight activity undertaken by staff includes generating ideas and policy approaches, researching policy suggestions of the members, writing policy statements, and formulating outlines upon which legislation can be used. A Member's interest or concern often focuses staff activity on a policy area or idea; subsequent staff work results in specific policy suggestions, and actions. Members and staff may be in continuing communication, or staff may proceed independently, identifying issues and generating policy approaches. Usually, members depend on staff and the congressional support agencies for assistance.

Oversight involves staff most especially in program evaluation and investigation activities. Other oversight activities, such as hearings, heavily involve the members. But even in this instance staff may spend days arranging for a hearing, contacting witnesses, writing the Member's statements and so on. The Members generally determine the subject of the hearing but may not be deeply involved again until the actual day of the hearing.

Staff are also active in providing constituent services. The representative function of Congress cuts across all three areas of policymaking: foresight, legislative development and oversight; in addition, constituent service work such as casework and federal projects assistance links the Congressman and his constituents on specific matters which may involve one of the three phases of policy making, or may not involve "policy" at all. Other constituent service matters,

154

such as newsletters, correspondence, and press releases may serve several goals: representation, education (regarding policy and/or federal government actions), self-advertisement and so forth. Most of the specific activity of serving constituents devolves on staff. Processing of casework and mail has become increasingly routinized, particularly in Senate offices; in many cases, the activity is performed by nonprofessional aides, with supervision by a higher-level professional. Staff also greet constituents, often talk with them or speak to constituent groups, and take them on tours of the Capitol. Staff (most usually professional aides) also handle most of the federal projects work, meeting with local, state, and federal agency personnel, and working out details of grants or of legislation. Congressmen tend to be more involved in federal projects activity than in casework, but in both instances the staff perform the bulk of the activity. Although involvement in press and correspondence matters varies between the houses and among offices, here again staff usually draft, write and process the office communication, with general supervision or perhaps only final approval from the Congressman.

Our objective in this chapter is to view staffing from a broader, systemic perspective, to present a few of the common themes, and in this way to indicate linkages between Congressional staffing and the wider external environment.

IMPACT OF TECHNOLOGY

A major external factor that has influenced staff and Members' behavior is technological developments, the impact of which extends to need for scientific assessment of technological programs, to more precise and measureable program impact, to hiring experts, and to use of the new technology in performing traditional Congressional operations.

Advances in technology both through social and scientific invention have affected the way members and staff perform their jobs. For instance, the development of computers and related technology,[1] now allows the member, assisted by staff, to communicate with a large portion of his constituents on a regular basis. Automatic typewriters and signature machines allow two or three persons to produce hundreds of "personal" letters each day.

Computer terminals in offices give Congressional staff access to a great deal of information. The status of bills pending before Congress, legislation sponsored and co-sponsored by members, indices including the *New York Times* and various Library of Congress data files are available.

The General Accounting Office can now provide members and staff with detailed lists and evaluation of programs by committee. Through developments like these, the utilization of technological advances helps to reduce the information and analytical gap that exists between the legislative and executive branches.

Congress has been slow to adopt many of the technological and scientific improvements but has been even slower to use social invention. For example, until the mid-seventies management and social program evaluation advances received almost no attention on Capitol Hill. Congressional management practices have been reviewed by the Commission on the Operation of the Senate and the House Commission on Administrative Review. Social program evaluation received a major boost when Title VII of the Congressional Budget and Impoundment Control Act of 1974 was enacted. A division has been established within GAO, in part to assist with Congressional utilization of program evaluation inventions. The rapid pace of technological development tests the skills and ingenuity of both members and staff as well as the viability of the congressional institution.

BUREAUCRACY OR PERSONAL TEAM

All staff groups (''in-house'' and support agency) contribute to what we see as an expanded (and expanding) role for professional staff. There are concomitant tensions between a large number of professionals and the personalized, generalist culture of Congress with a long tradition of direct participation in a multitude of decisions by the principal actors: the Senators and the Representatives.

Arguments that the staffs of Congress are ''little bureaucracies'' have merit generally when staff is outside a member's span of control. As Lewis Dexter has so poignantly noted, a personal staff team differs from other bureaucratic staffs.[2] Bureaucratic norms such as promotion on the basis of merit, seeking formal professional achievement, encouraging a standard pattern of careers, and rigorous selection procedures have less application in the Congressional setting than elsewhere. Norms such as personal loyalty, persistence, courtesy, rewarding initiative, and less concern with formal assigned duties and tasks are also characteristic of most personal and committee staffs; thus these staffs function as a personal team.

Parallels between the courts of kings, assistants to presidents and generals, and the staffs of Senators and Representatives are clear. As we have noted, staff organizational structure is often flat, and the member has direct access to most of his professional staff. These staff adhere to the norms of courtesy and loyalty much more than the apprenticeship norms that characterize most bureaucracies.

Bureaucracy is sometimes used as a synonym for large staffs. Large staff groups do have elements of bureaucracy but are basically a mix of professionalism and what we have called personalism. Typical bureaucracy will, we doubt, ever exist throughout Congress (although some groups may be more bureaucratic than others).

The legislative branch does not, and we believe should not, match the executive branch in numbers. (If this were to occur, Washington would simply have two large bureaucracies, each with all the typical behavior patterns of a large, complex organization.) The legislative branch has unique functions. With multiple access points, various decision centers, and a flat organizational structure, Congress is able to assure that a variety of views will be heard in the course of the decision process.

However, staffs have increased and presently exhibit some elements of bureaucracy.[3] Staff specialization has increased as larger staffs have permitted a division of workload not previously possible. One consequence has been that almost all Senators now have committee staff, or personal committee aides, who give detailed attention to specific legislative matters within the jurisdictions of a Member's committee. At the same time, particularly on Senate personal staffs and some committee staffs, departmentalization is occurring. On Senate personal staffs legislative, mail, constituent-services, and press departments are being organized; a "chief LA" or "chief press assistant" heads the department and reports directly to an administrative assistant. Consequently, professionals work directly with Senators and Representatives less frequently.

Management of staffs is becoming an important aspect of a Congressman's job. On the Senate side, personal staffs average about thirty employees, with some as large as sixty or seventy. Committees, and some subcommittees, have similarly large staffs. These offices, and even the personal staffs of the House, require more coordination of personnel, and more precise lines of authority and responsibility than has been the case in the past. Congressmen have been slow to realize, however, the need for management skills, both for personal staff and for committee staff. Congress often operates on a limited time frame and in a pressure atmosphere; new committees are staffed and studies and legislation produced in this way. Congress needs, and in some instances is beginning to move toward, planned schedules of work with lead-time to assist analysis and consideration. But overall, Congress needs to focus more on management of present resources.

A tension continues to exist between the professionalism of experts and the demands of a personalized and often partisan working environment. In 1946, the Special Senate Committee reporting bill S. 2177, which became the Legislative Reorganization Act, provided for permanent, professional committee aides appointed by committees after "certification" of qualifications by a Director of Congressional Personnel. Both the provisions for certification and for a Director of Personnel were struck during Senate debate, but the issue of defining professionalism remains. Congress does not have a tenure or merit appointment system for its professional legislative aides. Most members of Congress do not want such a system, and a formal Civil Service system could be expected to have significant dysfunctional consequences. One of the major arguments against a Congressional Civil Service system is that office and committee staff are performing personal political tasks, which violates basic bureaucratic norms. Staffing has often been looked on as personal assistance. In the early years of personal staff, secretaries and clerks were paid from personal funds. In addition, the political culture of the Hill would work against appointment solely on a Civil

Service merit and recruitment system, in our view. For many staff jobs, assessment of political intelligence and judgment as to public reaction may be important information needs. It may be that some nonpartisan jobs require less skills of this type. But even on nonpartisan committee staffs, there is often a responsiveness to the priorities of the chairman and a need for political expertise which could be absent if the "permanent professionals" *proposed* in 1946 were indeed appointed.

Certain legislative staffs are bureaucracies in the Weberian sense: the support agencies, for instance. Attempts to make personal staffs more bureaucratic are aimed at changing the basic structure of the staff-member relationship.

In summary, a true legislative bureaucracy exists composed of the support agencies and parts of the legislative secretariat. There are also 535 member offices and over 100 committee and subcommittee staffs, increasing in size and with some elements of bureaucratic behavior, especially expertise and specialization, but they continue to function as personal teams.

There is an ever-present tension between staff increase and the traditional world of Capitol Hill—generalist, clubby, devoted to the role of the individual actor. Bureaucracy and bureaucratization is perceived as a less than congenial organizational arrangement for Congress. For many, the executive branch hierarchy results in delayed decisions and a layering between experts and decision makers. A Congressional bureaucracy is unacceptable.

THE NATURE OF STAFF

Noting that personal and committee staff on the whole are not bureaucrats, can they be nonpartisan, expert, a professional, and so on. The concepts are complex, thus causing confusion about what best describes staff.

And aides can be described by a number of adjectives—partisan, activist, entrepreneurial,[4] expert, educator or advocate, professional, core support or personal support, policy designer, and specialist or generalist. Of course, these terms have many meanings, reflecting various dimensions of the Congressional milieu and staff attributes.

Staff tend to be partisan both in their orientations and activity. Being a Democrat or Republican is an important factor in the staff equation. Because of the political implications of most staff activity, a strong sense of and affiliation with a political party seems to provide a base for making decisions and taking action in the congressional office and committee setting. In addition, since staff are appointed to their position by a partisan, they may be expected to and, indeed do, reflect their patron. On some committees, the staff is hired as non-partisan, but these tend to be exceptions.

Activist or entrepreneurial staff are often the norm on Capitol Hill. Our data show that professional staffs are high activity persons. Second, the general staff personality type identifies staff as being high on leadership and on total interaction initiated. He or she may also test high on persistence, dominance, sophistication, and leadership. All these qualities as well as the data on communications and activity lend substantial support to the claim that staff are active and often activist.

Can a professional staff member be an entrepreneur? Our answer is yes. A number of the qualities which are common to activists also characterize entrepreneurs. They have ideas, and initiate legislation. They establish useful contacts and communications. They persist in following through on strategy. They, many times, serve as conduits to members and other staff, often drawing on their own expertise and professional training.

Along a different dimension, staff also serve as educators—tutoring their boss on substantive issues. Hearings, briefing books, conversations, interviews, speeches, are all used by staff in educating members. After all, if the member cannot articulate a concept, propose an amendment, or debate a vital point, then no matter what staff do, little can be accomplished. But how much of an advocate is the staff member? Without a doubt some staff members are strong advocates even to the extent of being propogandists, but on the whole they brief their bosses relying on their own knowledge, expertise, and perception of the member's ideology.

Congressmen must deal with the tension between the generalist norms of the Hill and need for expertise. Most Congressmen want to retain the personal contact with aides without too many intervening layers of hierarchy; at the same time, they recognize the need for expert assistance.

By education most professional staff are specialist, either being attorneys, or with other professional training. Our data show that aides in the more recently recognized jobs, such as legislative assistants, have, on average, more education (as measured by degrees awarded) and more specialized training than earlier recognized positions, such as AA. In addition, staff of the newer support agencies (OTA, CBO) are highly educated and have extensive training. Overall, a larger proportion of professional aides on the Hill now have advanced, specialized training than previously. But in their work staff are often called on to be generalist–specialists. For instance, a tax attorney may find himself working on unemployment or food stamps legislation and shortly thereafter on international trade matters.

Should there be more staff diversity? We think so. Although we would not argue for a staff which should primarily supplement legislator training, a diversity of expertise is important. Technical and scientific staff, program and business analysts, and so forth can bring added informational and analytic expertise. Among Congressmen, the percentage of lawyers and the mix between training in the law and other fields varies over time and by region.[5] The needs of Congress may also vary. It would be a mistake, we believe, to mandate specific types and numbers of staff. The activities of Congress may change over time; certainly the emphasis varies, and to some degree the role of the legislature is fluid; staffing should be also. But Congress does need staff with various kinds of training and background.

What is the professional staff member? Our definition of the professional Congressional staff member is based on salary, job title, activity, and professional recognition (see Appendix). Training, experience, and peer nomination are also components.

In another sense the development of norms, standards, and codes of behavior may characterize the development of a professional cadre. Congressional staff cannot be considered a profession, but they are often members of a profession—law, medicine, political science.

SENATE–HOUSE COMPARISON

The House is becoming more like the Senate, according to many observers. Larger staffs contribute to the similarities, as does wider distribution of resources. What are the implications of this for staffing and for the role of the House vis-à-vis the Senate? Several points can be made:

- as staffs increase, managerial procedures and skills will be needed;
- staffs, particularly personal staffs, as they become more specialized, are likely to become more professional, that is, tenure may rise and specific training can be expected to increase;
- increasing parallelism in legislative processing may occur;
- the Senate–House balance, with the Representatives often the specialists and the Senators the generalists, may shift slightly. It is possible that the House will move in the direction of the Senate—that is, will become less specialist and personally knowledgeable. The present situation is the reverse, rather surprisingly, we find, of earlier eras. Rogers reports that in the 1920's, Senators were expected to revise and "fix up" the often inadequate legislation sent over from the House.[6]

Overall, the message is, how can Senators and Representatives use staff most effectively and within the traditions of the Congressional environment; that is, how can Senators and Representatives meet the needs of working with larger staffs while keeping the traditional direct relationships.

DEMOCRATIZATION OF CONGRESS

Both the House and Senate have undergone major reform throughout the 1970s. These have tended to equalize power, influence, and resources within the respective houses. The impact on staff has been dramatic. Legislative staffs now exist in nearly every office. A freshman Representative in the 95th Congress, for instance, hired three legislative assistants, one legislative correspondent, and a legislative secretary. He expects and will have a voice in the way his committees do business. In the House, committee staff have been given to subcommittee chairmen and ranking members and to all members of several Committees. Almost all junior Senators utilized personal committee staff appointed under S. Res. 60 for their committee work.

The apprenticeship period of earlier years is lessening. Rohde, Ornstein, and Peabody[7] have described this in the Senate; Fox has similar data from his Senate personal staff study.[8] In the House, for example, Representative Joseph Fisher (D-Va.) participated actively in shaping the work of the Ways and Means Committee during his first term; freshman Representative Bob Krueger (D-Tex.) took an active lead in the debate over deregulation of natural gas. The reduced impact of seniority is also evident in the distribution of subcommittee chairmanships, and in the House, new election procedures for committee heads. Participation by all is made possible and is expected. Specific changes make the distribution of staff resources more equitable.

Each Senator and Representative has larger personal staffs, including an increase in staff salary allotments and (for Representatives) in the permitted maximum number of employees. The control of committee staffs becomes less important when professional assistance is available elsewhere.

Staffs, better prepared, more specialized, and more engaged in legislative activity, are participating more fully in the analysis and evaluation of information for shaping the contents of legislative decisions. They are also actively involved in the strategy of legislative action. House personal staffs have taken the lead in working on Floor strategy for end-the-war amendments, House reform, and other issues. Senate aides were largely responsible for defeating two of President Nixon's Supreme Court nominees, for hammering out an acceptable version of the Congressional Budget and Impoundment Control Act of 1974, and for various of the recent changes in procedure and resources distribution. Sheer numbers are one reason for this activity. But another, and more fundamental, cause is the expertise of aides and an acceptance of their role on the part of the principals in the Congressional arena: Senators and Representatives.

What of the future? Various staff groups may require less adherence to the personal loyalty norm. Certainly this will be true of support agency staffs and some core committee staffs. Anticipating a greater participation in committee business by all committee members, it may be that committee staff will become somewhat less personally oriented. We foresee that personal staffs will continue to be appointed as at present, with training and experience as important factors but with party, region, and ideology often being critical, as well.

We would hope that there will be more uniformity of jobs—descriptions, content, and title—so that movement between jobs on Capitol Hill will be facilitated. A more uniform salary structure, among committee and personal staff offices, between the houses, and also among personal offices, would be helpful.

Staff will continue to increase, but we would predict that the growth would be slower than in recent years and with more emphasis on management of existing staff.

Continued emphasis on more equitable distribution of staff resources seems likely. This may occur through devices similar to S. Res. 60 or by a wider distribution and sharing of power positions. Presently more than half the Senate is in a first or second term. Both houses in 1977 have large freshman classes. A high proportion of members in low seniority groups, less knowledgeable about Chamber traditions and hence less bound by them, can be expected to continue and, perhaps, expand the emphasis on equal participation by all. Fairer distribution of staff seems a likely result. Who gets staff can be expected to affect power distribution and policy output. There is some evidence that Senators and Representatives with personal committee staff or increased legislative assistance through recent control of committee resources are bringing high-quality analysis to Congressional decison making.

We are in a period of transition, as Congressional staffers increase in numbers, expertise, and involvement in a widening range of activities and issues. The chief Congressional actors, the Senators and Representatives, both as individuals and groups, are searching for optimum ways of using added staff resources.

Added staff are extra resources. Although their main function may be to bring greater analytical capability to the decison-making process, their presence makes inevitable an increased staff impact on policy. As in most organizations, the questions of staff role in policy making and control of staff are central issues for debate. In the future, the productive utilization of staff resources will be a vital component of Congressional action.

NOTES

1. Robert Lee Chartrand, "Modeling on Capitol Hill: The Congress Forges Ahead Using Computerized Analysis," SIAM NEWS, A publication of Society for Industrial and Applied Mathematics, August 1976, pp. 1 and 4.

2. Lewis A. Dexter "Court Politics." Also see Neville Williams: *All the Queen's Men: Elizabeth I and Her Courtiers* (London: 1976) and Evans, "The Invisible Men Who Run Congress."

3. A symposium on Congress, Marginal Districts, and the Electoral Connection appears in *The American Political Science Review* June, (1977). Included is an article examining the relationship between Congressional staffing of constituent services and the decline in marginal districts by Morris P. Fiorina.

4. See David E. Price, "Professionals and Entrepreneurs: Staff Orientations and Policy Making on Three Senate Committees", *Journal of Politics,* 33 (1971), 316–336.

5. Roger H. Davidson, in Kornberg and Muloff, ed., *Legislatures in Developmental Perspective.*

6. Lindsay Rogers, *The American Senate* (New York: Alfred A. Knopf, 1926).

7. David Rohde, Norman Ornstein, and Robert L. Peabody, "Political Change and Legislative Norms in the U.S. Senate," paper presented at American Political Science Association Annual Meeting, 1974.

8. Fox, "Personal Professional Staff."

Appendix

Additional data can be found in Harrison W. Fox, Jr., "Personal Professional Staffs of U.S. Senators," unpublished Ph.D. dissertation, The American University, 1972, and Susan Webb Hammond, "Personal Staffs of Members of the U.S. House of Representatives," unpublished Ph.D. dissertation, The Johns Hopkins University, 1973.

FIGURE 1.   **Factors Involved in Congressional Staffing**

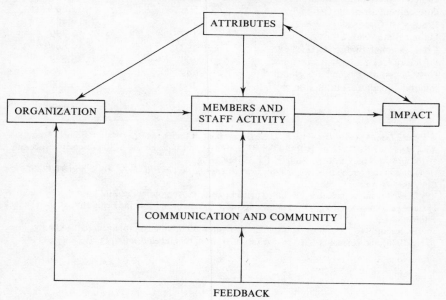

TABLE 1. Personnel Employed by the Legislative Branch, June, 1976, and Appropriations for Salaries and Expenses, 1976

	PERSONNEL[a]	SALARIES AND EXPENSES[b] (IN THOUSANDS)
Congress:		
House of Representatives	11,286	$227,537
Senate	7,009	123,068
Joint items		83,240
Architect of Capitol	1,926	76,142
Botanic Garden	57	1,253
General Accounting Office	5,126	141,541
Government Printing Office	8,508	153,869
Library of Congress	4,273	119,425
United States Tax Court[c]	197	6,799
Congressional Budget Office[d]	193	4,868
Office of Technology Assessment[d]	93	6,578
Cost Accounting Standards Board[c,d]	42	1,635
Federal Election Commission[c,d]	160	5,000
Total	38,870	$950,955

[a]Data from Manpower Division, U.S. Department of Labor, and Legislative Branch Appropriations *Hearings* FY 1977 on H.R. 14238, U.S. Senate and U.S. House of Representatives, Spring, 1976, and Appendix to U.S. Budget, FY 1978.

[b]House of Representatives, *Legislative Branch Appropriations Bill, 1977,* H. Report 94-1225, 94th Congress, 2d Sess., p. 59.

[c]These organizations are not included in the Legislative Appropriations Bill, but either by tradition or statute are considered legislative branch agencies and are included in the Legislative Branch budget estimates.

[d]H. Report 94-1225, pp. 2–3. Listed dollar figures are new budget (obligational) authority, Fiscal Year 1976, and personnel is estimated for 1976, from *Budget Appendix,* 7Y 1977, pp. 11–47.

TABLE 2. Growth of Committee Staff, 1947–1975: U.S. Senate and House of Representatives

	80TH 1947 Senate	House	85TH 1957 Senate	House	90TH 1967 Senate	House	92ND 1971 Senate	House	94TH 1975 Senate	House
Aeronautical & Space Sciences (Senate) / Science & Astronautics (House)	—	—	—	—	12	22	13	26	22	31
Agriculture	3	7	8	7	7	18	13	17	22	21
Appropriations	23	35	31	54	40	56	41	74	72	84
Armed Services	10	10	27	18	19	29	25	32	30	28
Banking & Currency	9	4	25	11	22	36	25	43	55	56
Budget	—	—	—	—	—	—	—	—	90	63
District of Columbia	4	6	6	6	10	12	27	17	33	29
Finance (Senate) / Ways & Means (House)	6	8	8	17	14	22	17	28	26	35
Foreign Relations (Senate) / Foreign Affairs, International Relations (House)	8	3	15	13	31	17	34	32	62	44
Government Operations	29	29	32	60	73	55	76	54	144	52
Interior	7	4	29	10	18	14	24	22	53	44
Interstate & Foreign Commerce	8	11	33	12	45	27	55	48	111	56
Judiciary	19	7	130	26	196	32	194	37	251	67

continued

TABLE 2., *continued*

	80TH 1947		85TH 1957		90TH 1967		92ND 1971		94TH 1975	
	Senate	*House*	*Senate*	*House*	*Senate*	*House*	*Senate*	*House*	*Senate*	*House*
Labor & Public Welfare (Senate)	9		18		45		82		150	
Education & Labor (House)		12		11		70		74		89
Post Office & Civil Service	46	6	31	11	19	32	23	38	25	56
Public Works	10	6	14	14	18	35	35	50	70	71
Rules & Administration (Senate)	41		55		18		15		29	
Rules (House)		4		3		5		6		9
Veterans	—	9	—	13	—	15	12	16	32	15
House Administration		6		9		6		30		61
Merchant Marine & Fisheries (House)		5		10		15		26		21
Standards of Official Conduct (House)		—		—		—		5		4
Internal Security (House)		10		43		48		53		39
Special & Select Committees	58	11	96	27	34	23	69	51	172	38
Total	290	193	558	375	621	589	780	779	1449	1013

Source: House: *Committee Reform Amendments of 1974*, Report of the Select Committee on Committees, U.S. House of Representatives to Accompany H. Res. 988, March 21, 1974, p. 357, and *Reports*, Clerk of the U.S. House of Representatives. Senate: 1947–1959—''Statistics on Senate Committee Staffs,'' American Law Division, February 19, 1963, The Library of Congress, Legislative Reference Service; 1960–1975, *Report of the Secretary of the Senate*, and, Temporary Select Committee to Study the Senate Committee System.

TABLE 3. Personal and Committee Staff* Employees of Congress (selected years)

YEAR	COMMITTEE		PERSONAL	
	Senate	House	Senate	House
1891[a]	41	62	39	—
1914	198	105	72	[b]
1930	163	112	280	870
1935	172	122	424	870
1947	290	193	590	1,440
1957	558	375	1,115	2,441
1967	621	589	1,749	4,055
1972	918	783	2,426	5,280
1977	1,184	1,868	3,903[c]	6,939

[a]1891–1947 House figures are based on authorized positions. Figures quoted for the House are based on clerk-hire payroll for a selected month during the year. Months vary. House committee staff in 1891 included 37 session clerks.

[b]No limit on number of staff; staff allowance of $1500/year per representative.

[c]Includes Personal Committee Aides (S. Res. 60).

Source: Reports of the Secretary of the Senate; *Congressional Record;* Hearings of the Subcommittee on Legislative Appropriations, U.S. House of Representatives, FY 1949–77; and statutes at large 1891–1935.

*Designated minority staff is as follows: Senate: 1959 (13), 1962 (51), 1965 (67), 1972 (147), and 1976 (228); House: 1951 (16), 1965 (53), 1972 (132), and 1976 (256). *Source:* G. B. Galloway, *The Legislative Process in Congress* (1955); Jt. Comm. on the Org. of Cong., Hearings (1965); H. Rept. 93–916 (Bolling Comm.); Sen. Comm. Syst. Comm.; Sen. Rep. Policy Comm.; and Fox (ed.), unpub. MS.

TABLE 4. State of Legal Residence of Staff Professionals

POPULATIONS[a]	SAME STATE AS SENATOR	OTHER STATE	UNDETERMINED	VA.	MD.	D.C.	OTHER
Senate personal staff							
Total population (N=481)	63.6%[b]	35.4%	1.0%	—	—	—	—
All respondents (N=244)	64.3	34.2	1.5	—	—	—	—
Committee staff							
All committees[c] (N=313)	—	—	—	24.3%	20.8%	19.8%	35.1%
Senate standing committees (N=126)	—	—	—	29.2	22.3	17.7	30.8
House standing committees (N=130)	—	—	—	19.8	21.4	19.0	39.8

[a]See pp. 204–205 for a discussion of the various populations observed.
[b]In percent. Of 244 Senate personal staff respondents, four, or 1.5 percent, did not respond to the question. Of 313 Committee respondents, 15, or 4.8 percent, did not respond to the question.
[c]"All committees" includes policy, campaign, select, joint, and special committees.

TABLE 5. Age of Staff Professionals

	UNDER 30	30–39	40–59	60 OR OVER	AVERAGE AGE
Senate personal staff					
Total population (N=481)	18.5%	42.4%	34.4%	4.7%	38.6
All respondents (N=244)	18.5	38.6	38.1	4.8	38.9
Not responding (N=237)	18.4	49.4	27.6	4.6	37.7
House personal staff (N=50)	46%	22%	32%*		
AA (N=22)	9	32	59		42
LA (N=18)	67	17	17		—
Other professional assistants (N=10)	90	10	0		—
Committee staff					
All committees[a] (N=313)	15.7%	40.5%	39 .1%	4.7%	40.0[b]
Senate standing committees (N=126)	18.3	46.7	30.8	4.2	37.8
House standing committees (N=130)	11.9	31.8	50.7	5.6	42.9

[a]"All committees" includes policy, campaign, select, joint, and special committees.
[b]Median: 37.4 all committees; 34.8 Senate standing committees; 43.2, House standing committees.
*Percent who are 40 or more.

TABLE 6.   Sex of Staff Professionals

POPULATIONS[a]	MEN	WOMEN
Senate personal staff		
Total population (N=470)	77.1%	22.9%
	(363)	(107)
All respondents	80.7	19.3
	(188)	(45)
Not responding	73.8	26.2
	(175)	(62)
House personal staff[b] (25 offices)	69.4	30.6
(N=62)	(43)	(19)
Committee Staff		
All committees (N=306)	89.2	10.5
	(273)	(33)
Senate standing committees		
(N=126)	84.9	15.1
	(107)	(19)
House standing committees		
(N=129)	92.2	7.8
	(119)	(10)

[a]See pp. 202–207 for a discussion of the various populations.

[b]The ratio of women to men (including professional and clerical positions) on personal staffs has remained fairly constant in recent years. In 1961, 63.5 percent of the total personal staff population were women, 36.5 percent were men; in both 1967 and 1971, 71 percent were women and 29 percent were men. These figures, compared to the above data for professionals, indicate that lower-level positions were filled almost exclusively by women.

Source: Records, Clerk of the House.

TABLE 7.   Intensity of Party Preference of Staff Professionals

PARTY PREFERENCE	VERY STRONG	STRONG	NOT SO STRONG	WEAK	TOTAL
Senators' Personal Staffs					
Democrat	54.1%	34.9%	9.2%	1.8%	100.0%
	(59)[a]	(38)	(10)	(2)	(109)
Republican	32.8	47.8	17.9	1.5	100.0
	(22)	(32)	(12)	(1)	(67)
Other	66.7	33.3	0	0	100.0
	(4)	(2)	(0)	(0)	(6)
Committee Staffs					
Democrat	43.9	39.8	13.1	3.2	100.0
	(97)	(88)	(29)	(7)	(221)
Republican	34.0	43.4	20.8	1.9	100.0
	(18)	(23)	(11)	(1)	(53)
Other	44.4	44.4	0.0	11.1	99.9
	(4)	(4)	(0)	(1)	(9)

[a]Number of staff.

TABLE 8.   Education of Staff Professionals

Position	No College	Some College	BA	Masters	JD or LLB	Ph.D.	MD
Senate							
AA	7%	5%	38%	14%	30%	5%	
(N=76)	(5)	(4)	(29)	(11)	(23)	(4)	
LA	1	1	25	13	52	8	
(N=87)	(1)	(1)	(22)	(11)	(45)	(7)	
House							
AA	10	14	41	15	18	2	
(N=265)	(26)	(36)	(109)	(39)	(49)	(6)	
LA	4.2	2.6	47	19	25	2.1	
(N=189)	(8)	(5)	(89)	(36)	(47)	(4)	
Committee Committee professional	4.5	—[a]	24.8	17.2[b]	45.0	7.6	0.7
(N=289)	(13)		(72)	(50)	(130)	(22)	(2)

[a]Not available.
[b]Includes one reported MBA.
Source: Derived from data in the *Congressional Staff Directory*, 1972, and respondents' replies.
Senate AA's have more law degrees and are slightly better educated (as measured by formal degrees) than House AA's. They also tend to be somewhat younger.

TABLE 9.   Jobs Held by Committee Professionals Just Prior to Committee Appointment (N=272)

	Percent of Respondents
Executive branch[a]	34.9
Other Congressional	29.8
Law (private practice)	8.8
Journalism	6.6
University: teaching or administration	4.4
Political, campaign	3.6
Business	3.3
Lobbyist	1.4
Other	2.6
First job	3.6

[a]Includes independent agencies. Excludes armed forces service, unless as a career.

TABLE 10.   Localism of Personal Staff Professionals House of Representatives (25 offices)

	ALL PROFESSIONALS WITH STATE TIES	AA's WITH DISTRICT TIES
Policy attitude of Congressman[a]		
(Conservative Coalition support scores)		
0–19 (9)[b]	53%	—
	(27)[c]	
20–79 (8)[b]	71	—
	(14)	
80–100 (8)[b]	76	—
	(17)	
Seniority of Congressman[d]		
Most senior quartile	71	60%
	(7)	(5)
Next most senior quartile	66	83
	(15)	(6)
Third most senior quartile	59[e]	71
	(20)	(7)
Most junior quartile	71	75
	(31)	(4)

    [a] As reported in *Congressional Quarterly,* weekly editions, and *Congressional Quarterly Almanac* (Washington, D.C.). Least conservative: 0–19; mid-range: 20–79; most conservative, 80–100.
    [b] Number of offices.
    [c] Number of staff members.
    [d] Most senior quartile: Democrats: have completed 8 or more terms; Republicans: 7 or more terms; next most senior quartile: Democrats: 5–7 terms; Republicans: 5–6 terms; third most senior quartile: Democrats: 3–4 terms; Republicans: 2–4 terms; most junior quartile: Democrats: in 3rd term or less; Republicans: in 1st or 2nd term.
    [e] May be skewed by one office with atypically large numbers of professionals, none from the district.

TABLE 11.   Previous Acquaintance of Professionals Prior to Joining Staff

	NUMBER OF OCCURRENCES
Senate personal staff	
Friend	14
Worked for his predecessor	3
Business and official positions	7
Reporter, newsman	20
Employee	11
Intern	8
Socially	11
Socially and professionally	5
Politically	16
Worked for another Senator	4
Professor, teacher	3
School, classmates	3

Committee staff	CONGRESS (N=313)	SENATE (N=148)[b]	HOUSE (N=144)[b]
Professional contacts, including former employer	49.2%	36.7%	60.7%
His personal staff	10.0	15.0	6.5
Political contacts	9.2	13.3	3.3
No response	56.9	57.4	56.3

[a]Adjusted frequencies. Percentages do not add to 100, as other previous acquaintance omitted.
[b]Omits party committees.

TABLE 12.   Person Appointing Committee Staff Employee[a]

	CONGRESS (N=313)	SENATE (N=148)[b]	HOUSE (N=144)[b]
Chairman or sub-committee chairman	75.2%	76.6%	77.9%
Ranking minority member	14.0	13.1	14.3
Full committee	0.7	0.7	0.7

[a]Adjusted frequencies.
[b]Omits party committees.

TABLE 13.   Tenure of Staff Professionals[a]

	LESS THAN 4 YEARS	4–10 YEARS	11–20 YEARS	MORE THAN 20 YEARS
Committee aides				
All committees (N=302)	49.7%	33.1	13.9	3.3
Senate committees[b] (N=148)	56.3	29.8	11.1	2.8
House committees[b] (N=144)	44.5	35.1	16.8	3.6
House personal staff				
Administrative assistants[c]	40.9	31.8	27.3	—

[a] Adjusted frequencies.

[b] Omits party committees.

[c] The tenure of AA's varies with the seniority of the Representative: for Representatives in the most senior quartile, 40 percent (2 of 5) had been on the staff as AA since the Representative's election; in the next most senior quartile, the comparable figure is 66 percent (4 of 6); in the third most senior quartile, 71 percent (5 of 7) have served since the Representative's election; in the most junior quartile, the comparable figure is 100 percent (4 of 4). (N=22)

TABLE 14. Staff Organization

	Responses				
	MEMBER	MEMBER	MEMBER		
	Type I Hierarchical	Type II Coordinative	Type III Individualistic	None or Missing	Total
Senate personal offices	35.6%[a] (67)[b]	18.1% (34)	43.7% (82)	2.7% (5)	100.1% (188)
House personal offices	40 (10)	(A)[c] (B)[d] 16 24 (4) (6)	20 (5)		100.0 (25)
Committee	62[a] (175)[b]	25 (71)	13 (36)		100.0 (282)

[a] In percent
[b] Number of staff members
[c] Subtype IIA

Congressman
AA   LA
All other staff

[d] Subtype IIB

Congressman
AA
Other professionals
All other staff

House offices in percent.
Number of House offices.

TABLE 15.   Personal Office Organization, by Party

| | SENATE (N=172 AIDES) | | | | HOUSE (N=25 OFFICES) | | | |
| | Republican | | Democratic | | Republican | | Democratic | |
TYPE OF OFFICE ORGANIZATION	% OF ALL R	% OF TYPE	% OF ALL D	% OF TYPE	% OF ALL R	% OF TYPE	% OF ALL D	% OF TYPE
Hierarchial (I)	43 (32)	51	32 (31)	49	50 (5)[a]	50	33 (5)	50
Coordinative A (IIA)	19 (14)	45	17 (17)	55	10 (1) } 50	25	20 (3) } 33	75
B (IIB)					40 (4)	66	13 (2)	33
Individualistic (III)	38 (28)	36	51 (50)	64	0	0	33 (5)	

[a] Number of offices. All other in parentheses are number of staff members.

TABLE 16.   Personal Office Organization, by Seniority

	HIERARCHICAL (I)	COORDINATIVE (II)	(IIA)	(IIB)	INDIVIDUALISTIC (III)
Senate[a] (172 staff aides)					
Nonranking	54.0% (34)[b]	71.0% (22)			56.4% (44)
Ranking minority	20.6 (16)	19.4 (3)			25.6 (14)
Chairmen	25.4 (13)	9.7 (6)			17.9 (20)
House (25 offices)[a]					
Most senior quartile	100 (5)[c]	0		0	0
Second most senior quartile	29 (2)	43% (3)	14%	29%	29 (2)
Third most senior quartile	43 (3)	43 (3)	0	43	14 (1)
Most junior quartile	0	67 (4)	50	17	33 (2)

[a] Senate: percent of that type of organization; House: percent of that seniority group.
[b] Number of staff members.
[c] Number of offices.

TABLE 17. Personal Office Organization, by Party and Seniority

SENIORITY	REPUBLICANS				DEMOCRATS			
	Hierarchial (I)	Coordinative (II)		Individualistic (III)	Hierarchial (I)	Coordinative (II)		Individualistic (III)
Senate (172 aides)								
Nonranking	39.0%[a] (16)[b]	26.8% (11)		34.1% (14)	30.5% (18)	18.6% (11)		50.8% (30)
Ranking minority/chairmen	48.5 (16)	9.1 (3)		42.4 (14)	33.3 (13)	15.4 (6)		51.3 (20)
House (24 offices)		(IIA)	(IIB)			(IIA)	(IIB)	
Most senior quartile	100[a] (2)[c]	0	0	0	100 (3)	0	0	0
Second most senior quartile	33 (1)	0	66 (2)	0	33 (1)	33 (1)	0	33 (1)
Third most senior quartile	66 (2)	0	33 (1)	0	25 (1)	0	50 (2)	25 (1)
Most junior quartile	0	50 (1)	50 (1)	0	0	50 (2)	0	50 (2)

[a]In percent of that seniority group.
[b]Number of staff aides.
[c]Number of offices.

181

TABLE 18.   Office Organization and Policy Attitude, House (24 offices)

POLICY ATTITUDE	HIERARCHIAL (I)	COORDINATIVE (IIA)	COORDINATIVE (IIB)	INDIVIDUALISTIC (III)
Least conservative	33%	33%	0%	33%
Mid-range	62	13	25	0
Most conservative	29	0	57	14

Source: As measured by 1971 conservative coalition support scores, in *Congressional Quarterly* (weekly editions) and *Congressional Quarterly Almanac, 1971* (Washington, D.C.·), least conservative: 0–19 (N=9); mid-range: 20–79 (N=8); most conservative: 80–100 (N=8).

TABLE 19.   Personal Office Organization, by Region (as percent of region)

REGION[a]	HIERARCHICAL (I)	COORDINATIVE (II)	INDIVIDUALISTIC (III)
East			
Senate	21.9%	40.6%	37.5%
	(7)[b]	(13)	(12)
House[d]	33	66	0
	(1)[c]	(2)	
South			
Senate	32.4	13.5	54.1
	(12)	(5)	(20)
House[d]	33	33	33
	(2)	(2)	(2)
Midwest			
Senate	22.2	11.1	66.7
	(4)	(2)	(12)
House[d]	30	40	30
	(3)	(4)	(3)
West			
Senate	47.1	12.9	40.0
	(40)	(11)	(34)
House[d]	67	33	0
	(4)	(2)	

[a]The states within each region are:

East: Connecticut, Delaware, Maine, Maryland, Massachusetts, New Hampshire, New Jersey, New York, Pennsylvania, Rhode Island, Vermont (11), and, for the House, West Virginia (12)

Midwest: Illinois, Indiana, Ohio, Michigan, Wisconsin (5), and, for the House also Iowa, Kansas, Minnesota, Missouri, Nebraska, North Dakota, and South Dakota (12)

South: Alabama, Florida, Georgia, Kentucky, Mississippi, North Carolina, South Carolina, Tennessee, Virginia, and, for the Senate, West Virginia, (10), and, for the House, Arkansas, Louisiana, Oklahoma, and Texas (13)

West: Alaska, Arizona, California, Colorado, Hawaii, Idaho, Montana, Nevada, New Mexico, Oregon, Utah, Washington, Wyoming (13), and, for the Senate also: Arkansas, Louisiana, Iowa, Kansas, Minnesota, Missouri, Nebraska, North Dakota, Oklahoma, South Dakota, and Texas (24)

[b]Number of staff members out of a total of 172.

[c]Number of offices, out of a total of 25.

[d]House offices within each type are distributed geographically as follows (in percent of each type): hierarchical: East, 10; South, 20; Midwest, 30; West, 40; Coordinative: East, 20; South, 20; Midwest, 40; West, 20; Individualistic; East, 0; South, 40; Midwest, 60; West, 0.

TABLE 20. Senate Personal Staff Perception of Interpersonal Relations with Role Senders

QUESTION:
PLEASE NOTE THE QUALITY OF YOUR WORKING RELATIONSHIP WITH THE FOLLOWING.

	VERY GOOD	GOOD	GOOD AND BAD	VERY BAD	DOES NOT APPLY	MISSING	TOTAL
Your Senator	80.3 % (151)	16.0% (30)	3.7% (7)	0% (0)	0 % (0)	0 % (0)	100.0% (188)
Your administrative assistant or equivalent	60.6 (114)	16.0 (30)	6.4 (12)	.5 (1)	10.1 (19)	6.4 (12)	100.0 (188)
Your legislative assistant or equivalent	64.4 (121)	20.7 (39)	3.2 (6)	.5 (1)	7.4 (14)	3.7 (12)	99.9 (188)
Rest of professional staff in your office	61.2 (115)	33.5 (63)	5.3 (10)	0 (1)	0 (14)	0 (7)	99.9 (188)
Rest of staff (secretaries, etc.)	52.1 (98)	41.0 (77)	6.9 (13)	0 (0)	0 (0)	0 (0)	100.0 (188)
Professional staff you know outside your office	41.0 (77)	46.8 (88)	10.1 (19)	0 (0)	1.1 (2)	1.1 (2)	100.1 (188)
Senators outside your office	21.3 (40)	51.1 (96)	6.9 (13)	1.6 (3)	18.6 (35)	.5 (1)	100.0 (188)

TABLE 21. Authority, Power, and Influence in the Pair Relationship: The Senator and His Personal Professional Staff (N=47)

Emotional Orientation	Symmetrical Relations of Influence	Asymmetrical Relations of Influence
Positive	(23)[a] We are mutual friends. The Senator influences me about as much as I influence him.	(20) I like to be with the Senator, but do not try to be like him.
		(6) In many ways I try to be like the Senator.
		(8) I follow the Senator's example and command.
Ambivalent	(2) We sometimes get along, but other times we have an antagonistic relationship.	(5) Because it is expected on Capitol Hill, I do what the Senator tells me.
		(13) Many times I do what the Senator tells me to do because he is an expert.
		(4) Because the office of Senator is an important position, I do what he tells me.
Negative	(0) Both of us fear and have hostility toward each other.	(0) I undertake tasks for the Senator, because I fear that he may be hostile.
Indifferent	(8) We do things equally for each other without emotional involvement.	(9) I undertake tasks for the Senator without emotional involvement.

POWER[b] AUTHORITY

[a] Numbers within parentheses represent the positive responses made to the statement. Also the total number of responses is more than 47 because of multiple responses.

[b] "All relations portrayed are those of influence; those within the broken line are also relations of power. Note the limited set of relations subsumed under authority." Schermerhorn, p. 9.

	Authority	+	Power	+	Influence
Pair relationship =					
(Formula) 98 =	30	+	17	+	51
			(excluding authority relationships)		(excluding power and authority relationships)

Source: Modified from Richard A. Schermerhorn, *Society and Power* (New York: Random House, 1961).

TABLE 22. Professional Staff Activities Performed Within the Senate Office

QUESTION: PLEASE NOTE HOW OFTEN YOU ENGAGE IN THE ACTIVITIES BELOW.	RESPONSE							Mean[c]	Total
	Once Each Hour	Once A Day Or More	Once A Week Or More	Once A Month Or More	Once A Year More Or Less	Not At All	Missing		
Activities									
With Senator in committee	1.6[a] (3)[b]	17.0 (32)	29.8 (56)	18.6 (35)	12.3 (23)	19.7 (37)	1.0 (2)	9.51	100.0 (188)
Writing Floor remarks and speeches	3.2 (6)	20.3 (38)	35.7 (67)	16.0 (30)	5.3 (10)	18.1 (34)	1.6 (3)	8.97	100.2 (188)
On legislative research, Bill drafting, and reading and analysing Bills	8.0 (15)	37.2 (70)	20.2 (38)	11.1 (21)	3.7 (7)	17.0 (32)	2.7 (5)	8.24	99.9 (188)
With lobbyist and special interest groups	2.1 (4)	36.7 (69)	39.3 (74)	13.3 (25)	0.5 (1)	6.4 (12)	1.6 (3)	7.70	99.9 (188)
Investigation and oversight	9.0 (17)	25.6 (48)	22.9 (43)	18.1 (34)	4.3 (8)	12.8 (24)	7.5 (14)	8.35	100.2 (188)
Handling constituency problems: projects	33.0 (62)	34.1 (64)	19.7 (37)	7.9 (15)	1.1 (2)	2.7 (5)	1.6 (3)	6.22	100.1 (188)
Handling constituency problems: casework	17.6 (33)	23.4 (44)	25.0 (47)	10.6 (20)	6.9 (13)	14.4 (27)	2.1 (4)	8.08	100.0 (188)

								Mean	Total
Visiting with constituents in Washington	10.1 (19)	35.1 (66)	36.2 (68)	10.1 (19)	2.6 (5)	4.3 (8)	1.6 (3)	7.28	100.0 (188)
On pressure and opinion mail	22.3 (42)	39.9 (75)	21.2 (40)	5.8 (11)	2.6 (5)	5.9 (11)	2.2 (4)	6.71	99.9 (188)
On letters of congratulation and condolence	4.3 (8)	23.9 (45)	22.8 (43)	19.7 (37)	3.2 (6)	25.0 (47)	1.0 (2)	9.29	99.9 (188)
On correspondence other than described	19.1 (36)	43.6 (82)	20.3 (38)	5.8 (11)	1.6 (3)	5.9 (11)	3.7 (7)	6.74	100.0 (188)
On requests for information	14.9 (28)	36.7 (69)	21.8 (41)	10.1 (19)	2.7 (5)	11.7 (22)	2.1 (4)	7.36	100.0 (188)
On opinion ballots	1.1 (2)	8.5 (16)	18.7 (35)	23.4 (44)	15.5 (29)	28.7 (54)	4.3 (8)	10.84	100.2 (188)
On press work radio, TV	16.0 (30)	26.6 (50)	26.6 (50)	13.3 (25)	2.2 (4)	13.3 (25)	2.1 (4)	7.85	100.1 (188)
Mailing government publications	2.7 (5)	5.8 (11)	12.7 (24)	20.2 (38)	6.4 (12)	48.4 (91)	3.7 (7)	11.41	99.9 (188)
Campaign	8.0 (15)	20.2 (38)	16.5 (31)	5.9 (11)	11.8 (22)	26.0 (49)	11.7 (22)	9.53	100.1 (188)
Write magazine articles, books, and speeches other than those for Senate floor use	3.2 (6)	6.9 (13)	16.0 (30)	27.1 (51)	13.8 (26)	30.9 (58)	2.1 (4)	10.62	100.0 (188)

[a]In percent.

[b]Number of staff members in this category.

[c]Mean calculated on basis of the following values: once each hour, 4; more than once a day, 5; once a day, 6; more than once a week, 7; once a week, 8; more than once a month, 9; once a month, 10; more than once a year, 11; once a year, 12; less than once a year, 13; and not at all, 14.

TABLE 23. Personal Senate Staff Specializations, by Intensity of Activity and the Number of Differentiated Roles

Intensity of Activity Engaged In	Many Differentiated Roles					A Few Differentiated Roles					Mainly Undifferentiated Roles				
	I					*II*					*III*				
	Exclusive Generalist					*Exclusive Multi-specialists*					*Exclusive Specialists*				
	ROLE TYPES[d]					ROLE TYPES					ROLE TYPES				
	1	2	3	4	5	1	2	3	4	5	1	2	3	4	5
High[a]															
Person A	VH	VH	VH	VH	VH										
Person B	VH	VH	VH	VH	VH										
Person C						L	M	VH	VH	VH					
Person D						VH	M	H	M	VH					
Person E											VH	VH	L	L	L
Person F											L	M	L	VH	L

Middle[b]

IV Nonexclusive Generalist	ROLE TYPES				
	1	2	3	4	5
Person G	M	M	M	M	M
Person H	M	M	L	M	M

V Nonexclusive Multispecialists	ROLE TYPES				
	1	2	3	4	5
Person I	M	L	L	L	M
Person J	L	M	L	L	L

VI Nonexclusive Specialists	ROLE TYPES				
	1	2	3	4	5
Person K	L	M	L	L	L
Person L	M	L	L	L	L

Low[c]

VII "Nonparticipant"	ROLE TYPES				
	1	2	3	4	5
None Were Found	"L"	"L"	"L"	"L"	"L"

[a] VH designates the highest 15 percent of the population, and H designates the highest third of the population.
[b] M designates the middle third of the population.
[c] L designates the lowest third.
[d] Role Types are identified as follows: 1. Interactor; 2. Supporter; 3. Corresponder; 4. Advertiser; and 5. Investigator.
Source: Modified from Bruce J. Biddle and Edwin J. Thomas (eds.). *Role Theory: Concepts and Research* (New York: Wiley, 1966), p. 34. All persons identified are actual staff members.

TABLE 24.   Role Types within Senate Offices: Four Cases

		ROLE TYPE				
OFFICE	PERSON	Inter- actor	Sup- porter	Corre- sponder	Adver- tiser	Investi- gator
A	One	L[a]	VH	M	H	M
	Two	L	L	M	VH	L
	Three	M	H	VH	H	VH
	Four	M	H	L	M	M
	Five	L	M	L	L	M
	Six	L	L	H	H	VH
B	One	VH	H	M	M	L
	Two	L	M	M	VH	L
	Three	M	VH	M	L	L
	Four	L	H	L	L	L
	Five	L	L	H	L	L
C	One	M	L	L	H	M
	Two	M	H	VH	L	M
	Three	M	L	M	H	L
	Four	H	L	M	M	M
D	One	VH	L	L	H	H
	Two	L	H	M	M	L
	Three	H	M	L	L	H
	Four	M	L	M	VH	L
	Five	H	VH	M	L	H
	Six	M	L	L	L	M
	Seven	M	L	L	VH	L

[a]L=Low, M=Medium, H=High, VH=Very High. These indicate relative activity within a specific role type. The population was divided into thirds (low, medium, and high) for each role type, with VH representing a person in the top 15 percent of frequency of role activity.

TABLE 25. Perception of How Own Behavior Affects Others: Subpopulation of Senate Personal Professional Staff Members (in percent)

QUESTION:
FOR THE FOLLOWING PERSONS
THAT YOU HAVE COME IN
CONTACT WITH, HOW DOES
YOUR BEHAVIOR USUALLY
AFFECT THEM?

	MOSTLY POSITIVE	SOME POSITIVE	NONE	SOME NEGATIVE	MOSTLY NEGATIVE	NO CONTACT	MISSING	TOTAL
Your Senator	63.8% (30)[a]	29.8% (14)		4.3 % (2)			2.1% (1)	100.0% (47)
Your LA or equivalent	46.8 (22)	31.9 (15)	4.3% (2)	2.1 (1)			14.9 (7)	100.0 (47)
Your AA or equivalent	42.6 (20)	31.9 (15)	2.1 (1)				23.4 (11)	100.0 (47)
Rest of professional staff	57.4 (27)	31.9 (15)	4.3 (2)	4.3 (2)			2.1 (1)	100.0 (47)
Rest of staff (secretaries, etc.)	55.3 (26)	31.9 (15)	2.1 (1)	6.4 (3)			4.3 (2)	100.0 (47)
Professional staff outside your office	31.9 (15)	55.3 (26)	2.1 (1)	2.1 (1)		4.3% (2)	4.3 (2)	100.0 (47)
Senators outside your office	25.5 (12)	23.4 (11)	31.9 (15)			12.8 (6)	6.4 (3)	100.0 (47)

[a]Number of staff.

191

TABLE 26. Expectations for Staff Role Behavior: Activities and Memberships

Questions	RESPONSES OF SENATE PERSONAL STAFF RESPONDENTS						
	Absolutely Must	Should	May or May Not	Should Not	Absolutely Must Not	Missing	Total
Take an active part in the Senator's campaign	27.1% (51)[a]	38.3 (72)	28.2% (53)	2.7% (5)	2.1% (4)	1.6% (3)	100.0% (188)
Join nonpartisan staff organization on Capitol Hill	1.1 (2)	14.4 (27)	83.5 (157)	.5 (1)	0 (0)	.5 (1)	100.0 (188)
Join organizations that try to influence public policy such as Common Cause	0 (0)	4.8 (9)	75.5 (142)	13.8 (26)	4.3 (8)	1.6 (3)	100.0 (188)
Join partisan staff organization	.5 (1)	10.1 (19)	87.2 (164)	1.6 (3)	0 (0)	.5 (1)	99.9 (188)
Join state organizations on Capitol Hill such as Florida State Society	0 (0)	24.5 (46)	73.9 (139)	1.6 (3)	0 (0)	0 (0)	100.0 (188)
Register to vote in the Senator's home state	8.5 (16)	32.4 (61)	56.9 (107)	.5 (1)	0 (0)	1.6 (3)	99.9 (188)

[a] Number of staff.

192

TABLE 27. Professional Staff Activity within Committees

QUESTION: PLEASE NOTE HOW OFTEN YOU ENGAGE IN THE ACTIVITIES BELOW.	ONCE EACH HOUR	ONCE A DAY	ONCE A WEEK OR MORE	ONCE A MONTH OR MORE	ONCE A YEAR MORE OR LESS	NOT AT ALL	MISSING	MEAN[a]	TOTAL
With congressmen in committee: Hearings	5.8%[b] (18)	13.1% (41)	34.9% (109)	30.7% (96)	5.1% (16)	4.5% (14)	6.1% (19)	8.46	100.0% (313)
With congressmen in committee: Markup	6.1 (19)	2.2 (7)	23.6 (74)	32.6 (102)	16.9 (53)	12.8 (40)	5.7 (18)	9.78	100.0 (313)
With congressmen in committee: Conference	5.1 (16)	1.6 (5)	9.3 (29)	27.8 (87)	32.5 (102)	17.9 (56)	5.8 (18)	10.70	100.0 (313)
With congressmen in committee: Executive Session	5.8 (18)	2.5 (8)	18.9 (59)	31.3 (98)	16.6 (52)	16.0 (50)	9.0 (28)	10.03	100.0 (313)
Writing floor remarks, speeches, and opening statements	2.2 (7)	16.7 (52)	39.3 (123)	26.2 (82)	5.4 (17)	5.4 (17)	4.9 (15)	8.53	100.0 (313)
On legislative research, Bill drafting, and reading and analyzing Bills	14.1 (44)	36.8 (115)	24.3 (76)	11.1 (35)	4.1 (13)	5.8 (18)	3.8 (12)	7.31	100.0 (313)
With lobbyist and special interest groups	2.9 (9)	27.2 (85)	39.6 (124)	15.6 (49)	4.8 (15)	6.7 (21)	3.2 (10)	8.14	100.0 (313)
Investigation and oversight	10.5 (33)	34.8 (109)	21.4 (67)	16.3 (51)	5.5 (17)	6.4 (20)	5.2 (16)	7.70	100.0 (313)
Handling constituency problems: projects	4.8 (15)	20.5 (64)	20.1 (63)	25.5 (80)	11.2 (35)	15.0 (47)	2.8 (9)	9.18	100.0 (313)
Handling constituency problems: casework	2.6 (8)	12.1 (38)	13.4 (42)	21.1 (66)	11.8 (37)	35.8 (112)	3.2 (10)	10.72	100.0 (313)

continued

193

TABLE 27. Professional Staff Activity within Committees *(continued)*

QUESTION: PLEASE NOTE HOW OFTEN YOU ENGAGE IN THE ACTIVITIES BELOW.	ONCE EACH HOUR	ONCE A DAY	ONCE A WEEK OR MORE	ONCE A MONTH OR MORE	ONCE A YEAR MORE OR LESS	NOT AT ALL	MISSING	MEAN[a]	TOTAL
Visiting with constituents in Washington	1.0 (3)	6.1 (19)	24.0 (75)	21.7 (68)	16.0 (50)	28.4 (89)	2.9 (9)	10.63	100.0 (313)
On pressure and opinion mail	3.5 (11)	24.9 (78)	25.6 (80)	19.5 (61)	5.7 (18)	17.6 (55)	3.2 (10)	9.01	100.0 (313)
On correspondence other than described	7.7 (24)	34.2 (107)	25.5 (80)	13.4 (42)	2.5 (8)	8.6 (27)	8.0 (25)	7.79	100.0 (313)
On requests for information	17.9 (56)	38.7 (121)	27.2 (85)	9.9 (31)	.9 (3)	1.9 (6)	3.5 (11)	6.72	100.0 (313)
On opinion ballots	0.3 (1)	1.3 (4)	5.1 (16)	15.7 (49)	20.5 (64)	49.8 (156)	7.3 (23)	12.36	100.0 (313)
On press work, radio, TV	3.8 (12)	14.4 (45)	24.9 (78)	19.5 (61)	8.9 (28)	24.0 (75)	4.5 (14)	9.75	100.0 (313)
Mailing government publications	2.6 (8)	13.8 (43)	13.5 (42)	11.2 (35)	5.1 (16)	47.9 (150)	6.2 (19)	11.07	100.0 (313)
Campaign	0.6 (2)	2.5 (8)	2.6 (8)	5.5 (17)	8.6 (27)	74.4 (233)	5.8 (18)	13.14	100.0 (313)
Writing magazine articles, books, and speeches other than those for floor use	0.3 (1)	2.9 (9)	13.8 (43)	31.6 (99)	23.0 (72)	25.2 (79)	3.1 (10)	11.00	100.0 (313)
Supervising clerical staff	31.3 (98)	25.0 (78)	9.9 (31)	4.6 (15)	1.6 (5)	24.6 (77)	2.9 (9)	7.82	100.0 (313)
Supervising professional staff	17.9 (56)	20.8 (65)	9.9 (31)	3.8 (12)	2.6 (8)	41.2 (129)	3.8 (12)	9.52	100.0 (313)
Working with another committee	3.5 (11)	15.4 (48)	32.9 (103)	27.2 (85)	10.5 (33)	7.0 (22)	3.5 (11)	8.87	100.0 (313)

[a]See Table 22, note c, for calculation of the means.
[b]Number of staff aides.

TABLE 28.   Professional Committee and Personal Staff Activities (selected)

QUESTION: PLEASE NOTE HOW OFTEN YOU ENGAGED IN THE ACTIVITIES BELOW.	SENATE STANDING COMMITTEES (N=126)[a]	HOUSE STANDING COMMITTEES (N=130)[a]	SENATE PERSONAL (N=188)[a]
With Congressman in committee hearings	5.60[b]	4.97	—
Writing floor remarks, speeches, and opening statements	5.30	5.38	5.97
On legislative research, bill drafting, and reading and analyzing bills	3.73	4.58	5.24
With lobbyists and special interest groups	4.57	5.25	4.70
Investigation and oversight	4.14	4.78	5.35
On correspondence other than described	4.64	4.78	3.74
On requests for information	3.69	3.47	4.36
Supervising clerical staff	4.56	4.94	—
Working with another committee	5.66	6.19	—

[a]Number of staff members.
[b]Mean calculated on basis of the following values: once each hour, 1; more than once a day, 2; once a day, 3; more than once a week, 4; once a week, 5; more than once a month, 6; once a month, 7; more than once a year, 8; once a year, 9; less than once a year, 10; and not at all, 11.

TABLE 29. Communication Patterns: Personal Professional Staffs of Senators

Type of Contact	Once an Hour or More	Once a Day or More	Once a Week or More	Once a Month or More	Once a Year More or Less	Not at All	Missing	Total
Senator	45.7% (86)	47.8% (90)	4.8% (9)	0.5% (1)	0% (0)	0% (0)	1.0% (2)	99.8% (188)
Constituents	35.1 (66)	42.6 (80)	16.5 (31)	3.7 (7)	0.5 (1)	0 (0)	1.6 (3)	100.0 (188)
Journalists	14.4 (27)	33.0 (62)	35.1 (66)	10.1 (19)	2.1 (4)	2.1 (4)	3.2 (6)	100.0 (188)
Staff in your senate office	93.1 (175)	4.3 (8)	0.5 (1)	0 (0)	0 (0)	0 (0)	2.1 (4)	100.0 (188)
Staff in other Senate offices	10.6 (20)	64.3 (121)	20.3 (38)	1.0 (2)	0.5 (1)	0.5 (1)	2.7 (5)	99.9 (188)
Staff in House office	.5 (1)	18.1 (34)	44.7 (84)	29.8 (56)	3.7 (7)	2.1 (4)	1.0 (2)	99.9 (188)
Bureaucracy	21.8 (41)	46.3 (87)	21.8 (41)	5.9 (11)	2.7 (5)	0 (0)	1.6 (3)	100.1 (188)
Committee staff (Senator's committees)	13.3 (25)	49.5 (93)	27.7 (52)	6.4 (12)	0.5 (1)	1.6 (3)	1.0 (2)	100.0 (188)
Committee staff (other committees)	2.7 (5)	25.6 (48)	45.2 (85)	19.7 (37)	2.7 (5)	2.7 (5)	1.6 (3)	100.2 (188)
Committee staff in House	0 (0)	5.4 (10)	21.3 (40)	45.2 (85)	14.9 (28)	11.2 (21)	2.1 (4)	100.1 (188)
Staff in Executive Office of the President	1.1 (2)	16.5 (31)	23.9 (45)	34.6 (65)	14.4 (27)	8.5 (16)	1.0 (2)	100.0 (188)

TABLE 30.   Communication Patterns: Professional Committee Aides and Senate Personal Staff

Type of Contact	Senate Personal Staff (N=188)	Senate Committee Staff[a] (N=126)	House Committee Staff[a] (N=130)
Senator	2.02[b]	3.98	7.90
Representative	—	7.36	2.88
Constituents	2.68	4.78	5.50
Press	4.01	4.35	4.68
Senators' personal staff	1.10	2.37	4.95
Representatives' staff	5.37	5.68	2.76
Bureaucracy	3.22	3.20	3.30
Own committee staff	3.53	1.38	1.35
Other Senate committees	4.91	3.90	5.13
Other House committees	7.01	5.57	4.46
Presidential office staff	6.31	7.45	7.70

[a]Standing Committees only.

[b]Mean calculated on basis of the following values: once an hour, 1; more than once a day, 2; once a day, 3; more than once a week, 4; once a week, 5; more than once a month, 6; once a month, 7; more than once a year, 8; once a year, 9; less than once a year, 10; not at all, 11.

TABLE 31.   Information Sources: Professional Committee Aides[a]

Information Source	Senate Committee Aides (N=126)	House Committee Aides (N=130)
Executive Department personnel	4.42[b]	4.18
CRS	5.69	5.80
Committee consultants	8.68	8.91
Labor groups	8.33	8.47
Business groups	7.38	7.43
Farm groups	9.40	9.50
Other interest groups	6.09	6.67
GAO	7.42	7.31
Presidential staff	8.64	8.78
Volunteer experts	7.63	8.29

[a]Standing committees only.

[b]Mean calculated on basis of the following values: once an hour, 1; more than once a day, 2; once a day, 3; more than once a week, 4; once a week, 5; more than once a month, 6; once a month, 7; more than once a year, 8; once a year, 9; less than once a year, 10; not at all, 11.

TABLE 32. Measures of Senate Staff Size and Committee Output

RANK BY STAFF SIZE	SENATE COMMITTEES, RANKED ACCORDING TO NUMBER OF STAFF, MOST TO LEAST[a]	RANK IN NUMBER OF COMMITTEE MEETINGS (INCLUDES HEARINGS) 1975
1	Judiciary	2
2	Labor and Public Welfare	6
3	Government Operations	10
4	Budget	13
5	Commerce	4
6	Appropriations	1
7	Foreign Relations	5
8	Public Works	8
9	Banking, Housing and Urban Affairs	7
10	Interior and Insular Affairs	3
	Rules and Administration	13
12	Armed Services	8
13	Finance	12
14	Agriculture and Forestry	11
15	Special Committee on Aging	18
	Select Committee on Small Business	15
17	Post Office and Civil Service	19
18	Aeronautical and Space Sciences	16
19	Veterans Affairs	17
	Select Committee on Nutrition and Human Needs	21
21	District of Columbia	20

[a]Includes subcommittee staff.

[b]Derived from ratio of number of measures reported by a committee to number of measures referred to the committee.

Source: Derived from data on staff numbers, Temporary Select Committee to Study the Senate Committee System, U.S. Senate and *Legislative Activity Source Book, U.S. Senate,* Committee Print, Commission on the Operation of the Senate, U.S. Senate, 1977, and Sourcebook data, Commission on the Operation of the Senate, Mimeo, 1976.

RANK IN NUMBER OF HEARINGS 1975	NUMBER STAFF/ NUMBER HEARINGS		NUMBER STAFF/ NUMBER MEETINGS		RANK: LEGISLATIVE INDEX[b]
	Rank	Ratio	Ratio	Rank	
2 (179)	13	0.87	.59	12	13
5 (126)	14	1.00	.72	15	13
6 (106)	14	1.00	.88	16	15
12 (54)	18	1.60	1.13	19	16
3 (138)	9	0.59	.39	10	9
1 (287)	2	0.25	.23	3	2
7 (101)	8	0.57	.32	6	4
9 (80)	10	0.60	.33	7	12
8 (99)	4	0.41	.28	4	10
4 (129)	1	0.23	.14	1	6
17 (19)	17	1.58	.38	9	1
9 (80)	3	0.36	.20	2	6
13 (51)	7	0.55	.33	7	18
11 (61)	5	0.43	.30	5	6
16 (20)	16	1.10	1.10	17	—
14 (50)	6	0.44	.42	11	—
19 (9)	19	2.10	1.12	18	10
15 (22)	12	0.84	.67	13	3
18 (19)	11	0.70	.67	13	16
21 (3)	21	4.70	3.50	21	—
20 (6)	20	2.20	2.33	20	5

TABLE 33.   Activity and Communications Comparison: Senate Standing Committees with Largest and Smallest Staffs[a]

	Three Largest Staffs[b]	Three Smallest Staffs[c]
Communications		
Bureaucracry	4.0[e]	4.3
Other Senate committees	4.0	3.3
Other House committees	5.3	5.0
Presidential staff	6.9	8.0
Senators	4.1	3.0
Constituents	4.2	4.0
Senators' staff	2.6	3.0
Measures Reported[d]	31.3	2.6
Number of Hearings[d]	140	14
Number of Meetings[d]	199	18

[a]Mean (average) reported for each group of committees.

[b]Mean size: 129; mean number professionals: 76.

[c]Mean size: 14; mean number professionals: 8.

[d]1975.

[e]Mean score for communications frequency calculated on the basis of the following values: once an hour, 1; more than once a day, 2; once a day, 3; more than once a week, 4; once a week, 5; more than once a month, 6; once a month, 7; more than once a year, 8; once a year, 9; less than once a year, 10; not at all, 11.

Source: 1974 Fox and Hammond survey data; Secretary of the Senate, *Report; Legislative Activity Sourcebook, 1975,* Commission on the Operation of the Senate, Committee Print, 1977.

TABLE 34. Cosponsorship, House of Representatives, by Type of Office Organization, Seniority, Policy Attitude, and Number of Staff (25 offices)[a]

By Office Organization	
Hierarchical	33.5[b]
Coordinative	50.9
Individualistic	62.4
By Seniority	
Most Senior	32.4
Second Most Senior	34.2
Third Most Senior	54.1
Most Junior	65.3
By Policy Attitude[c]	
Liberal	72.5
Moderate	36.6
Conservative	27.3
By Number of Professional Staff	
3 or more	58.4
2	50.8
1	29.0
By Total Number of Staff[d]	
13–14	63.4
11–12	42.2
10 or less	24.1

By Number of Professional Staff, Controlling for Policy Attitude

	Staff	Cosponsorships
Liberal	1	44
	3 or more	73
Moderate	1	27
	2	52
	3 or more	28
Conservative	1	17.5
	3 or more	28

[a]Based on number of measures sponsored or cosponsored by Representative, 92d Congress, 1st Session (1971).

[b]Mean (average) number of measures sponsored or cosponsored.

[c]Based on Conservative Coalition Support Score, *Congressional Quarterly*, 1971. Liberal = 0–19; Moderate = 20–79; Conservative = 80–100.

[d]April 1971 payroll; includes both field office and Washington, D.C., staff.

Research Methods

HOUSE OF REPRESENTATIVES PERSONAL STAFFS

The interviews in which the data on personal staffs in the House were obtained by Susan Hammond were mainly conducted during the 92nd Congress (1971–1972).[1] They were semi-focused, lasting from half an hour to about two hours in length. In each interview, certain specific topics were covered, although not always in the same order nor with exactly the same wording. Notes were taken and as soon as possible afterward were transcribed fully.

With only two exceptions all the professionals in each of the twenty-five offices in the sample were interviewed; a majority of the Congressmen were interviewed also. The study was set up in this way in order to draw on the insights and experiences of all those involved in legislative and policy functions. Because office staffs are "small groups," it was deemed important to interview not only the AA in each office, but also the other professional staff people and Congressmen. A staff member's perceptions of office organization and role will vary, just as Congressmen's perceptions do.[2] The interview data support this decision: the additional interviews in each office filled in gaps and added insights which give a much fuller and more accurate picture than one interview only. It was also found that a first interview gave the researcher a basis of data which was helpful in eliciting additional information from those in the same office who were interviewed subsequently. All respondents were promised anonymity.

Professionals were chosen on the basis of duties. In most instances, the professionals in a Congressional office are clear: The administrative assistant, the legislative assistant, the press assistant are usually delineated by title as professional staff aides. In the case of lower-level staff (legislative secretaries, for example) and quasiprofessionals such as case workers, the professional function is not so clear: these staff were interviewed if it became clear that their staff colleagues in the office regarded them as professionals with some policy input. If it was clear from initial interviewing that lower-level personnel, in spite of a title, actually functioned in a routine secretarial position, they were not interviewed. (In any given office, interviews averaged two to four.)

Salary levels were not used in order to determine which staff should be interviewed. In contrast to the Senate, where this is a viable method,[3] House salaries at professional levels below the administrative assistant position may be below $15,000 or even $12,000. Hence although payroll data were used for portions of the analysis, they were not a definitive criterion in determining which persons to interview.

A total of seventy-one interviews with persons in the sample offices were conducted, fifty-eight with staff and thirteen with Congressmen. Ten additional interviews, with personal and committee staff, were also conducted, making a total of eighty-one interviews in all. Additionally, there has been continuing contact with staff and Congressmen on the Hill, both those in the sample offices and others. The material from the persons outside the sample has assisted in sharpening perceptions of the research data but has not been included in specific analysis. Work on the staff of Congressman William H. Meyer of Vermont during the 86th Congress (1959–1960) afforded an opportunity to view the operations of Congress first hand.

Except for four offices included in a pilot study conducted in 1969–1970, the offices surveyed were chosen using a table of random numbers for the first office and taking every *n*th office thereafter, using a list of members of the House of Representatives, 92nd Congress. The four pilot study offices were not chosen at random, as for only four this did not seem feasible. They do represent a party balance (two from each party) and some variation in seniority, region, and policy attitude.

The party ratio in the House of Representatives at the start of the 92nd Congress (January 1971) was 225(D), 180(R) or 59 percent (D), 41 percent (R). This is reflected in the 15(D), 10(R) [60 percent (D), 40 percent (R)] ratio of the offices in the sample.

TABLE A-1.   House Members and Sample, by Region and Party

	REPUBLICANS IN HOUSE	%	REPUBLICANS IN SAMPLE	%	DEMOCRATS IN HOUSE	%	DEMOCRATS IN SAMPLE	%
Total	180	41	10	40	255	59	15	60
East	49	27	1	10	73	29	2	13
South	31	17	2	20	88	34	4	27
Midwest	70	45	5	50	55	22	5	33
West	30	17	2	20	39	15	4	27

Note: The states were divided by regions according to the commonly accepted practice. *See,* for example, Barbara Hinckley, *The Seniority System in Congress* (Bloomington: Indiana Univ. Press, 1971) p. 26, n.2. Eastern states are: Connecticut, Delaware, Maine, Maryland, Massachusetts, New Hampshire, New Jersey, New York, Pennsylvania, Rhode Island, Vermont, West Virginia; Southern states are: Alabama, Arkansas, Florida, Georgia, Kentucky, Louisiana, Mississippi, North Carolina, Oklahoma, South Carolina, Tennessee, Texas, Virginia; Midwestern states are: Illinois, Indiana, Iowa, Kansas, Michigan, Minnesota, Missouri, Nebraska, North Dakota, Ohio, South Dakota, Wisconsin; Western states are: Alaska, Arizona, California, Colorado, Hawaii, Idaho, Montana, Nevada, New Mexico, Oregon, Utah, Washington, and Wyoming.

The sample also closely reflects the seniority distribution in the House during the 92nd Congress. By region, the sample under represents the East and South, and slightly over represents the West and Midwest.[4] The East is the most under represented in the distribution: slightly more than twice as many Congressmen from the East should have been interviewed (seven rather than three) to mirror House distribution exactly. The South is only very slightly underrepresented—by three percentage points. Actually, interviewing even one more Congressman from the South would have overrepresented the South by one percentage point, so that this is not significant. The overrepresentation is less skewed, as it is divided between the Midwest and the West.

Distribution of the sample choice was based on reflecting the distribution of House membership according to three critera, in descending order of priority: party, seniority, and region. The sample closely reflects the party and seniority distribution. Although it does not mirror the distribution by region, if there are significant differences in staffing by region, these should appear in the data.

By occupation, the sample also clearly reflects the distribution in the House as a whole.[5] Payroll data for the analysis were taken from the official records of the Disbursing Office of the Clerk of the House, U.S. House of Representatives. The historical data on clerk-hire are from a variety of written sources. The *Congressional Record* (and indices thereto), committee calendars, committee hearings, and the Statutes at Large were used, often cross-checking one source against another, from 1888 through 1976.

SENATE PERSONAL STAFFS

The Populations

The Senate personal staff research was carried out by Harrison Fox. The original list of Senate personal professional staff members included the names of 490 individuals. These names were selected from the *Report of the Secretary of the Senate*[6] and Brownson's *1971 Congressional Staff Directory*.[7]

General questionnaires were sent to staff members (92nd Congress), and twenty-two were not returned for the following reasons: not in Washington office; deceased; no longer with Senator, etc. Thus 468 staff members were given an opportunity to return questionnaires and 244 (52.1 percent) responded. Of these, 188 (40.1 percent) cooperated by returning a completed question-naire(s) and 56 (12.0 percent) refused their cooperation. In over ninety Senate offices, at least one staff member responded. Of the staff members returning completed questionnaires, thirteen chose not to be identified.

An in-depth questionnaire was sent to ninety-eight staff members who on the general questionnaire indicated a willingness to cooperate further. One of these questionnaires was returned because the staff member had left the Senate. Thus ninety-seven staff members had an opportunity to complete the in-depth questionnaire and forty-nine (50.5 percent) returned the questionnaire. One of these did not complete the questionnaire, and another's response was received too late for processing. Thus responses from forty-seven staff members were included in the analysis of the in-depth questionnaire.

Listed below are the various populations and numbers in these populations (*n*) that are mentioned in the text.

Population	N=
Original list of staff members	490
Loss	22
Population sent general questionnaire	468
Not responding to general questionnaire	237
Responding to general questionnaire	244
Cooperative (answering) identified	175
Cooperative (answering) unidentified	13
Uncooperative	56
General questionnaire plus unidentifiable responses	481
General questionnaire plus two (2) unidentifiable responses who could be identified for some purposes	470
Staff members sent the in-depth questionnaire	98
Loss	1
Not responding to the in-depth questionnaire	48
Responding to the in-depth questionnaire	49
Cooperative and processed	47
Uncooperative	1
Received too late for processing	1

Interview and Observation Procedure

Semi-focused interviews[8] were carried out with professional staff members in several Senate offices—preferably with those who had answered the questionnaires. During these interviews probes were made for general comments and interpersonal relationships within the office, office organization, and the interviewee's personal attributes and role behavior. One purpose of the interviews was to test the "surface" validity of the responses given on the general questionnaire—particularly to those questions dealing with staff activities. Another purpose was to gather information that "can't be placed on a closed interview form" by a respondent. Interviews were carried out with eleven professional staff members in four Senate offices. These interviews have been supplemented by over five years of participant observation of the Senate staff subsystem.

Robert F. Bales's small group observation techniques[9] provided a useful focus for seeking insights into professional staff members' personalities and interpersonal behavior. Working with Dr. Morley Segal's freshman class at American University enabled a set of interpersonal behavior observational skills to be perfected.

The in-depth questionnaire includes questions from which a personality profile can be developed. Both the interviews and observations were greatly aided by the personality profiles.

COMMITTEE STAFF

The committee staff research was conducted during the 93rd Congress (1973–1974). A questionnaire was sent to all professional staff of Senate and House committees in the spring of 1974. All standing, select, and special committees were included; party committees, such as policy and steering, were also included, although the analysis focuses primarily on standing committee personnel.

Committee professionals were defined by title, using the *Congressional Staff Directory*. An effort was made to include all nonclerical employees, and titles such as staff assistant were therefore considered as describing professional positions. According to the replies, this seems to have been an accurate assumption except in a few isolated instances.

Eight hundred eighty-nine questionnaires were sent to committee professionals, 387 in the Senate, 428 in the House, and 74 to joint committee personnel. A follow-up letter and a second questionnaire were sent six weeks later to those who had not returned the questionnaire.

Three hundred thirteen replies were received, a 35.2 percent response rate. One hundred forty-eight (38.2 percent) Senate aides responded, 144 (33.6 percent) House aides. The response rate of joint committee personnel was 21.6 percent (16 responses). In both Houses, the response rate of aides on standing, select, and special committees was higher than that of party committee aides.

Senate: party committees, 27.8 percent response; standing, select, and special committees, 38.8 percent.

House: party committees, 27.3 percent response; standing, select, and special committees, 34 percent.

A number of aides added comments to the questionnaire, explaining and expanding upon their responses. These were very helpful. The survey questionnaires were also supplemented by semi-focused interviews conducted with a small sample of respondents during the 93rd and 94th Congresses.

The response rate for the different staff positions is as follows:

Responses, By Position, to Committee Staff Survey

	% OF TOTAL RESPONSES	N
Staff Director	3.8	12
Deputy Director	4.2	13
General, Chief Counsel	1.9	6
Counsel, Attorney	12.1	38
Assistant to Counsel	2.2	7
Research Assistant	8.3	26
Professional Staff Member	14.1	44
Assistant to Chief Counsel	14.7	46
Economist	3.2	10
Minority Staff	21.7	68
Minority Counsel	1.6	5
Assistant Chief Clerk	4.2	13
Systems Analyst	1.0	3
Press Secretary	1.9	6
Investigator	0.6	2
Consultant	2.9	9
Unknown	1.6	5

NOTES

1. In the four offices included in the pilot study, interviewing was done in the 91st Congress with follow-up during the 92nd.
2. See Raymond Bauer, Ithiel de Sola Pool and Lewis A. Dexter, *American Business and Public Policy* (N.Y.: Atherton Press, 1963) for perceptive discussion of this point with regard to Congressmen.
3. See Fox, "Personal Professional Staffs."
4. Without the pilot study offices, the random sample of N remaining is not significantly more representative of the entire House membership.
5. See Appendix a, Hammond," House of Representatives Staffs" for further discussion of occupational distribution.
6. Published twice yearly by the U.S. Senate, Government Printing Office, Washington, D.C.
7. Charles Brownson, *Congressional Staff Directory* (Washington, D.C., 1971).
8. Interviews were conducted according to the method suggested in Lewis A. Dexter's *Elite and Specialized Interviewing* (Evanston, Ill.: Northwestern University Press, 1970).
9. *Personality and Interpersonal Behavior.*

Select Bibliography

Select Bibliography

BOOKS

Bailey, Stephen K. (1950) *Congress Makes a Law*. New York: Columbia University Press.

Bibby, John and Roger H. Davidson. (1972) *On Capitol Hill: Studies in the Legislative Process* (1972) 2nd Ed. Hinsdale, Illinois: The Dryden Press.

Biddle, Bruce, J., and Edwin J. Thomas (eds.). (1966) *Role Theory: Concepts and Research*. New York: Wiley.

Breslin, Janet E. (1976) "Constituent Service" in *Senators: Offices, Ethics, and Pressures*, Commission on the Operation of the Senate, Committee Print, Washington, D.C.: Government Printing Office.

Brownson, Charles B. *Congressional Staff Directory*. Washington: The Congressional Staff Directory, 1959–1977.

Citizens Conference on State Legislatures. (1971) *State Legislatures: An Evaluation of Their Effectiveness*. New York: Praeger.

Clapp, Charles L. (1963) *The Congressman: His Work as He Sees It*. Washington, D.C.: The Brookings Institution.

Cleveland, James C. (1966) "The Need for Increased Minority Staffing," in *We Propose: A Modern Congress,* (ed.) Mary McInnis. New York: McGraw-Hill Book Co.

Cooper, Joseph. (1970) *The Origins of the Standing Committees and the Development of the Modern House*. Rice University Studies. Vol. 56, No. 3.

Congressional Quarterly. (1971) *Congressional Quarterly's Guide to the Congress of the United States*. Washington, D.C.: Congressional Quarterly, Inc.

Davidson, Roger. (1969) *The Role of the Congressman*. New York: Pegasus.

———. David M. Kovenoc, and Michael K. O'Leary. (1966) *Congress in Crisis: Politics and Congressional Reform*. Belmont, Calif.: Wadsworth Publishing Co.

———. and Walter J. Oleszek. (1977) *Congress Against Itself*. Bloomington, Indiana: Indiana University Press.

DeGrazia, Alfred (ed.). (1966) *Congress: The First Branch of Government*. Washington, D.C.: The American Enterprise Institute for Public Policy Research.

211

Dexter, Lewis A. (December, 1968) "Book Reviews and Notes." Review of D. Katz and R. L. Kahn, *The Social Psychology of Organizations* (Wiley). *American Political Science Review,* LXII, p. 1036.

———. (1969) *The Sociology and Politics of Congress.* Chicago: Rand McNally.

Eidenberg, Eugene and Roy D. Morey. (1969) *An Act of Congress.* New York: W. W. Morton.

Ellwood, John W. and James A. Thurber. (1977) "The New Congressional Budget Process," in *Congress Reconsidered.* New York: Praeger.

Fenno, Richard F. (1966) *The Power of the Purse: Appropriations Politics in Congress.* Boston: Little, Brown and Company.

Fiorina, Morris. (1977) *Congress, Keystone of the Washington Establishment.* New Haven: Yale University Press.

Form, William H. "Occupations and Careers," *International Encyclopedia of the Social Sciences,* XI, 245–254.

Fox, Harrison W. Jr. and Susan Hammond (1975) "The Growth of Congressional Staffs," in *Congress Against the President,* Harvey C. Mansfield, Sr. (ed.), *Proceedings of the Academy of Political Science,* Vol. 32, No. 1.

———. (1975) "Legislative Staffs and Legislative Change," in James J. Heaphey and Alan P. Balutis (eds.) *Legislative Staffing: A Comparative Perspective.* New York: Halsted Press, Wiley.

Fox, Harrison W. Jr. and William H. Foskett (1976) "Program Evaluation: A Manual for Legislators and Legislative Staffs" in *Legislative Oversight and Program Evaluation,* Subcommittee on Oversight Procedures, U.S. Senate Government Operations Committee, May and *Congressional Oversight: Methods and Techniques,* Subcommittee on Oversight Procedures, U.S. Senate Government Operations Committee, July.

Galloway, George B. (1953) *The Legislative Process in Congress.* New York: Crowell.

Gillespie, David F. (Fall, 1970) Review of Nicos P. Mouzeles, *Organization and Bureaucracy: An Analysis of Modern Theories* (Aldine). The New Scholar, II, 251–253.

Greenstein, F. I. and Michael Lerner (eds.). (1971) *A Source Book for the Study of Personality and Politics.* Chicago: Markham.

Griffith, Ernest S. and Francis Valeo (1975) *Congress, Its Contemporary Role* (5th ed.). New York: New York University Press.

Gross, Bertram M. (1953) *The Legislative Struggle.* New York: McGraw-Hill.

Gross, Neal, W. S. Mason, and A. W. McEachern. (1958) *Explorations in Role Analysis: Studies of the School Superintendency Role.* New York: Wiley.

Hammond, Susan Webb. (1975) "Characteristics of Congressional Staffers" in James J. Heaphey and Alan P. Balutis (eds.), *Legislative Staffing: A Comparative Perspective.* New York: Halsted Press, Wiley.

———. (1976) "The Operation of Senators' Offices" in *Senators: Offices, Ethics, and Pressures.* Commission on the Operation of the Senate: Committee Print. Washington, D.C.: Government Printing Office.

———. Harrison W. Fox, Jr., Richard Moraski, and Jeanne B. Nicholson. (1976) "Senate Oversight Activities" in *Techniques and Procedures for Analysis and Evaluation,* Commission on the Operation of the Senate, Committee Print. Washington, D.C.: U.S. Government Printing Office.

Harris, Richard. (1971) *Decision*. New York: E. P. Dutton.

Huitt, Ralph K. (1965, 1973). "The Internal Distribution of Influence: The Senate" in *The Congress and America's Future,* David B. Truman (ed.). Englewood Cliffs, N.J.: Prentice Hall.

Huitt, Ralph K., and Robert L. Peabody. (1969) *Congress: Two Decades of Analysis*. New York: Harper and Row.

Jewell, Malcolm E., and Samuel C. Patterson. (1976) *The Legislative Process in the United States*. 2nd ed. New York: Random House.

Kahn, Robert L., and others. (1964) *Organizational Stress: Studies in Role Conflict and Ambiguity*. New York: Wiley.

Kammerer, Gladys M. (1949) *The Staffing of the Committees of Congress*. Lexington: University of Kentucky.

_____. (1951) *Congressional Committee Staffing Since 1946*. Lexington: University of Kentucky.

Katz, Daniel and R. L. Kahn. (1966) *The Social Psychology of Organizations*. New York: Wiley.

Keefe, William J., and Morris S. Ogul. (1973) *The American Legislative Process: Congress and the States*. 3rd ed. Englewood Cliffs, N. J.: Prentice-Hall.

Kilpatrick, Franklin P., Milton C. Cummings, Jr., and M. Kent Jennings. (1964) *Sourcebook of a Study of Occupational Values and the Image of the Federal Service*. Washington, D.C.: Brookings Institution.

Kingdon, John W. (1973) *Congressman's Voting Decisions*. New York: Harper & Row.

Kofmehl, Kenneth. (1962) *Professional Staffs of Congress*. West Lafayette, Ind.: Purdue University Press. (Also, 1977, 3rd Edition).

Laird, Melvin, ed. (1968) *Republican Papers*. Garden City, N.Y.: Doubleday Anchor.

Madron, Thomas W. (1969) *Small Group Methods and the Study of Politics*. Evanston, Ill.: Northwestern University Press.

Manley, John F. (1970) *The Politics of Finance: The House Committee on Ways and Means*. Boston: Little, Brown and Co.

Marvick, Dwaine. (1967) "Political Recruitment and Careers," *International Encyclopedia of the Social Sciences,* XII, 273–282.

Matthews, Donald R. (1954) *The Social Background of Political Decision-Makers*. Garden City, N.Y.: Doubleday.

_____. (1960) *U.S. Senators and Their World*. New York: Vintage.

McConachie, Lauros G. (1898) *Congressional Committees*. New York: Crowell.

Milbrath, Lester. (1963) *The Washington Lobbyists*. Chicago: Rand McNally.

Ornstein, Norman J. (1975). "Legislative Behavior and Legislative Structures: A Comparative Look at House and Senate Resource Utilization" in *Legislative Staffing: A Comparative Perspective,* James J. Heaphey and Alan P. Balutis (eds.). New York: Halsted Press, Wiley.

Patterson, Samuel C. (1970) "Congressional Committee Professional Staffing: Capabilities and Constraints," in *Legislatures in Developmental Perspective.* Alan Kornberg, and Lloyd D. Musof (eds.). Durham, N.C.: Duke University Press.

Peabody, Robert L. and Nelson W. Polsby (eds.). (1969) (1977) *New Perspectives on the House of Representatives*. 2nd & 3rd ed. Chicago: Rand McNally.

Price, David E. (1972) *Who Makes the Laws*. Cambridge: Schenkman Publishing Co.

Price, Hugh D. Review of Kenneth Kofmehl, *Professional Staffs of Congress* (Purdue University Press). *American Sociological Review*, XXVIII, 5 (October, 1963), 858–859.

Redman, Eric. (1973) *The Dance of Legislation*. New York: Simon & Schuster.

Riegle, Donald, with Trevor Armbrister. (1972) *O Congress*. Garden City, N.Y.: Doubleday & Co., Inc.

Rieselbach, Leroy N. (1973) *Congressional Politics*. New York: McGraw Hill.

Ripley, Randall B. (1975) *Congress: Process and Policy*. New York: W. W. Norton & Company.

Robinson, James A. "Staffing the Legislature," in *Legislatures in Developmental Perspective*. Alan Kornberg, and Lloyd D. Musof, eds. Durham, N.C.: Duke University Press.

Rokeach, Milton. (1970) *Beliefs, Attitudes, and Values*. San Francisco: Jossey-Bass.

Rosenthal, Allan. (1974) *Legislative Performance in the States*. New York: The Free Press.

Saloma, John S. (1969) *Congress and the New Politics*. Boston: Little, Brown and Co.

Schermerhorn, Richard A. (1961) *Society and Power*. New York: Random House.

Tacheron, Donald G., and Morris K. Udall. (1966 & 1970) *The Job of the Congressman*. Indianapolis: Bobbs-Merrill.

Ulmer, S. Sidney (ed.). (1970) *Political Decision-Making*. New York: Van Nostrand Reinhold.

Wahlke, John, Heinz Eulau, and John Ferguson. (1963) *The Legislative System*. New York: Wiley.

Wilensky, Harold L. (1956) *Intellectuals in Labor Unions*. Glencoe, Ill.: The Free Press.

Wilson, James Q. (1973) *Political Organizations*. New York: Basic Books, Inc.

PERIODICALS

Allport, F. H. "The Structuring of Events: Outline of a General Theory with Applications to Psychology," *Psychological Review*, LXI (September, 1954) pp. 281–303.

Alpern, M. David with Stephan Lesher, "The Hidden Power Elite," *Newsweek* (January 17, 1977), pp. 20–22.

Berry's World, "My Staff came up with more foolish ways to spend money than YOUR staff!," *Washington Star News* (August 21, 1974).

Bowsher, Prentice, "The Speaker's man: Lewis Deschler, House Parliamentarian," *The Washington Monthly* (April, 1970), pp. 22–27.

Braden, Tom. "The Hidden Fifth Estate," *The Washington Post* (March 20, 1976), p. A 15.

Butler, Warren H. "Administering Congress: The Role of the Staff," *Public Administration Review*, XXVI (March, 1966) pp. 3–13.

"Capitol Hill Staffs: Hidden 'Government' in Washington," *U.S. News and World Report* (April 4, 1977), pp. 37–40.

Cochrane, James D. "Partisan Aspects of Congressional Committee Staffing," *Western Political Quarterly*, XVII (June, 1964), pp. 338–348.

"Congress Taps its Library for Science Help." *Chemical and Engineering News* (January 1967), pp. 30–33.

"Consumer Group to 'Train' Senate Staffers," *Industry Week* (December 16, 1974), p. 55.

Dewar, Helen. "Elephant Rides Go with Hill Press Job," *The Washington Post* (June 29, 1975), pp. B 1 and 8.

Dexter, Lewis A. "The Representative and His District," *Human Organization*, 16, pp. 2–13 (1947).

Drew, Elizabeth B. "The Politics of Auto Safety," *Atlantic Monthly*, (October, 1966), pp. 95–102.

Editorial, "Empire Building on the Hill," *The Washington Star* (April 6, 1976), p. 10.

Evans, Rowland, Jr. "The Invisible Men Who Run Congress," *Saturday Evening Post* (June 8, 1963), pp. 13–17.

Ford, Gerald R. "Congressional Minority Staffing," *Good Government*, LXXXIII (Spring, 1966), pp. 11–12.

Froman, Lewis H., Jr. "Organization Theory and the Explanation of Important Characteristics of Congress," *American Political Science Review*, LXII (June, 1968), pp. 518–526.

Garb, Gerald, and Cleon Harrell. "The Economist and the State," *Quarterly Review of Economics and Business*, VI (Winter, 1966), pp. 25–30.

Gwirtzman, Milton S. "The Bloated Branch," *New York Times Magazine* (November 10, 1974), 30–31, 98, 100–102.

Graves, Brook W. "Legislative Reference for the Congress of the U.S.," *American Political Science Review*, XLI (April, 1947), pp. 284–293.

Hattery, Lowell, and Susan Hotheimen. "The Legislator's Source of Expert Information," *Public Opinion Quarterly*, XVIII (1954), pp. 300–303.

Issacs, Stephen. "The Capitol Game," *Washington Post* (Feb. 16, 1975), A1, 4; (Feb. 18, 1975), A 1, 12; (Feb. 19, 1975), A 1, 9; (Feb. 20, 1975), A 1, 6; (Feb. 21, 1975) A 1, 6; (Feb 23, 1975) A 1, 12; (Feb. 24, 1975) A 1, 4.

House of Representatives Commission on Information and Facilities. *Staff*, 94th Congress, Issues 1–3 (1975–1976).

Johnson, Haynes. "Congressional Staffs: The Third Branch of Congress," *The Washington Post* (January 18, 1970), pp. 1 A and 17 A.

Judge, John F. "Standing Staffs, The Invisible Empire," *Government Executive* (May 1974), pp. 67–69.

Kammerer, Gladys M. "The Record of Congress in Committee Staffing," *American Political Science Review*, XLV (December, 1951); pp. 1126–1136.

Kampelman, Max M. "The Legislative Bureaucracy: Its Response to Political Change, 1953," *Journal of Politics*, XVI (August, 1954), pp. 539–550.

King, Larry L. "Washington's Second Banana Politicians," *Harper's*, CCXXX (January, 1965), pp. 41–47.

Kofmehl, Kenneth Theodore, "COSPUP, Congress and Scientific Advice," *Journal of Politics,* XXVIII (February, 1966), pp. 100–120.

Landauer, Jerry. "Capitol Hill Salaries Are Often Baffling-But Are Always High," *The Wall Street Journal* (June 1, 1972), pp. 1 and 18.

MacPherson, Myra. "The Power Lovers," *The Washington Post* Potomac (September 28, 1975), pp. 10–13, 18, 20–26.

Madden, Richard L. "Congress Master Mechanics: The Committee Chiefs of Staff," *The New York Times,* (March 3, 1974), p. L 45.

Malbin, Michael J. "Congressional Staffs—Growing Fast, But in Different Directions," *National Journal,* (July 10, 1976), pp. 958–965.

Manley, John F. "Congressional Staff and Public Policy-Making: The Joint Committee on Internal Revenue Taxation," *Journal of Politics,* (Nov., 1968), pp. 1046–1067.

Meller, Norman. "Legislative Staff Services: Toxic, Specific, or Placebo for the Legislature's Ills," *Western Political Quarterly,* XXX (June, 1967), pp. 381–389.

————. "The Policy Position of Legislative Service," *World Political Quarterly,* V (1952), pp. 109–123.

Miller, Kay. "Sex Discrimination Charged," *Capitol Hill Forum* (June 16, 1975), pp. 1 and 8.

Neustadt, Richard E. "Approaches to Staffing the Presidency: Notes on FDR and JFK," *American Political Science Review,* LVII, 1 (December, 1963), pp. 855–864.

Oberdorfer, Don. "Vast Ghostland of Washington," *New York Times Magazine* (April 26, 1964), pp. 24, 26, and 98.

Patterson, Samuel C. "The Professional Staffs of Congressional Committees," *Administrative Science Quarterly,* XV (March, 1970), pp. 22–37.

Pipe, G. Russell. "Congressional Liaison: The Executive Branch Consolidates Its Relations With Congress," *Public Administration Review,* XXVI (1966), pp. 14–24.

Price, David E. "Professionals and 'Entrepreneurs': Staff Orientations and Policy-Making on Three Senate Committees," *Journal of Politics,* XXXIII, 2 (May, 1971), pp. 316–336.

Rich, Spencer. "Slowly, Women are Climbing to New Heights on the Hill," *The Washington Post* (March 4, 1973), p. A 3.

————. "Women Hold Fewer Top Senate Jobs," *The Washington Post* (June 8, 1976), pp. A 1 and 9.

————. "Senate Committee Staff Tenure Depends on Who's Chairman," *The Washington Post* (November 18, 1976), p. A. 55.

————. "An Invisible Network of Hill Power," *The Washington Post* (March 20, 1977), pp. E 1, 5, 9 and 10.

Ridgeway, James. "Advising Congress," *New Republic,* CLV (July, 1966), pp. 17–18.

Rogers, Lindsay. "The Staffing of Congress," *Political Science Quarterly,* LVI (March, 1941), pp. 7–22.

Schlossberg, Kenneth. "The Ablest Men in Congress," *Washingtonian,* III, 4 (August, 1968), pp. 61–63, 72–75.

"Sexists in the Senate?" *U.S. News and World Report* (July 21, 1975), p. 22.

Shelton, Isabelle. "Senate Salaries Sexist, Political Caucus Says," *Washington Star News* (June 16, 1975), p. A-3.

Sherrill, Robert. "Who Runs Congress?" *New York Times Magazine* (November 22, 1970), pp. 52–88.

Teixeira, Linda. "Congressional Fellows—Professional Interns," *Capitol Hill Forum* (September 22, 1975), pp. 3 and 8.

Thomas, W. C. "Generalist vs. Specialist Careers in a Municipal Bureaucracy," *Public Administration Review,* XXI, 1 (1961), pp. 485–521.

Walker, Connecticut. "Mr. Miller Goes to Washington: The Power Behind the Powers," *Parade* (November 30, 1975), pp. 16–18, and 19.

Wallace, Robert A. "Congressional Control of the Budget," *Midwest Journal of Political Science,* III (May, 1959), p. 163.

Welsh, John. "Science Advice: New Division for Science Policy Research Set Up in LRS to Aid Congress," *Science,* CXLV (September, 1964), pp. 1162–1164.

"Where Tax Bills Run the Gauntlet," *Business Week* (June 11, 1966), pp. 106 and 111.

Wyden, P. "Ghosts on Capitol Hill," *Newsweek,* January 28, 1957, p. 33.

Wyner, Alan J. "Staffing the Governor's Office." *Public Administration Review,* vol. 30, no. 1 (1970), pp. 17–24.

UNPUBLISHED WORKS

Arnold, John. (Spring, 1971) "The Defense Subcommittee of the House Appropriations Committee," Washington Semester Paper, American University.

Balutis, Alan P. "Legislative Staffing: Does It Make a Difference?" (1976) Paper, Symposium on Legislative Reform and Public Policy, University of Nebraska.

Capitol Hill Women's Political Caucus. (1975) "Sexists in the Senate?" A Study of Differences in Salary by Sex Among Employees of the U.S. Senate."

Dexter, Lewis A. (1976) "Court Politics: Presidential Staff Relations as a Special Case of a General Phenomenon," Paper, American Political Science Association Annual Meeting.

Eidenberg, E. (1966) "The Congressional Bureaucracy." Unpublished PhD dissertation, Northwestern University.

Fenno, Richard F. (1975) "Congressmen in Their Constituencies: An Exploration," Paper, American Political Science Association Annual Meeting.

Fox, Harrison W. Jr. (1972) "Personal Professional Staffs of U.S. Senators." Unpublished PhD Dissertation, The American University.

_____. (1973) "Information and Analytical Needs of the Senate Office," Paper, Annual One Day Symposium of the Association for Public Program Analysis.

_____. (1973) "Activities, Roles, and Positions of U.S. Senate Personal Staff Professionals," Paper, Conference of the National Capitol Area Political Science Association.

_____. (1973) "Congressional Reform: A Survey of the Alternatives " (with Joe Wir kelmann).

_____. (1974) "Performing Research, Formulating Statements, and Drafting Legislation: A Manual."

———. (1974) "Oversight: Is Congress Doing Its Job?" Paper, Annual Meeting of the American Political Science Association.

———. (1976) "Congressional Evaluation: Recent Developments," Paper, The Evaluation Network, St. Louis, Missouri.

———. (1977) "Evaluation, Research and Congressional Oversight: A Case Study of a General Phenomenon," Paper, American Association for the Advancement of Science.

———. and Susan Webb Hammond (1974) "Congressional Staffs and Congressional Change," Paper, APSA Annual Meeting.

———. (1976) "Committee Professional Staffs: Attributes, Activities and Communication Patterns." Paper, American Political Science Association Annual Meeting.

———. (1976) "Recent Trends in Congressional Staffing," Paper, Southern Political Science Association Annual Meeting.

———. and Jeanne Nicholson. (1977) "Foresight, Oversight, and Legislative Development: A View of Congressional Policy Making," Paper, American Political Science Association Annual Meeting.

Hammond, Susan W. (1970) "The Office Staff of the Congressman: Organizational and Recruitment Patterns". Unpublished MA thesis, The Johns Hopkins University.

———. (1973) "Personal Staffs of Members of the House of Representatives," Unpublished PhD dissertation, The Johns Hopkins University.

———. (1974) "The Changing Role of the Personal Professional Staff in Congressional Decision-Making," Paper, American Political Science Association Annual Meeting.

Loomis, Burdette A. (1976) "The Congressional Office as a Small (?) Business: Members of the Class of 1974 Set Up Shop," Paper, American Political Science Association Annual Meeting.

Macartney, John David. (1975) "Political Staffing: A View from the District." Unpublished PhD. dissertation, UCLA.

Nass, Martin Barry (1966) "A Career-Line Study of Senate Administrative Assistants." Unpublished M.A. Thesis, Syracuse University.

Ornstein, Norman Jay. (1972) "Information, Resources and Legislative Decisionmaking: Some Comparative Perspectives of the U.S. Congress." Unpublished PhD dissertation. The University of Michigan.

Patterson, Samuel C. (1967) "Congressional Committee Professional Staffing: Capabilities and Constraints." Paper, Planning Conference of the Comparative Administration Group Legislative Services Project.

Peabody, Robert L. (1963) "Organizational Theory and Legislative Behavior: Bargaining, Hierarchy and Change in the U.S. House of Representatives." Paper, American Political Science Association Annual Meeting.

Rohde, David W., Norman J. Ornstein and Robert L. Peabody. (1974) "Political Change and Legislative Norms in the United States Senate," Paper, American Political Science Association Annual Meeting.

Rundquist, Paul S. (1976) "Senate Personal Committee Staff: A First Year Appraisal." Paper, American Political Science Association Annual Meeting.

Segal, Morley (1965) "The Role and Function of the Legislative Staff in the California Assembly." Unpublished PhD dissertation, Claremont Graduate School and University Center.

Thomas, Cynthia and Lynda Carlson. (1971) "Interaction Among Staff Members in the Indiana Delegation: A Preliminary Study." Paper, Southern Political Science Association Annual Meeting.

CONGRESSIONAL DOCUMENTS

U.S. Congress

Joint Committee on the Organization of Congress, 79th Congress, 2nd Session: Hearings (March–June, 1945); Report (S. Rept. 79–1011). Government Printing Office: Washington, D.C., 1945–1946.

Joint Committee on the Organization of Congress, 89th Congress, 1st Session: Hearings, Symposium, Interim Reports, Final Report. Government Printing Office: Washington, D.C., 1965–1966.

U.S. House of Representatives

Commission on Adminstrative Review, (95th Congress) Interim Report, H. Rept. 95–178 and Final Report, H. Rept. 95–272.

Committee on Rules, Hearing, Legislative Reorganization Act of 1970, and Report, H. Rept. 91–1215.

Select Committee on Committees, 93rd Congress: Hearings, "Committee Organization in the House" (93rd Congress, 1st Session, 1973), 3 vol. H. Doc. 94–187, 94th Congress, 1st Session.

Final Report, Committee Reform Amendments of 1974, H. Rept. 93–916 (93rd Congress, 2nd Session, 1974). (Select Committee on Committees)

U.S. Senate

_____. Debate on S. Res. 60, Personal Committee Aides, *Congressional Record*. June 9–June 12, 1975.

Commission on the Operation of the Senate

_____. Final Report, *Toward a Modern Senate*. (94th Congress, 2nd Session, 1976). S. Doc. 94–278.

_____. Studies (7 volumes) (94th Congress, 2nd Session, 1976). Committee Prints. Government Printing Office: Washington, D.C.

Temporary Select Committee to Study the Senate Committee System

———. First Staff Report (94th Congress, 2d. Session, 1976). Committee Print.

———. Hearings (94th Congress, 2d Session, 1976). Committee Print.

———. "Structure of the Senate Committee System." First Report with Recommendations, 1976. Committee Print.

———. "Operation of the Senate Committee System: Staffing, Scheduling, Communications, Procedures and Special Functions." Second Report with Recommendations, 1977. Committee Print.

Index